Every Child Is Special

Quality Group Care for Infants and Toddlers

Rena Shimoni

Mount Royal College, Calgary
Hebrew University, Jerusalem

Joanne Baxter

Mount Royal College, Calgary

Judith Kugelmass

Hebrew University, Jerusalem

ADDISON-WESLEY PUBLISHERS LIMITED

Don Mills, Ontario • Reading, Massachusetts
Menlo Park, California • New York • Wokingham, England
Amsterdam • Bonn • Sydney • Singapore • Tokyo
Madrid • San Juan

This book is dedicated to our ever supportive and patient husbands:

Yakhin, Dave, and Sonny

and to our children:

Tammy, Galit, Orit, Chelsea, Carissa, Ronit, Oren, and David.

Canadian Cataloguing in Publication Data

Shimoni, Rena, 1948–
   Every child is special

Includes bibliographical references and index.
ISBN 0-201-58552-9

1. Day care centers. 2. Child care services.
I. Baxter, Joanne M. (Joanne Marlena), 1955–
II. Kugelmass, Judy W. III. Title.

HV851.S55 1992   362.7'12   C92-093314-9

Production Editor: Elynor Kagan
Design and Page Layout: Joseph Chin

Printed and bound in Canada.

B C D E F   WC   98 97 96 95 94

Contents

Foreword

It is a great pleasure to write a foreword for *Every Child Is Special.* It is a pleasure on several levels:

- First, it is extremely satisfying to see the growing number of Canadian early childhood publications that are becoming available not only for Canadian audiences, but for broader, international readership as well.

- Second, it is gratifying to see the growing breadth and depth of a pool of Canadian child-care expertise formed by skilled practitioners and instructors who have completed graduate-level degrees and are now making significant contributions to early childhood literature.

- Third, it is always a pleasure to recommend to the field and to students a strong, well-organized and imminently useful text to assist all of us in our quest for quality care for children.

Rena Shimoni, Joanne Baxter, and Judith Kugelmass have developed a text that blends research with practice, theory with application. As part of the continuum that recognizes each child as a special child, the special-needs child is integrated into the text. The degree of thoughtful consideration evident in that integration is apparent in other aspects of the book as well. The chapters aim for a blend of research, case examples, material for reflection, and practical application guidelines. Such a format, while particularly appropriate for a student audience, can also serve well the needs of a more diverse readership, including professional caregivers, parents, and parent educators.

The range of topics covered in these twenty chapters is impressive, and reinforces the volume's encompassing utility. From toilet training to parent support, from play to program evaluation, a broad array of issues, concerns, and guidelines is clearly presented in a non-technical format. The sections of the volume move from a broadly based perspective on infant and toddler caregiving issues, through more focused chapters on program and child development, to conclude with critically important (and too often neglected) chapters on working with parents and program evaluation. The organization of the volume echoes the development of many professional caregivers, from a general interest in the topic, through the challenges of creating developmentally appropriate programs, to the need to evaluate the effectiveness of those programs.

I welcome this volume and applaud its authors not only for the evidence it provides that the field of early childhood education and care is alive and well in Canada, but for the broader contributions a volume such as this makes to our more universal striving to ensure that all children receive high quality care in their earliest years.

Alan R. Pence
School of Child and Youth Care
University of Victoria

About This Book

All caregivers working with infants and toddlers want to provide the kind of care that promotes healthy development. All parents want their children to be in care that is of the highest quality. This book was designed to provide guidance and assistance to those providing care. It is geared to caregivers working with infants and toddlers and to students in training programs who intend to work with this age group. We hope that this book will also be of assistance to directors of centers, and to those who are responsible for monitoring the quality of care. Although the focus is center care, much of the content is relevant to family day-home settings as well. Parents who want to know about care of infants and toddlers that is respectful and developmentally appropriate will also find the book informative.

Group care for infants and toddlers on a wide scale is a relatively new social phenomenon. There has been an increase, as well, in the demand for day care for children with special needs. Chapters 1 and 2 address some of the concerns about the appropriateness of group care for infants and toddlers. As these concerns are best addressed by providing care of high quality, Chapter 3 outlines the essential components of a quality program.

The foundations of quality care lie in the program philosophy and the goals set for the children. These are discussed in Chapter 4. Chapter 5 identifies some of the key issues that are relevant to the planning of quality programs for infants and toddlers.

Essentially, for much of the day, infants and toddlers are playing with people — mainly the caregiver but also other children — and with things — toys and equipment. After a brief description of play in Chapter 6, Chapters 7 through 13 discuss each area of child development. These chapters describe how the caregiver can protect, support, enrich, and observe the lives of children in each developmental area.

Much of the care of very young children revolves around the routines of arrival, departure, mealtime, naptime, diapering and dressing, and toileting. Chapters 14 to 18, therefore, describe how routines can become an essential component of the quality program if they are based on an understanding of each child's developmental needs.

The final section of the book is devoted to two broader aspects of group care that are central to the provision of a quality program. Chapter 19 is devoted to working with parents of infants and toddlers in group care, and Chapter 20 discusses the evaluation of programs.

• • •

This book took ten years to evolve. We would like to tell its story, and, at the same time, to acknowledge the key players in its growth and development. The book began at a small department at the Hebrew University of Jerusalem in Israel, called the Schwartz Early Childhood Graduate Training Program. Dr. Miriam Rosenthal, Director of the Schwartz Program, obtained funding from the Joint Distribution Committee-Israel to develop training material for staff working with infants and toddlers. It was she who brought Rena and Judy together to develop this project.

We prepared two trainer's manuals, one on routine caregiving and a second on organizing the environment for play. Both have been widely used in day-care and family day-care training programs, and are available in both Hebrew and Arabic. Sections of these manuals have been adapted and incorporated into this book. For these parts Rena and Judy both express appreciation to the Joint Distribution Committee-Israel and gratitude to Dr. Rosenthal and the team at the Schwartz Program for their support.

While Judy continued to develop this training project in Israel, Rena came to Canada and worked as a consultant for a large integrated child development center. The training manuals were adapted for use in Canada. Most of the adaptations were made necessary by the cultural differences among adults. The needs of infants and toddlers — for warmth, security, and a responsive, interesting environment — differ little with geography. Providence Child Development Center gave Rena an opportunity to learn much about working in an integrated setting. Deep down, she believed that, if we are really committed to the idea that every child is special and programs should try to adapt to children rather than vice versa, the boundary between special-needs children and those called normally developing becomes cloudy indeed.She sought the counsel of Joanne, who specialized in special education.

Joanne and Rena worked together in developing a model for integrated quality day care. Essential to this model is the belief that all infants and toddlers have very special needs that must be met in quality care settings. Some children require extra help and support as a result of physical or developmental disabilities. Successful integration is possible provided that caregivers' commitment to individualized care is backed by additional knowledge. Our thanks go to Terry Creighton, Executive Director of Providence Child Development Center, for his support and patience. We also wish to acknowledge the support of the Child Care Initiative Fund in the preparation and development of materials.

Joanne and Rena continued to work together at Mount Royal College in Early Childhood Education and Rehabilitation Studies. This is where the final stages of the book evolved. The materials were field tested with students working in day-care centers in Calgary. The Academic Development Center funded this part of the project and Billie Shepherd, Coordinator of the Early Childhood Program at Mount Royal College, provided a tremendous amount of assistance and support.

Two years later it occurred to Rena that, through the combined efforts of Judy, Joanne, and herself, the material could become a book. Beth Bruder of Addison-Wesley Publishers thought so as well. We thank her for her enthusiasm and confidence, and Elynor Kagan for the work she has put into seeing this project through. We are deeply indebted to Cindy Crane who typed and retyped the endless number of revisions and adaptations with an amazingly positive attitude. Special thanks go to the staff, parents, and children of the Providence Child Development Center in Calgary and the Centenary/Seven Oaks Child Care Center in Scarborough (a center operated by the Municipality of Metropolitan Toronto), where the photographs for the book were taken.

• • •

This book represents the combined efforts of three authors who span three generations. Judy is a grandmother, Rena's daughters are in their teens, and Joanne's daughters are preschoolers. We have mothered our own children in different cultures and in different times. We hope that the diversity in our academic backgrounds and our personal lives has enriched the pages of this book.

Good caregiving begins in the heart, and that special feeling cannot be learned through reading a book. But we hope our combined efforts will assist those who care to appreciate the value of their work, and will provide some guidelines for ensuring that infants and toddlers receive the best care possible.

Rena Shimoni
Joanne Baxter
Judith Kugelmass

PART I FOUNDATIONS

Before we can explore infant and toddler programs in depth, we need to discuss a number of preliminary topics. The first chapter focuses on the question, Should infants and toddlers be in group care? Next, Chapter 2 explores the appropriateness of having children with special needs in integrated group-care settings. Both of these issues have been widely debated.

Regardless of all the debates, there *will* be infants, toddlers, and children with many varying needs in group-care settings, and there *is* consensus that every attempt must be made to provide quality care. Therefore, Chapter 3 defines the characteristics of a quality center.

The program of a quality center is built upon a clear program philosophy and program goals. Chapter 4 deals with this topic. Chapter 5 raises some of the overriding issues that must be considered in planning and implementing all quality programs. Topics such as the importance of health and safety, the importance of a primary caregiving system, and the importance of the physical environment are discussed.

Part I will provide caregivers with the foundations on which quality programs can be built.

Should Infants and Toddlers Be in Group Care?

Objectives

- ❖ To discuss the concern over infant and toddler day care in a historical context.
- ❖ To discuss the major concerns regarding day care for very young children.
- ❖ To address these concerns through a discussion of research findings.

Opening Thoughts

If you had an infant or toddler, would you consider group care a good option if you were returning to work? Why or why not?

Comments on Opening Thoughts

- ❖ Whether or not you think that group care is ideal, there is a growing demand for day care for infants and toddlers.
- ❖ There is a strong connection between people's values (e.g., the belief that women need or have the right to work) and their views on day care.
- ❖ It is very difficult to examine the pros and cons of day care without considering the kind and quality of that care. ❐

Infants and Toddlers in Group Care

Conversation between two mothers:

Mrs. Davies: I had an offer to return to work last week that was quite tempting. But I would never put my baby in a day-care center. I've heard too many bad things can happen there.

Mrs. Ying: Day care is the best thing that ever happened to my family. Johnny loves it there, and I love being back at work.

Day care for infants and toddlers is a controversial issue that often arouses heated and emotional debates. Television programs, newspaper articles, and many books have been devoted to questions such as: What effect will being in group care have on infants and toddlers? What kind of care is best for babies?

Understanding the pros and cons of day care for infants and toddlers has been likened to "wandering in the wilderness with signposts pointing every which way" (Wingert & Kantrowitz, 1990: 71). Even among professionals and researchers in the field of early childhood, infant day care raises uneasy feelings and hesitancy in some and confidence and optimism in others.

Hesitancy about infant and toddler group care is well rooted in our history. Day-care centers in Canada date back to 1850, when they were grim, "barren and cheerless." They were seen as a very last resort for families in extreme poverty or for "pathological" families (O'Brien Steinfels, 1973). Most of these centers provided minimal custodial care that was concerned with children's basic needs for survival — food, clothing, and shelter.

Until approximately thirty years ago the idea of placing infants and toddlers in a group-care setting was generally unacceptable in most western societies. The mother's role was to be at home and care for her children. Pediatricians, psychiatrists, psychologists, and other child welfare professionals considered infants very vulnerable and in need of the attention and love of their mothers full time. They believed that separation from the mother could cause the child emotional damage. Reports that described developmentally delayed, apathetic children who were raised in residential settings — mostly orphanages — led to the conclusion that the damage to the children's development was caused essentially by the lack of mother love (Bowlby, 1951). Although this view has now been largely refuted, child-care experts at that time concluded that day care could be as damaging to the child as those orphanages were. This early research into the effects of out-of-home care reinforced the "ethic of mothercare" (Pence, 1990) that was largely unchallenged until the 1960s.

In the 1960s and 70s attitudes began to change. The belief that early childhood programs could have a lasting positive effect on children and families was gaining ground in North America (Braun & Edwards, 1972), and many leading psychologists and educators began to see day care as a challenge and opportunity to improve the lives of children. Several model programs were established in Canada (Fowler, 1980) and the United States (Willis & Ricciuti, 1975; Provence et al., 1977; Caldwell, 1972). The development of these model day-care programs marked the transition from custodial care to quality care.

Simultaneously, many social changes were occurring. There were fewer extended families, single parenthood increased, economic needs and/or expectations altered, and the women's movement changed the life-style of many women. All of these factors resulted in the massive increase in the number of working women and demand for day-care services. The number of day-care centers increased rapidly, but the quality ranged tremendously.

Doubts about day care linger. Some of these doubts can be attributed to the fact that many today still believe that mothers should stay home with their children. But other doubts stem from specific concerns about the effect of day care on child development. These concerns have become a major focus of child development research. Research does not attempt to question the beliefs about motherhood, but it can help clarify some of the fears and concerns about how day care affects children. Some of the major concerns associated with group care of infants and toddlers relate to the physical health, the emotional and social development, and the intellectual and language development of the children.

The aim of day-care programs is no longer custodial care but quality care.

Health Concerns

Babies need to be in a safe and healthy environment. Avoiding the risks of accidents, contamination through close contact between small children, and inadequate nutrition must be of paramount concern in any setting for infants and toddlers. Medical research into group-care settings has indicated that some of these concerns are well founded. Coughs, colds, influenza, and gastrointestinal diseases tend to occur more among young children who attend group-care settings (Aronson, 1982). While little has been written about accident rates in group care, it is known that many preventable accidents do occur (Weiser, 1991).

The safety of the children in day care has become a major concern in the early childhood field, and there are now several sources of information and guidelines (Shapiro et al., 1988) which, if followed, can minimize the risk of accidents. Similarly, excellent guidelines for ensuring that children receive a healthy diet are available (Network of the Federal/Provincial/Territorial Group on Nutrition & National Institute of Nutrition, 1989; Shapiro et al., 1988). In low-quality centers where caregivers do not take precautions, the health of children is indeed at risk. However, if the guidelines are followed diligently, group care can safeguard the physical health and safety of young children.

Concerns for Social-Emotional Well-Being

Given the widely held view in our society that babies should be raised at home with their mothers, it is not surprising that parents and experts continue to express concern about babies being away from their mothers for many hours a day. Parents may wonder whether their babies will receive the loving attention that they need. Well-known experts have published emotional pleas suggesting that group care should be avoided. Penelope Leach, for example, answers the question of whether an infant can receive the kind of care he or she needs in child care by stating: "It is actually impossible within an employment situation. To replace a mother with an employee (e.g., a caregiver) cannot be done..." (Leach, 1984: 9). Burton White talks about the need of small children to be with "someone who is absolutely nuts about them ... someone who loves them, no matter what" (White, 1984: 8). These statements seem to point to the need for infants to be with their mothers full time. However, it is possible to agree with them without ruling out the possibility of effective, quality day care. Infants in day care do mostly have "somebody special" or "someone who is nuts about them" — their parents. Day care does not replace the family. Furthermore, research has suggested that infants can and do form secure attachments with their caregivers (Goosens & van IJzendoorn, 1990), who can make them feel that they are special.

One of the main questions that researchers have been attempting to answer concerns the effect of the infant's temporary daily separation from his or her "special people" on emotional and social development.

We do not have clear answers to this question yet. A major review by Belsky (1986) concluded that healthy emotional development may be at risk for infants under one year of age who spend more than twenty hours a week in out-of-home care. Not surprisingly, the risk is much higher in poor-quality centers. Belsky's interpretation has caused a major debate and has been challenged by other researchers (Clarke-Stewart, 1988; Thompson, 1988) who claim that we do not yet have sufficient evidence to draw that conclusion, and that more research is needed before clearer answers are available (Sroufe, 1988).

Another concern that has been raised relates to social development. Some researchers (Belsky, 1986) suggest that infants and toddlers in group care may be more aggressive, less compliant, and have more behavior problems during their preschool years. Others (Clarke-Stewart, 1988; Field et al., 1988) suggest that infants who have been in day care may display more self-confidence and sociability than children reared at home, and that, if the center provides quality care, there is little reason to be concerned.

Concerns for Intellectual and Language Development

Thirty years ago, few people even considered the importance of intellectual development in the early years. Understanding and learning were thought to begin when children entered school. This approach changed in the 1960s with the realization that the early years of life are crucial in establishing the foundations of learning and that young children need a stimulating environment (Hunt, 1961). The notion that early learning experience is essential has been carried to such an extreme that some parents subject babies in the womb to lessons in music and speech, and newborns are shown flashcards to teach them to read! The pressure to succeed in school is so prevalent that the concern for group care to provide infants with experiences that promote their intellectual development is a serious one.

Intellectual development, like other areas of development, has been the subject of ongoing research. Generally speaking, day care has been given a "clean bill of health" regarding the intellectual development of children. Clarke-Stewart (1988) cites evidence

The early years of life are crucial in establishing the foundations of intellectual development.

that suggests that infants in day care score higher on intelligence tests than home-reared children, but suggests that the difference between home-reared and day-care children is not significant in the long run. Grusec and Lytton (1988:453) have summed up the evidence by saying that "it seems that most ordinary day care centers provide a sufficiently stimulating intellectual diet to ensure adequate (intellectual) development of their charges. The enrichment programs ... seem to advance the intellectual ability of disadvantaged children." However, poor-quality programs that have little to offer children in the way of enrichment have been shown to be detrimental to the intellectual development of children (McCartney et al., 1982; Schwarz, 1983). High-quality care can be a suitable environment for infants and toddlers to grow and learn.

Can a group-care setting ensure the healthy development of infants and toddlers? We do not have definitive answers. Given the concerns about day care, the simplest solution might be to decide that babies should stay at home. But, as one researcher has stated, "Whether infants and toddlers belong in child care at all is no longer an issue" (Howes, 1987). They *are* in child care.

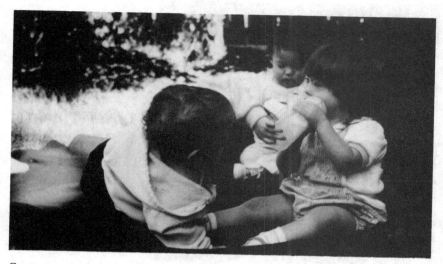

Some researchers suggest that infants may gain self-confidence and sociability in day care.

A look at Canadian demographic trends supports the view that child care is and will be needed as a support service for families. The divorce rate has increased more than 600 percent in the last twenty-five years; the number of single-parent families is increasing sharply; one in three children has a mother in the work force; one out of every five children lives in poverty (Doxey, 1990). Therefore, even those experts who have expressed concerns about day care have agreed that it is an issue that cannot be ignored. And, although researchers differ on the interpretations of some of the findings, they agree on one major point: if babies and toddlers are to be in day care, their well-being is ensured only if the centers provide high-quality care. Unfortunately, we know that many infants and toddlers spend their days in centers that provide substandard care that is detrimental to their development (Whitebook et al., 1990; Children's Defence Fund, 1989). The fears regarding poor-quality care are valid indeed. While researchers must continue to learn more in extended studies about how day care affects children and families, we have an urgent responsibility to learn what constitutes quality care and how we can best provide it.

PRACTICAL APPLICATION

1. Prepare a short talk to a group of new parents who ask for advice on whether or not their infant or toddler should be in day care.

2. What are some of the unanswered questions that you would like day-care researchers to address? Write a letter to a group of day-care researchers stating what questions they should be addressing, and why these questions are important.

3. Find two or three newspaper or magazine articles about day care. What view of day care is presented in these articles? Do you agree with this view? Why or why not?

Should Infants and Toddlers with Special Needs Be in Integrated Group Care?

Objectives

❖ To discuss the appropriateness of integrated group care for infants and toddlers with special needs.

❖ To address the myths and fears surrounding the integration of children with special needs in day care.

❖ To discuss the conditions in which successful integration of infants and toddlers can occur.

Opening Thoughts

How do you think that attitudes toward people with disabilities have changed within the past decades? How do you think those changes in attitudes apply to very young children?

Comments on Opening Thoughts

❖ While society's attitudes toward people with disabilities are changing, many myths and fears prevail.

❖ The appropriateness of integrated group care for infants and toddlers with special needs is a topic that has received attention only recently.

❖ Many factors influence the successful integration of special-needs children into group programs. ❐

Defining Special Needs

Linda is being carried by her mother with Elaine, her older sister, following. Debbie, the caregiver, looks up, smiles, and says, "Good morning." "You'd better be on guard this morning," says Linda's mother. "She hasn't had a bowel movement yet, and we are expecting a big one." Both adults chuckle as Debbie extends her arms to Linda. "Let's give you some breakfast."

Debbie places Linda in her highchair, hands her a piece of toast, and says, "There — you can munch on this while I get Sarah ready for breakfast." Linda's mother, seeing that her daughter is happily settled and eating, waves goodbye and leaves for work.

Linda has Down's syndrome. Ten years ago, this scene would never have occurred because a child with special needs would never have been in a group-care setting with non-disabled children. Older children with special needs were educated in separate schools, and babies and toddlers stayed at home or received specialized care in institutions. These arrangements were viewed as necessary since it was believed that disabled or developmentally delayed children needed special services and treatment. Myths and fears have perpetuated the segregation of disabled children and adults in a variety of educational and recreational settings.

Perhaps we should begin this discussion by defining what we mean by "children with special needs." It is a difficult term because, as anyone who works with infants and toddlers knows, they all have needs that are different or special. Some babies are more upset than others when their parents leave and need more attention, others may come to the center with a diaper rash and need very frequent changing, and so forth. However, when a child has special needs that are related to a physical or mental disability, he or she may need more help and support than is normally required. This is the manner in which the term "special needs" has been traditionally used (Canning & Lyon, 1990). Labeling a child as having "special needs" sometimes can set that child apart, and it may be preferable not to use the term. However, the intention of its use in this book is to focus on working with such children so that caregivers will feel more confident. Indeed, we use the label with the goal of helping caregivers to integrate children with special needs.

In the 1960s, as the positive effects of early intervention became well known, early education programs became available for preschool children with special needs. The principles and techniques of early intervention for disadvantaged children were shown to benefit children with disabling conditions. Years of research have verified that early stimulation is important for young children with developmental delays or disabilities. Similarly, lack of remedial programming can lead to the development of other problems (Meisels & Shonkoff, 1990).

While early intervention programs for children with special needs have been demonstrated to be effective, the premise upon which they are based has been questioned. In these programs, children are identified by their condition. The program then focuses on "fixing" the defect or the problem. This primary focus on the deficit can fail to take into account the whole child and the need to foster all aspects of development. Furthermore, this emphasis has led to the belief that children with special needs will not benefit from normal developmental experiences such as play. As a result, play — which is considered essential to the healthy growth and development of "normal" children — has not been considered a beneficial activity in early intervention programs (Canning & Lyon, 1990). The belief that prevailed was that children with disabling conditions are more different from than like their non-disabled peers (Widerstrom, 1986); thus they were thought to require a different early learning environment. This belief has helped to perpetuate segregation.

Integrating Children with Special Needs

As a result of educational initiatives in the United States and Canada, along with increased legal pressure, integration for children with special needs has recently become a hotly debated

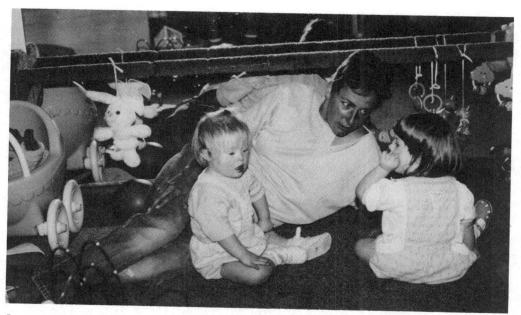

Integration is based on the belief that all disabled people — even disabled children from the youngest age — have the right to be included in all aspects of society.

issue. The pressure to integrate stems from the Principle of Normalization (Wolfensberger, 1972). Essentially, this principle upholds the right of all disabled people to be included in all aspects of society, and this includes children from the very youngest age. While few debate the principle, there are those who are concerned that putting the principle into practice is not as easy as some would wish.

Should infants and toddlers with special needs be in group care with their non-disabled peers? This question is a major concern to parents and professionals. All the issues raised in the previous chapter about the effects of day care on the development of infants and toddlers may be of particular concern for parents of infants and toddlers with special needs. In an attempt to answer the question, we need to look at some of the fears and concerns surrounding the issue of integration.

Concerns about Integration

The fears surrounding integration tend to fall into two major categories. First, there are concerns regarding the ability of group-care settings to meet the requirements of children with special needs. In other words, will these children be taken care of in a manner that will help them reach their potential in all areas of development? Second, since children with special needs require extra attention, there is a concern that the rest of the children will not receive the attention they require. If caregivers need to be involved in lengthier feeding sessions, or if helping a toddler with a disabling condition to get dressed takes longer, will the other children be deprived of the caregiver's precious time? Another associated worry that arises sometimes is how the "normally developing" children will be affected by the presence of a child with special needs.

Although little research has been done on integrated infant and toddler settings, many studies of preschool settings have concluded that children with special needs in high-quality integrated settings make equivalent or more progress than in segregated settings. That is, children with special needs in integrated settings showed as much or more progress in academic skills, speech, and cognitive and motor development than similar children in segregated settings (Appoloni & Cooke, 1978; Bailey & Wolery, 1984; Guralnick, 1976). In addition, studies have demonstrated that progress is also seen in social areas (Guralnick, 1976). Children with special needs in integrated settings developed skills in interacting with others. Finally, the studies carried out showed no ill effects on the normally developing children in the groups. Their development was in no way hampered by the presence of children with special needs, nor did they pick up any maladaptive behaviors (Bricker & Bricker, 1973). The children with special needs in these studies were not the only ones who were positively affected. The attitudes of teachers, caregivers, and parents of other children tended to be positively affected as well. Negative views of children with special needs changed, and children with special needs came to be viewed as more like all the other children (Bricker & Bricker, 1978; Guralnick, 1976, Bailey & Wolery, 1984).

It must be stressed, however, that the majority of research on integration has focused on children with relatively mild disabling conditions. These included mild mental disabilities, visual impairment, or physical disabilities. One cannot jump to the conclusion that children with multiple or severe disabilities would thrive in an integrated setting.

Making Integration Work

It is very difficult to define exactly which children with which disabling conditions would benefit from an integrated setting, as successful integration depends on much more than the specific disability. Some children — for example, those with Down's syndrome — integrate very well. Others may require more specialized care. Decisions to integrate depend on factors relating to the personality and temperament of the child, attitudes of parents and staff, resources available at the center, and so on. However, disabling conditions that would likely be seen in an integrated setting might include Down's syndrome, visual or hearing impairments, or cerebral palsy.

Studies have repeatedly shown that integration works only if support services are available (Bailey & Wolery, 1984; Guralnick, 1976). Children with special needs cannot just be "dumped" into an integrated setting. Professional resources such as psychologists, physiotherapists, speech pathologists, or occupational therapists may be required to ensure that the infant or toddler receives optimum care. These professionals usually provide guidance and assistance to the caregiver in addition to working with the child and family.

Successful integration depends as well on the knowledge and attitudes of the caregivers. One parent related an incident where her developmentally delayed non-verbal daughter was left in substitute care. When the mother left, the little girl started to scream, and continued until she returned. The caregiver panicked and could not determine what the child wanted. Upon her return, the mother asked if the child had been given her bottle. Although a normal response to an infant who is crying would be to offer a bottle, it did not occur to the caregiver to consider this response. Because the child was disabled, the caregiver responded to her differently than to a normal child. Parents may well be

Children with special needs are not the only ones to benefit from integrated settings. Other children are positively affected too.

concerned that their child with special needs will not be understood by the caregivers.

While research has indicated, as we have seen, that integration does not have a negative effect on the normally developing children in the group, the needs of all the children must be considered. Realistically, infants and toddlers with severe disabilities such as total blindness or physical immobility require intensive care. This may deprive the other infants and toddlers of the attention they require unless extra staff is continuously available.

It is clear that there is no simple answer to the question, Should infants and toddlers with special needs be in group care settings? Yet infants and toddlers with special needs are increasingly going to be in group care. First, more and more of their mothers are joining the work force, like the mothers of their non-disabled peers. Second, and extremely important, many disabling conditions in children are not identified during infancy and toddlerhood. Thus, infants and toddlers with disabilities such as minor developmental delays, visual or hearing impairment, or

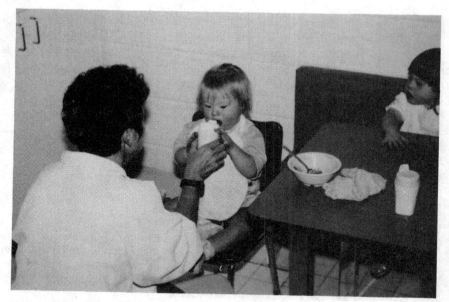

Young children with special needs will, like all children, benefit from group care, providing it is of high quality.

language delays may well be in group care before anyone recognizes that they have special needs. The role of the caregiver in early detection of special needs is of paramount importance. Our task, then, is to consider not whether, but how, the special needs these of infants and toddlers can be met in group care.

Since the attitudes of caregivers are often the most crucial factor in making integration work, one of the purposes of the following chapters is to dispel some of the myths and fears that surround disabling conditions. We also hope to demonstrate that children with special needs are more like their peers than they are different. It is our aim to help caregivers feel comfortable in interactions with special-needs children by providing practical tips and supplementary resources. It is beyond the scope of this book to provide guidelines for working with infants and toddlers who require highly specialized care, as these children would be less likely to be integrated, and would be more likely to benefit from an early intervention program.

The infants and toddlers with special needs who are referred to in this book will — like all children — benefit from group care, providing that it is of high quality, and providing that attention and concern for the individual needs of all children is the top priority. The following chapter discusses the concept of quality care.

PRACTICAL APPLICATION

1. Observe an infant or toddler with a disabling condition in a group-care setting. Then observe a non-disabled child. In what ways are the children similar?

2. What information do you think it is necessary to have before deciding on whether the needs of an infant with special needs could be met in a particular group setting?

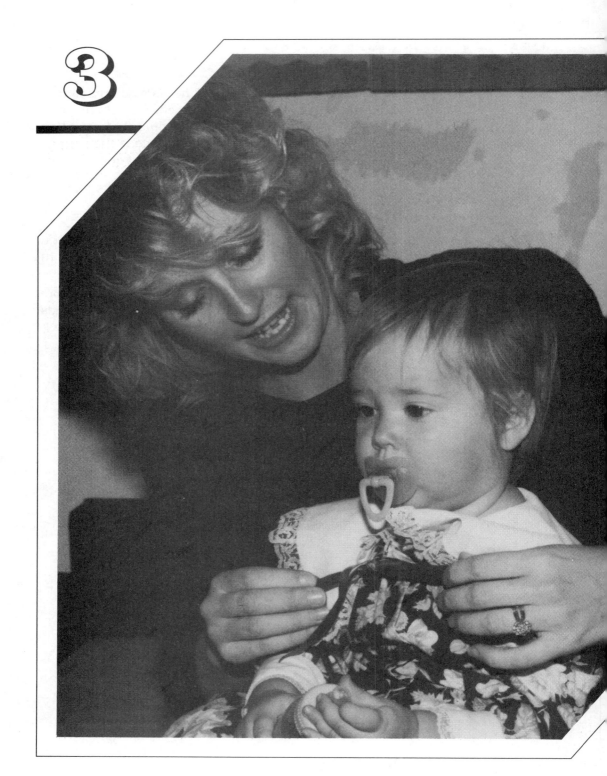

Defining Quality Care

Objectives
- To describe the essential components of quality care.
- To discuss the factors that facilitate the implementation of quality care.

Opening Thoughts
What are some of the different ways you use the term "quality"? What is a quality experience, a quality of life, a quality relationship, or a quality product? How do your ideas about quality relate to the quality of care in a group setting for infants and toddlers?

Comments on Opening Thoughts
- It is difficult for people to agree on what is meant by the term "quality."
- Different views of quality may arise from different value orientations and from religious or cultural backgrounds or preferences.
- In spite of these different views, it is necessary to have a clear understanding of the essential components of quality care for infants and toddlers. ❐

What is Quality Care?

The word "quality" raises many associations. But however defined, it carries with it the message of something that is good — something better than average, or even excellent. While we all want quality care for all children, at all ages, we know that very young children, under two years of age, *must* be in high-quality programs that are designed to meet their special needs.

The standards or criteria for what constitutes quality group care for infants and young toddlers have been determined by a combination of what we call professional judgment and research data.

When the early models of day care were planned in the 1960s and 1970s, program developers had few examples to learn from and had to design their programs based on the best knowledge available. We are in debt to these early programs for many of the standards and principles of practice that we now accept. Today, we continue to rely upon professional judgment in our decisions about quality care. However, during the past twenty years, a growing body of research has helped us to confirm some of these professional opinions. Research has helped us to see the relationships among the characteristics of a center, the group, the caregiver, and child outcomes (the way children behave and how they develop while in day care).

Experts in early childhood have made great strides in determining the components of quality care (Lero & Kyle, 1985; National Academy of Early Childhood Programs, 1984; National Center for Clinical Infant Programs, 1988). The definition of quality care is not static; it will change and adapt as new knowledge becomes available and should adapt to "ongoing societal changes" (Canadian Child Day Care Federation, 1990). However, we now can say that there is general consensus among experts on the subject. We can also say that it has been convincingly demonstrated by research that the development of young children is affected by the quality of the care they receive. Children who attend high-quality centers develop more optimally than those in medium- or low-quality centers. The National Academy of Early Childhood Programs defines a quality early childhood program as:

... one which meets the needs of and promotes the physical, social, emotional and cognitive development of children and adults — parents, staff and administrators — who are involved in the program.

Each day of a child's life is viewed as leading toward the growth and development of a healthy, intelligent and contributing member of society (NAECP, 1984: 7).

The components of a quality program that are proposed by the Canadian Child Day Care Federation (1990) are:

❑ health and nutrition;

❑ safety;

❑ child development and the learning environment;

❑ interactions and relationships;

❑ group size and ratios;

❑ coordination of home and programs; and

❑ management of child care services.

These components can be divided into two categories. One category includes things that should be happening. Under "interactions and relationships," for example, it is stated that "the interactions among all persons in a child care setting reflect mutual respect, trust, and cooperation." The second category includes "things that help make these things happen." Management of child-care services, for example, includes staff training, group size, and child-staff ratio. In other words, interactions that reflect mutual respect are more likely to occur when "the things that help it happen," such as appropriate staff-child ratio, group size, and staff training, are in effect.

The National Center for Clinical Infant Programs focuses on and reinforces the importance of these components, with special emphasis on the role of the caregiver and his or her interactions with the child. "It is important that infants and toddlers be able to know and trust the familiar, consistent adult who takes care of them..." (NCCIP, 1988: 9). This suggests the need for a loving caregiver who understands child development, is flexible, respectful of individual differences, and committed to the individual care of each child. In addition, the caregiver must be able to work cooperatively with parents, guard the health and safety of

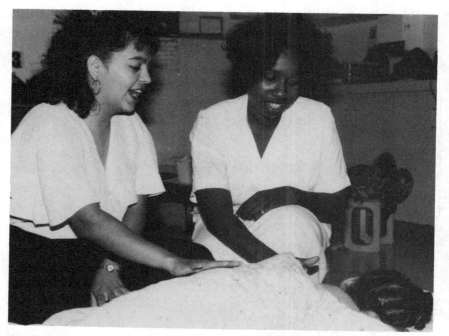

Staff training is a crucial element in the provision of quality care.

each child, and provide developmentally appropriate opportunities that encourage exploration and learning.

The caregiver's role is so central that, not surprisingly, it is often said that the quality of a program can be no better than the quality of caregivers. But caregivers, as dedicated and as competent as they may be, need to be backed by people, policies, and conditions that help them do their job (Whitebook, 1990; Phillips, 1987).

Below is a brief overview of some of the conditions that help the caregiver make quality care happen.

Center Size

In quality child care, smaller is usually better (Caldwell, 1982; Roupp et al., 1979). The larger the center, the more effort seems to be expended in organizational matters, and staff seem to interact more with each other and less with the children.

Group Size

Large groups of children result in a lower quality of care, even when the child-staff ratio is low. Again, it seems that when more adults are in the same room, they tend to talk to each other more and interact with the babies less. The Canadian Child Day Care Federation recommends a maximum of six infants (up to the age of one year) and eight toddlers to a room.

Child-Staff Ratio

Ratio seems to be a key determinant of quality care. When any caregiver has more than three infants to care for, the likelihood of meeting each child's needs for focused attention, cuddling, holding, and conversation decreases. Lower ratios (fewer children per staff member) are often related to more positive interactions between the children and the caregivers (Honig, 1985).

Staff Training

Staff in infant and toddler centers who have training specifically in child development and early childhood education tend to engage more in the kinds of interactions that promote language and intellectual and social development (Whitebook et al., 1990).

Staff Turnover

High staff turnover is linked to lower quality care (Whitebook et al., 1990). Not surprisingly, staff who receive higher wages tend to remain at the same center for longer periods.

If the conditions recommended above are met, they will help to promote the healthy development of children. While this has been substantiated by research, common sense will tell us that children get more individual attention when there are three in a group than when there are five, and that staff who are hoping to leave a center because the salary is too low cannot provide babies and toddlers with secure, consistent care or develop relationships of trust with the children and their parents.

Usually, however, caregivers and parents have little control over decisions regarding group size, staff ratio, or hiring policies.

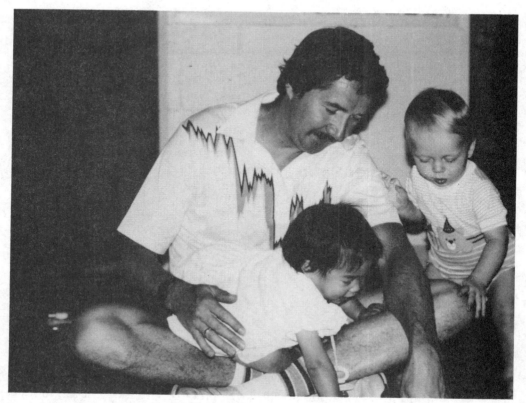

Low child -staff ratios are key to quality care.

In Canada, provincial and territorial governments are responsible for the regulation of child-care programs and have jurisdiction over child-care standards (Yeates et al., 1990). Regulations vary from province to province. For example, the child-staff ratio for children up to twenty-four months of age ranges from 7:1 in New Brunswick to 3:1 in British Columbia. Governments have regulatory power to establish and apply standards and to use sanctions against programs that fail to meet standards. Such power could, theoretically, ensure a high quality of care. This is not, however, the case. In fact, the regulatory system in many of the provinces provides only a minimal standard (Yeates et al., 1990).

The responsibility of ensuring high-quality care is so great, and the need to ensure quality care so vital, that it cannot be left to individual caregivers or centers or governments. The Canadian Child Day Care Federation states that quality child care occurs "when there is a shared partnership between parents, service providers, training institutions, provincial territorial associations, and governments, who together carry out supplementary responsibilities related to the children's care" (CCDCF, 1990: 17). The financial, professional, and moral support of society at large is necessary in order for quality care to occur. With this backing, caregivers will be able to live up to their responsibility to learn how to provide rich and nurturing daily experiences in the child-care setting, and to work cooperatively with parents to ensure the quality care that all children deserve.

PRACTICAL APPLICATION

1. Ask two different parents of infants or toddlers in group care to list five qualities that they looked for when choosing a day-care center. How do those qualities compare with the characteristics of quality care that have been described in this chapter?

2. The components of quality care can be divided into "things that should be happening" and "things that help make those things happen." Look at the components of quality care listed on page 25. Which components would fall into each category, and why?

4

Philosophy and Goals of a Quality Program

Objectives

❖ To describe what is meant by program philosophy and goals.

❖ To describe the relationship among beliefs, knowledge, and values in philosophy and goals.

❖ To review briefly some of the concepts of development basic to infant and toddler programs.

Opening Thoughts

Think about the very general ideas you hold about children. Now complete the following phrases:

I believe that children are _____ .

I believe that children should _____ .

I believe that children need _____ .

Think about your response to these questions and then try to determine where your beliefs or ideas stem from.

Comments on Opening Thoughts

❖ People have very different ideas about what children are like.

❖ Our beliefs about children and what they should or will become are derived from many sources.

❖ Professionals working with infants and toddlers need to be aware of their beliefs about children, both personal beliefs and those derived from knowledge of child development. ❐

Philosophy and Goals

Johnny, who is fifteen months old, takes a large red crayon from the table, waddles over to the door of his room at the center, and draws a bright red "picture" on the door. Jennifer, his primary caregiver, approaches Johnny and in a calm but firm voice says, "Johnny, I see that you want to draw a big picture. We don't draw on the doors. Come with me and I'll give you a large paper." Jennifer takes Johnny's hand and guides him to a low table. "Here, Johnny. You can draw another picture on this paper." Jennifer points to the paper to direct Johnny's attention.

Mary, a beginning student, watches Jennifer and Johnny, and then says to Jennifer, with great surprise in her voice, "Why did you do that? He did that on the door on purpose. Why didn't you show him that you were angry and take the crayon away from him? He'll do it again and he won't learn."

Jennifer and Mary have very different views of what Johnny was doing and how to react to his behavior. Jennifer sees Johnny as a young toddler experimenting with a new skill who does not yet understand that the norms of his society do not accept drawing on doors. Jennifer believes that the way to change Johnny's behavior is to acknowledge his new skill and firmly but positively direct him to an acceptable place to draw. Mary, on the other hand, regards Johnny's behavior as intentionally bad. She believes that the best way to correct the behavior is to show anger and "teach" him by taking away the crayon.

In this example Jennifer shows an understanding of the developmental capabilities of a fifteen-month-old and his need for positive guidance. Mary acts more upon conventional notions.

The education and socialization of very young children is not a modern phenomenon, but something that has gone on for centuries in all societies, in all cultures, in all types of families. Adults have always had conceptions of what children are like, what kinds of adults they want them to become, and how they should be directed in order to become that way. These conceptions have always been influenced by the traditional, religious, and cultural values dominant in a particular society, at a particular time in history. We are all familiar with sayings that reflect "educational" points of view. "Spare the rod and spoil the child," "Children should be seen and not heard." Attitudes have passed from parent to child, from generation to generation.

Our own views of what children are like, what we want them to become, and how we believe they should be treated are also strongly influenced by our own life experiences. We began to learn our attitudes and beliefs very early in life. We learned from the way we were treated and the way we responded in our own families, in our schools, and with our friends. We were influenced by our religion, by the people in our neighborhood, by the radio, television, and newspapers that we read. Some of us had experience with children — we cared for them, played with them, and observed them.

Today, however, we have an advantage over previous generations. In addition to our own personal experiences, we have access to a large body of empirical (based on experiment and observation) and theoretical knowledge that has been gathered over the past fifty years by clinical and research methods. This information helps us understand what children are like; how they grow, develop, and learn; and what factors influence the rate and direction of their development. We do not have to rely only on our own subjective experiences and feelings to understand, educate, and socialize children.

All professionals who work with and are concerned about infants and toddlers agree that our goals for them should be based in large measure upon what we have objectively and systematically learned by studying children. This knowledge should be applied in the ways we organize children's experiences and relate to them in quality care. This attitude has been termed the developmental approach to educational practices.

The objective of every person who works with infants and toddlers in a quality child-care center is to acquire as much knowledge as possible about child development. This knowledge grows through professional education and experience, and then becomes part of our values and beliefs.

No matter how much knowledge we gain, however, our behavior will still be influenced by the values and beliefs we have absorbed since we were children. This is because knowledge and

beliefs are interrelated. The way we interpret knowledge is affected by our beliefs and what we believe can be altered and modified
by the knowledge we gain. The combination of professional
knowledge and personal values forms the basis of an educational
philosophy.

Since each of us has had a different life experience, no two
caregivers can come to a child-care center with identical educational philosophies. This is natural — and individual differences
between adults must be respected just as we must respect differences in children. Nevertheless, quality programs are not built
upon the personal goals and philosophies of individual caregivers. The development of a program for infants and toddlers
requires communication, discussion, and agreement among staff
members. While minor differences among staff members are
healthy, people with very different sets of goals and philosophies
cannot develop sound programs for children. Vulnerable babies

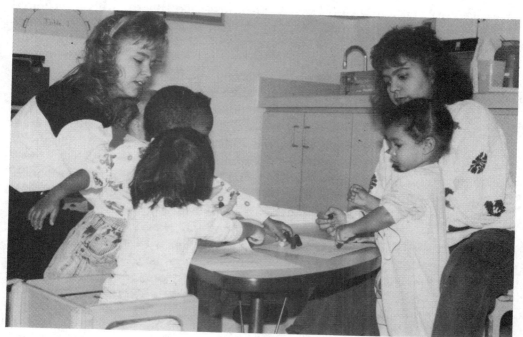

The development of a quality program requires agreement among staff members about goals and philosophy.

must learn to deal with the differences between home and the center. It is not fair to ask them to learn to adjust to staff members who have very different expectations and different approaches. Clarification of goals and philosophy is an essential step in the development of a program. It should also be an interesting and creative staff experience (Feeney et al., 1991; Center for Child and Family Studies, 1988).

One of the ways to ensure that staff can build a solid program with well-formulated goals and philosophy is to provide caregivers with a common knowledge base and with guidance in translating goals and knowledge into everyday practice. Much of this book attempts to do just that. Before we proceed, however, we must discuss the importance of goals and review some developmental concepts that we should keep in mind as we read through the remaining chapters.

The Goals for Children

If we are going on a trip, we cannot decide which road to take if we are not sure of our destination. The goals of a program tell us where we are going. They tell us what the program is going to attempt to achieve through the experiences it offers the children while they are at the center (Langenbach & Neskora, 1977). Goals state what we want the children to become and what we want them to learn.

A quality program is not static. It must change as children grow and develop. If we know where we are going, if our goals are clear, we can change and adapt the social and physical environment without losing sight of what we want to achieve. Goals are like signposts that give direction to our decisions (Dittmann, 1973).

As mentioned in the previous chapter, the primary goal of all quality centers is to support and facilitate the healthy development of each individual child. Quality programs share a holistic ("whole view") of the child, and are committed to formulating goals that relate to the child's physical, emotional, social, cognitive, and language development. A quality program cannot focus only on emotional development and neglect physical development, or only on physical development and neglect the child's language development. Program developers formulate goals for each area of development, and then plan social and physical environments that offer experiences which can help the children reach the goals.

The goals of a program are drawn, as we have suggested, from two main sources. The first is the program developers' knowledge of child development. This knowledge has come from psychologists, sociologists, anthropologists, and others who study children, their families, and their communities. It provides an understanding of children's needs and allows us to define developmentally appropriate goals.

The second main source for definition of goals are the personal, social, and cultural values of the program developers. These goals describe the kind of child and, in the long run, the kind of adult that the program will try to develop.

Evans (1971) has suggested that most lists of goals are a mixture of philosophical, social, and psychological thought. Let us examine some of the goals suggested by Huntington, Provence, and Parker (1973) for children from birth to three. On this list we find familiar goals that one might expect in most developmentally appropriate programs, for example:

❑ gain increasing control of body systems
❑ increasing awareness of self as a separate identity
❑ a sense of effectiveness and competence.

However, in addition to these goals, we also find:

❑ hope and faith and a belief that the world is, by and large, a good place
❑ the ability to trust others and be trustworthy; to develop a sense of responsibility
❑ the ability to be flexible and open to new ideas, new feelings, new people (Huntington, Provence, & Parker, 1973: 16).

Clearly, this set of goals combines both developmental understanding and social values. The goals reflect the thinking of early childhood specialists living in a democratic society in the twentieth century. This list of goals would not have been presented a century ago, or in goal statements in other societies, or even in

Both independence and the capacity to trust are important developmental goals.

the goal statements of some early childhood programs today. In other programs we might find an emphasis on equality of sexes, or group consciousness, or religious and cultural customs. It is very important that we recognize that goals are reflections of our cultural and social attitudes.

Because goals reflect values as well as knowledge, it is imperative that both parents and caregivers be involved in the formulation of the goals. At least, they should be informed and given the opportunity to discuss the goals of a program. If parents or caregivers do not agree with program goals, the children will find themselves being socialized in two very different worlds. For some children, this may be confusing and may cause stress.

Willis and Ricciuti (1975) had parents in mind when they suggested developmental goals for their program. The following list provides us with a good example of goals that relate to all areas of development and are appropriate to children under the age of two.

The qualities most parents would like to see nurtured in their young child are the same whether the infant spends most of the time at home or in a day care setting. The following list is not intended to provide a detailed description of the "super-toddler," but outlines some important characteristics of the one-and-a-half to two-year-old child that are influenced by early experiences:

1. A sense of belonging to the family, primary attachments to parents and other family members.

2. The capacity to trust people, to feel secure when away from home and with people other than family members. Security implies that the child trusts that his or her parents will return after departures, and trusts the person in whose care he or she has been placed by the parents.

3. Enjoyment of people, both adults and other children; sensitivity to others and the capacity to interact effectively.

4. A curiosity about the world; the ability to take pleasure in learning and exploring; self-confidence that leads to persistence in overcoming obstacles.

5. Autonomy and independence, the ability to think and act with pleasure by oneself.

6. A sense of oneself as an important person who is cared about, who is able to direct his or her own behavior to some extent (for example, in coping with distress or initiating appropriate social behavior), and who has an effect on the social and physical world (mastery).

7. The ability to comprehend language and events, to begin to be able to express oneself in a way that can be understood; the capacity to solve simple problems.

8. An appropriate level of competence in the areas of locomotion and motor coordination (Willis & Ricciuti, 1975: 2-3).

Note that this list of goals is phrased in general, psychological terms that are appropriate for a group of children rather than an individual child. They are also long-range goals (Schwartz & Robison, 1982), and it is clear that many babies and toddlers will only begin to reach, but cannot fully achieve, these goals during their first two years.

Use of Objectives

Some program developers (Langenbach & Neskora, 1977; Caldwell & Rorex, 1977) feel that general, long-range goals are basic to program development, but are too abstract and not appropriate to the needs of the individual child. Concepts such as positive self-image or curiosity are open to interpretation and can be used differently by each caregiver or parent. These program developers suggest that it is important to define what we mean when we use abstract goals by breaking them down into smaller, clearer agreed-upon behaviors, called objectives. For example, if our goal is to help children become independent, our objectives might be: can remove socks, can put hand into sleeve, can use spoon, etc. Objectives are the small steps that the child makes on the road to achieving the long-range goals of the program (Schwartz & Robison, 1982).

The use of behavioral objectives allows the caregiver to think and plan for each individual child, according to his or her particular needs, level, and rate of development. However, in order to use objectives wisely, the caregiver must have a very good understanding of developmental sequences and know the child very well. The child should lead us; if we observe, the child will tell us where he or she can go next. Objectives for each child can and should be determined with the child's family. Great caution must be taken not to use objectives like test items or something that children will be artificially pushed toward. Doing so could only create tension for parents, caregivers, and children. Objectives, like goals, are tools to help guide caregivers as they plan for and relate to the child. Used in any other way they can be a danger.

While goals and objectives form an essential part of a program's foundation, "they do not tell caregivers what to do or not to do.... Implementation of goals requires a thorough knowledge of infant development and an open mind about the best way to achieve these ends" (Dittmann, 1984: 2–3).

Guiding Concepts of Development

We have suggested that knowledge about how infants and toddlers develop should serve as the basis of our educational philosophy and our principles of practice. We are indeed fortunate to have today a large body of knowledge that can guide us. Much of this knowledge has been organized into theories that describe, explain, and predict patterns of behavior (Bee, 1989; Kaplan, 1991).

It would be impossible to summarize all of this knowledge. Our aim here is to point to a few principles of development that are particularly important to the creation of a quality child-care program.

The Influence of Nature vs. Nurture, or Heredity vs. Environment

For generations philosophers and psychologists have argued over what is the most important influence in a child's development. Do the child's inborn, inherited characteristics have the greatest effect on his or her development, or are the child's experiences with people, things, and events more influential? Today, this question is still a research issue, but most psychologists and educators agree that both heredity and environment are important. It is the way that the child's genetic make-up interacts with the environment that will affect his or her development.

Maturation

Healthy children are born with powerful inner forces for growth and development. These inner forces are programmed in such a way that we can identify ages and stages that are common to most children. We are able to determine norms of development — that is, age ranges when we are likely to see the appearance of new abilities in all areas of development. These abilities can and should emerge naturally. They should not be artificially stimulated or pushed, but do require an environment that is supportive and encouraging. Knowledge of normative development is very important to educators as it helps us to know what to expect and how to plan a physical and social environment that is appropriate to the needs of the children in our groups.

Individual Differences

There are very large differences among babies in their biological make-up and rate of maturation from the moment of birth (and even before). While differences in rates of growth, walking, and talking have been recognized for many years, we now know that there are also differences in the way individual babies use their senses and their bodies and in the way they learn. One of the most important areas of difference is the temperamental or personality pattern of each child. Some infants are more active, others more passive; some more sensitive, others more resilient; some are persistent, others give up easily. There is evidence that these are inborn tendencies that, as all differences, must be recognized and respected. All parents and caregivers must develop observation skills that enable them to identify the specialness of each child.

The "Whole" Child

For research and descriptive purposes, different aspects of the child's development are usually described separately. For example, we speak of motor development, language development, social development, and so on. Infants and toddlers are whole children, and are not made up of segments. Their experiences affect all aspects of their development. The baby who is banging on a drum is having a sensory experience, learning to coordinate eye-hand movements, and learning that he or she can produce a sound. While it may be practical to identify different areas of development, we must make sure that we put the child back together again and see him or her as a whole person!

Development is Uneven

Not all areas of a child's development progress at the same pace. Some infants may acquire motor skills at a very early age, and begin to speak later than other children. Others may be able to feed themselves earlier than most, but may be more hesitant than others in social interactions. This sort of variation is normal, and should be respected. The pattern of variation occurs with all children, including those with special needs.

The Environment Affects the Child

The child's hereditary tendencies — for example, temperament and a unique, individual "program" for development — need to be fostered in a supportive and nurturing environment. The way children feel about themselves, the way they relate to people, and the way they learn to communicate and speak will depend on the environment in which they grow up. The love, respect, and security provided by the family is the most important environmental influence in the life of very young children. In addition, however, young children need an interesting and developmentally challenging physical environment in which to explore and play, and an adult who encourages, supports, and interprets their experiences for them.

The Child Affects the Environment

From an infant's first days, he or she has an effect upon the people in the environment, just as the people in the environment affect the child. The sex of the infant, the way the infant moves, smiles, or cries elicits different responses from the parent or caregiver. Babies are sensitive and can pick up the pleasure or displeasure they cause others. Adults must be aware of their feelings toward, and the way in which they respond to each and every child.

The Ecological Approach

There has been a general recognition of the prime importance of the family, especially the mother, in the infant or toddler's life. Today, children grow up in two-parent families, single-mother or single-father families, blended families, and families with a wide variety of life-styles, religions, and cultures. Though we do not yet fully understand the impact of differences in family structures on children, we must be aware of them and take them into account in learning about children's development. All families' lives are affected by the neighborhood in which they live, the workplace of the parents, and the nature and scope of available support services (such as day-care centers, schools, and health and recreation facilities). These aspects of family life are affected, in turn, by the social policies and ideologies prevalent in our society. An ecological approach recognizes that all these (and many more) interrelated factors ultimately affect the way in which each child develops.

In summary, this chapter has described a framework for establishing the philosophy and goals for a quality program. The program philosophy and goals provide the foundation and "signposts" that help keep us on track. Now that the foundation has been laid, we turn to specific issues that will guide us in implementing a quality program for infants and toddlers.

PRACTICAL APPLICATION

1. Collect and review the written philosophy statements of three infant and toddler programs.

   a) What similarities and differences can be found?

   b) How can these similarities and differences be accounted for?

2. Ask three parents what they want most for their infant or toddler in group care and what they think is important that the center provide. Now compare their response to your own opening thoughts about children.

5

Overriding Issues

Objectives

- ❖ To emphasize that each child should be treated as an individual.
- ❖ To discuss the importance of the group to infants and toddlers.
- ❖ To discuss the importance of a primary caregiving system.
- ❖ To address health and safety issues related to infants and toddlers in group care.
- ❖ To address cultural diversity and sensitivity in infant and toddler care.
- ❖ To emphasize the roles of the parent and the caregiver.
- ❖ To discuss the physical setting and its impact on infants and toddlers.
- ❖ To discuss the importance of time scheduling.

Opening Thoughts

Review the objectives above. Try to put yourself in the place of

- a) a child,
- b) a caregiver, and
- c) a parent.

What would your three most important objectives be in each case? Do priorities differ in each case? If so, why?

Comments on Opening Thoughts

- ❖ The important issues in quality care are interconnected. For example, cultural sensitivity will help to establish good relations with parents, and a primary caregiving system helps to maximize the health, safety, and individualized care of all children. ❑

This chapter will provide an overview of the essential considerations in a quality program for infants and toddlers. These concerns are so basic and important that they are reviewed here, and then referred to throughout the remainder of the book.

Individualized Care is Essential

This book is based on the belief that group care must provide individualized care. The central concern for caregivers must be to meet the individual needs of each and every child. Getting to know each child very well — through close observation, through trying different approaches and learning from the responses, and through spending time caring for and playing with each child — helps the caregiver develop a personal relationship with each one. Knowing what the child likes or dislikes and being familiar with the child's interests and routines is the basic information needed to suit the program to the baby, rather than the baby to the program.

The first step in individualizing care is getting to know the infants and toddlers. And understanding the differences among children is not enough. We have to use that understanding to guide what happens during the day. Will the baby who is having difficulty separating from his mother have a bit more of the caregivers' attention? Will the toddler who loves to play with water be rushed on to another activity, or allowed to pursue her interest? Will the toddler who knows no fear have a caregiver right beside her as she approaches the slide, and the one who needs encouragement receive it? And will every effort be made to ensure that each and every child has some "quality time" with the caregiver each and every day?

As adults, we tend to think of the need to be "fair" in terms of dividing things up equally, including the amount of attention each child receives. Often we hear caregivers express the concern that, if they let one child have something special or have extra time with the caregivers, this will not be fair to the other children. Infants and toddlers do not see the world that way. They need to have their own needs met, but they do not compare what they receive with other children. One very active toddler may need more time to play outside, while another may need more time on the caregiver's lap. Being fair to infants and toddlers means assessing what each child needs, and responding accordingly, rather than trying to distribute toys, time, and attention equally.

A Primary Caregiving System is Important

Infants and toddlers are very dependent on adults to ensure that their desires and needs are met. Meeting these needs, as we have discussed, requires caregivers who know the children on a very individualized and personalized level. This is the main reason why many experts in infant and toddler care (Weiser, 1991; Honig, 1985) recommend a primary caregiving system for this age group. In a primary caregiving system, each caregiver is assigned responsibility for a small group of two to three infants or three to four toddlers (the exact ratios will be determined by local regulations). The exact nature of the primary caregiver's responsibilities can vary, but they usually include getting to know each child in the small group very well and developing a special relationship; planning experiences that will be beneficial to the child; attending to routine care; being available to comfort the child; monitoring and evaluating progress and keeping records for the children in the group; and communicating with the parents (Weiser, 1991).

In any group situation all caregivers must observe and be sensitive to all children in the group. However, to develop that special relationship and to get to know the children very well, it helps to have responsibility for a limited number of infants and toddlers. Simple arithmetic dictates that it is easier to form a special relationship with three babies than with six. It is also less emotionally demanding on the caregiver.

Some day-care staff have expressed the concern that a primary caregiving system results in the baby becoming too attached to the caregiver. When the caregiver leaves temporarily (due to illness, for example) the baby suffers from separation and can be very distressed. Even when the caregiver is not absent, there will be times — shift changes and breaks, for example —

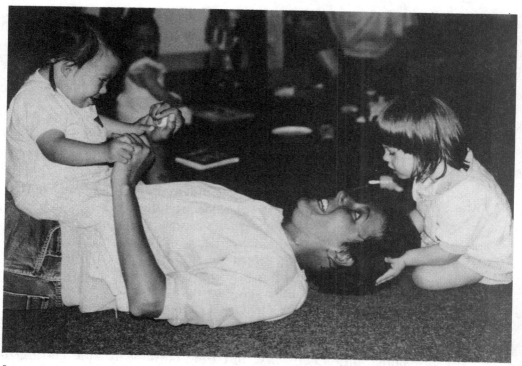

In a primary caregiving system, one caregiver is responsible for just a few children for whom she is special.

when another caregiver will fill in. There are children who respond with tears whenever their caregiver leaves the room, even for a coffee break.

There are no simple solutions for these problems. They can be minimized by gradual transitions between caregivers. The primary caregiver can be present while the baby warms to the replacement. Usually, in the course of time, the infants and toddlers become comfortable enough with all the caregivers to feel secure in the absence of their special one. Once the special attachment has been made to one caregiver, a transition to another caregiver should be made very gradually. Anyone who has worked with toddlers will tell you that many children assign themselves to primary caregivers, regardless of the decisions that adults make. Some infants are simply drawn to particular adults, and feel more comfortable with them. Decisions about which children should be with which caregiver can be altered sometimes if the change will result in a better match.

The Group Is Important

Even in a center that focuses on individualized care and a primary caregiver system, the fact remains that the child spends many hours with a group of children. The impact of group living on each individual child cannot be ignored. In addition to separation from family and familiar surroundings, the child in a group must adjust to the movement, smells, sounds, and competing needs of other children.

At one time it was thought that very little babies were not aware of all the things that were happening around them. While we do not know as yet what infants perceive and feel in a group situation, we do know that they do have the capabilities to be aware of things happening in their world. For some babies, the stimuli can be interesting; for others they can be a source of confusion and distress.

Older infants and toddlers certainly are not only aware, but are constantly interacting with, influencing, and being affected by the other children in the group. The group situation, however appropriate, often imposes an artificial sibling rivalry and demands for patience and sharing that are difficult for some children at early stages of development.

Caregivers who are aware of stresses can do a great deal to reduce their impact. Caregivers should be conscious of the way the physical setting is arranged, of the noise level, of the need to supply an abundance of toys and to avoid "herding" too many children together at one time in one place. They should also realize that group living can be a positive experience. Little children watch each other, imitate each other, explore together, romp together, laugh and have fun together. Sensitive caregivers see this aspect of group care and help the children capitalize on these positive experiences.

Older infants and toddlers are constantly interacting with, influencing, and being affected by the other children in the group.

Health and Safety Are Paramount

Protecting the very young from harm is a strong instinctive response. Parents' primary concern for their children is often to ensure that they are safe and healthy. When young children come into group care, we have a responsibility to place priority on health and safety. Infants and toddlers who are sick, who have received inadequate nourishment, or who have been injured, cannot enjoy even the most stimulating and interesting programs. The policy of each center must be to ensure that all required health and safety measures are routinely implemented (Shapiro et al., 1988). Policies should ensure both the creation of a healthy and safe setting and the establishment of routine pre-

ventative practices. Health and safety policies should aim to prevent infectious diseases and injuries, and to ensure that all children receive adequate nutrition.

Prevention of infectious diseases involves rigorous attention
to hygiene (Godwin & Schrag, 1988), the most important aspect of
which is regular handwashing. Good sanitation practices, including regular and frequent cleaning of all materials and toys, will
help limit the spread of germs. Well-ventilated rooms and plenty
of outdoor activities are also essential to good health.

The young child's activity, curiosity, and inability to understand or predict danger make a hazardous mix. Young children
need to be supervised constantly. Many accidents occur because
of a misuse of equipment (Shapiro et al., 1988). In addition,
infants and toddlers are constantly at risk from small objects
that can be swallowed, choked on, or inserted into noses or ears.
Caregivers need to scrutinize constantly all the equipment and
toys to foresee possible accidents. All toys and small objects need
to be looked at as a potential hazard. Strategies such as a primary caregiving system and dividing children into small groups can
make supervision an easier task.

While safety and health matters must always be taken into
account, we do not want sterile, uninteresting surroundings.
Greenman (1988) talks about a risk-free environment being a
boring environment, and that we certainly do not want. Wherever
children play, they risk the normal bruises, bumps, and minor
scrapes that can be minimized with good planning and supervision, but not totally avoided. We must, however, ensure that serious injuries do not occur. Many centers require that staff be
qualified in First Aid and CPR (cardiopulmonary resuscitation).
This requirement is highly recommended.

Good nutrition is essential to the healthy development
of infants and toddlers. Indeed, it is "central to establishing
the foundation for lifelong health" (Network of the
Federal/Provincial/Territorial Group on Nutrition, 1989).
The early years represent a time of changing nutritional
needs as infants begin to eat solids and finger foods and to
make choices about what they eat. Parents and caregivers
share the concern that the child should be provided with a
well-balanced and healthy diet. Excellent nutritional guidelines are available (Network of Federal/Provincial/Territorial Group

on Nutrition, 1989; Shapiro et al., 1988) and the nutrition policy of all centers needs to be carefully developed and followed.

The licensing requirements of all provinces and territories in Canada spell out standards for health, safety and nutrition. In addition, there are excellent resources (listed in the recommended readings) to help staff develop and implement a healthy and safe program for infants and toddlers.

Today we are becoming increasingly aware of the problem of child abuse. A discussion of the health and safety of young children would be incomplete if it ignored this issue.

Caregivers must be able to identify the possible symptoms of physical, emotional, or sexual abuse. Children are protected from abuse by criminal law (Bala et al., 1991) and there are child protection agencies with legal responsibilities to investigate and take appropriate action in every Canadian jurisdiction. These agencies vary from place to place, in name and in approach. Caregivers must be aware of current child welfare laws and resources in their particular area.

The care of young infants and toddlers involves close physical contact, often with private body parts (e.g., during diapering). Policies to ensure that young children are protected are essential. In addition, caregivers need to be protected against false accusations by developing practices that lessen the likelihood of suspicion. For example, diapering should occur in an accessible area where observation of the caregiver is possible.

Caregivers have a legal and moral obligation to protect the abused child (McFadden, 1986). Reporting a suspected case of abuse can be frightening. It may involve confronting a parent or asking very difficult questions. McFadden (1986) suggests that reporting abuse will be a bit easier if caregivers recognize that the family must be urgently helped, and if they realize that most parents who abuse their children *are* helped, rather than punished. In addition, the caregiver should keep in mind the best interests of the child who may not be able to speak for or help himself.

All caregivers working with infants and young toddlers are encouraged to learn about child abuse. Guidelines for recognizing signs of abuse are provided in Appendix A. Readers are also encouraged to refer to the recommended readings and attend training seminars on this topic.

The Environment Is Important

Children and adults are very much affected by the settings in which they live, work, and play. Our moods, behaviors, and relationships with people can be affected positively or negatively by our physical setting. Most adults are aware of this, and are capable of recognizing the need for a change of scenery when tired, stressed, or simply in the mood for something new. We know where we can go to "let off steam" (e.g., a squash court), to enjoy some peace and quiet (e.g., a library, or trail in the mountains), or to practice a new skill we have acquired (e.g., the computer room). Infants and toddlers are dependent upon adults to provide them with the benefits of a physical environment that will enhance the quality of their life and promote all aspects of their development.

The design of the physical environment for infants and toddlers has become an important issue among experts in early childhood (Lally & Stewart, 1990; Greenman, 1988). Although one often sees toddler centers designed very much like preschool centers, the needs of infants and toddlers are very different from those of three- and four-year-old children. Therefore, it is often recommended that the home setting be a model for group care (Greenman, 1988). But many homes are not designed to accommodate group living for children, and modeling centers after homes begs the question, What kind of home do we use as a model and still respect the economic and cultural diversity among families?

The environments of infant and toddler centers should attempt to provide the best of both worlds. The space to play freely and the availability of appropriate equipment that we associate with centers should be combined with the comfort, warmth, and opportunities for privacy that we associate with homes.

The exact plan for the physical setting will vary from center to center, based on the kind of building, the number of children, the budget, and the preferences of staff and parents. However, several principles for planning environments for infants and toddlers should be implemented in all settings.

First, all settings for infants and toddlers need to be safe and to promote good health. Attention must be paid to lighting, heat, ventilation, and elimination of safety hazards such as exposed electric outlets and reachable medicines or cleaning materials. The physical setting needs to be planned with efficiency in mind. For example, changing areas need to have their own sinks that are proper height for staff comfort, and the areas should be located near the bathroom (and away from eating areas).

Environments for younger children need to have an overall softness, with carpeted areas, stuffed animals, and cushions — cuddly things and things to cuddle on. (Note, though, that you should check the licensing requirements. Items such as stuffed animals and pillows have to be safe and washable.) It is very important that the setting have private spaces, where infants and toddlers can curl up alone or with the caregiver, away from the activities of the group. Low dividers, cubbies, and even firm cardboard boxes with a pillow in the bottom are useful for this purpose.

Environments for younger children need to have an overall softness.

It is equally important that the setting be interesting, to promote children's exploration and activity. Moving babies and toddlers require a lot of relatively uncluttered space to roam about in, and clear pathways to get from place to place. They need choices of toys and materials, set up in such a way as to maximize their control and promote feelings of competence — the "I can do it" feeling. This means that, when possible, they should be able to choose and help themselves to toys that they can play with successfully (Olds, 1982).

The design of the physical setting must keep the needs of adults as well as those of children in mind. The setting should say "Welcome parents" in a variety of ways. Decorations representing the cultural diversity of the families and caregivers should be present. A coffee machine and comfortable chairs give clear messages to parents that their presence is desirable. In addition, staff who work with children all day long need a comfortable room to retreat to. The playrooms, as well, should have adult-size furniture for comfort.

Weather permitting, maximizing outdoor time is physically and mentally healthy for adults and children alike. Outdoor areas for infants and toddlers need not be full of equipment. A grassy area for infants and toddlers (with provision for shade) and a hard surface for toddlers can provide hours of freedom and enjoyment. Most of the indoor equipment and toys should be easy to move outdoors. Fenced-off areas, high enough to prevent babies from being "run over" by older children, and low enough for toddlers to peep over, are advised.

Relevant suggestions for toys, equipment, and arrangement of space are provided in the individual chapters that follow. In addition, readers are encouraged to refer to the recommended readings on this topic for additional information.

Time Is Important

We live in a culture in which our daily experiences are, to a large extent, regulated by the clock. Infants and toddlers arrive at the center at a certain time of day and leave at a certain time. The child's experience between the time of arrival and departure will be greatly influenced by the way in which staff members organize the center's schedules.

The daily schedule will affect how much time the children will have to finish their meal or to enjoy the caregiver's company, how much time the caregiver will spend with each child when changing diapers, and when each child will be able to find and pursue a play activity to full satisfaction.

There is often a tendency to organize the schedule of an infant-toddler center according to the custom of the nursery school — a time to eat, to play, to sleep, to go outdoors (Cataldo, 1983). This type of schedule ignores the physiological and psychological needs of babies or young toddlers. Each child has an individual internal rhythm and schedule. As with all areas of development, learning to adjust the individual "clock" to conform to a group schedule requires maturation. Many children cannot do so until well after their first year, closer to the second (and for some, beyond that). Abruptly imposing an artificial schedule on a baby can cause frustration and distress. Each child's rhythm must be respected, and each child should be helped, slowly, to move toward a group schedule.

Evolving a schedule for an infant room is very difficult. Babies and toddlers do need to be fed, changed, and put to bed. Even when ratios are low, individual demands for attention can pull the caregiver in many directions. Caregivers have to use good judgment and prioritize their time and attention. It is wise to remember that infants and toddlers do not read the clock. Some babies need immediate attention, some can tolerate a reasonable waiting time. While regularity in schedules does give a child a sense of security in knowing what is likely to happen next, the predictability that babies really need is familiarity and consistency in the way the caregiver responds to them (Provence et al., 1977).

The schedule for each child must be adapted to take into account that child's schedule at home. For example, if an infant wakes up very early in the morning, he or she may well be ready for a nap immediately upon arrival. In addition, babies' schedules should change as they grow. What was appropriate at eleven months will not be appropriate at fifteen months.

While there are no recipes for evolving a time schedule for a baby and toddler room, certain principles can guide our decisions. We know that babies and toddlers need time to do what they are trying to do, we know that their transitions from activity to activity should not be rushed, we know that they have relatively short attention spans in most activities (not all, though — a toddler can often enjoy playing at the sink for many minutes) (Gonzalez-Mena, 1986). Time schedules should be linked to the developmental capabilities and tasks of the infancy and toddlerhood period.

Parents Are Important

More than with any other age group, in infant and toddler group care, communication and cooperation with the parents is absolutely essential. Parents and caregivers need to share information every single day because what occurs at home affects what occurs in the center, and vice versa. How much the child ate and slept, what he did, and how he felt are the kinds of information that parents and caregivers regularly share. Beyond that, because parents are the primary adults in a child's life, they have a right to know in detail what is occurring at the center, and to have some input as to what is happening with their child. They may have clear ideas about the kind of care they want for their children. Some, for example, may want a warm loving caregiver who provides lots of hugs and cuddles, while others may want the caregiver to focus more on activities. While caregivers certainly are guided by their own professional principles, parents' desires should be taken into consideration. At the very least, parents have a right to know what is occurring at the center, in order to determine if it is the right place for their child.

Group care can do much to support the parents — by providing information, by making sure the center is warm and welcoming, and by inviting (but not insisting upon) participation.

Cultural Diversity and Sensitivity Are Important

Canada is made up of many cultures, each bringing its own variety of customs, beliefs, foods, languages, and religious practices. Culture influences all aspects of development by shaping the child's behavior, interests, and attitudes (Chud & Fahlman, 1985). The cultural background of the children and their families will affect their expectations of the program, the way in which they participate in the program, and the benefits they reap from the program.

Canadian society has a tradition of valuing cultural diversity. Understanding and appreciating cultural differences helps us to clarify where the expectations of parents and of staff may differ, and enables a smoother transition for the child between home and center. Young children's trust and comfort may be upset by significant variations between center and home. Diet, routines, and expectations for children's behavior are areas that are often influenced by culture. It is therefore important to seek information about customs and practices at home and, where possible, to bring some of these into the center. For example, if children are learning a language other than English at home, it might be helpful to ask parents for some key words to help the child make the transition from home to center.

Our attitudes to people who are different from us are often so deeply ingrained that we are not always conscious of them. Therefore, a first step in having a culturally sensitive program is to examine our own attitudes and values. Next, we should aim to learn as much as possible about the cultures of the people with whom we have contact. We have to be cautious, however, that this knowledge is not used to stereotype. Reading about how one particular ethnic group celebrates holidays does not tell us how any particular family celebrates a specific festival. If certain childrearing practices are common in a particular ethnic group, it does not mean that every family in that group rears children in the same way. Indeed, the attitudes of children in all cultures are affected by the key people in their world (Phenice & Hildebrand, 1988), which is why it is so crucial for caregivers to accept differences.

Children, from very early ages, need to know and understand their own heritage as part of the development of self awareness and self esteem (Phenice & Hildebrand, 1988). As they get older they need to learn about the diversity of cultures that make up their world (Chud & Fahlman, 1985). Food, pictures, songs, and books that reflect the different cultures should be available in the center. Even if the infants and toddlers are too young to differentiate between the symbols of their own culture and others, it is important to set the stage for culturally sensitive programs at an early age. Parents, whom we have said need to feel welcome and accepted in the center, will more likely feel comfortable if their culture is represented and respected. Incorporating elements from other cultures not only serves the families well, it enriches and enhances the program and makes it a more interesting place for children, parents, and staff.

Caregivers Are Important

Caregivers share with parents one of the most important tasks in the world — nurturing and educating the next generation. The expectations of caregivers are high, and yet they are often not provided with wages and working conditions that they deserve (LaGrange & Read, 1990; Whitebook et al., 1990). As one writer humorously explained: Caregivers are expected to "raise our children according to the best theories...; to make them healthy, secure, intelligent, challenged ... while keeping track of their spare socks, wiping runny noses, cleaning potties, and ... not ever charging more than two dollars an hour" (Blum, 1983).

Caregivers work with young children because they are nurturing, giving people. They genuinely care about the children and are committed to meeting their needs. It is not unusual for caregivers to miss their lunch or coffee break because the center is short staffed, or even to come to work when they are unwell. This lack of attention to their own needs can lead to physical and emotional exhaustion, and indeed, there is a high rate of burnout among day-care workers (Whitebook et al., 1990).

A worker suffering from burnout tends to treat the people she is responsible for like objects and she finds it increasingly difficult to care about and for the children. Burnout occurs in situations where staff continually give of themselves to others.

In order to prevent burnout, caregivers must take care of themselves and advocate for their own needs. Centers should value their caregivers. They should meet the caregivers' needs for physical comfort. For example, changing tables should be high enough so that caregivers don't need to bend, and comfortable chairs should be available. Staff rooms should be pleasant and comfortable, so that time away from the children is refreshing, and every attempt must be made to honor coffee and lunch breaks. Caregivers sometimes have to set limits when expectations of them go beyond the call of duty.

Caregivers should have ongoing support from their supervisors or directors, and a chance to have input into policy decisions at the center. They should have a chance to further their knowledge and skills through in-service training, conferences, and workshops. Perhaps most important, the public should be made aware of the vital role that caregivers play in the lives of children and families.

PRACTICAL APPLICATION

1. After reading each of the issues described in this chapter, spend some time in your day-care center examining how each is considered.

2. Recommend where changes might be made and discuss why they would be an improvement.

▼▼▼▼▼▼▼▼▼▼▼▼▼

PART II PLAY TIMES,
OTHER TIMES

In Part I, the foundations of a quality program were discussed. The philosophy and goals of the program "set the stage" but they don't actually offer specific guidelines that will assist in providing quality care. This part will attempt to do just that, with an emphasis on promoting development in specific areas.

Essentially, much of a baby's day revolves around interactions with people (adults and other children) and things (toys, equipment, utensils). Many of these interactions occur during routine care times, which will be covered in Part III. The task now is to look at the rest of the day, and to ask how we can ensure that the child's interactions with people and things will indeed be meaningful experiences.

A major proportion of a child's interactions with people and things occurs during exploration, play, and activities. Therefore, this part begins with a discussion of play. The subsequent chapters review the developmental process in selected areas. Each chapter also discusses the role of the caregiver as we have defined it: to protect, support, enrich, and observe the infants and toddlers so that they can develop optimally while in group care. The caregiver's role is described in more detail at the end of Chapter 6.

The Importance of Play

Objectives

- ❖ To describe infant and toddler play.
- ❖ To discuss why play is so important to development.
- ❖ To describe the role of the caregiver in promoting play.

Opening Thoughts

Think about how young children play. List as many examples of play as you can.

Comments on Opening Thoughts

- ❖ It is likely that many examples of play that were given reflected activities of preschoolers — three-, four-, and five-year olds.
- ❖ The type of play in which infants and toddlers engage is not typically considered to be play.
- ❖ Adults have an essential role in facilitating play for infants and toddlers. ❐

Nine-month-old Shantel stares intently at Janet, her caregiver, who is changing her diaper. Shantel reaches out, grasps a corner of the clean diaper beside her, and brings it up to her face. Janet smiles and says, "Where is Shantel? Are you playing peekaboo with me?" She gently removes the diaper from Shantel's face, and in a surprised tone of voice says, "Here's Shantel!" Shantel laughs and repeats the game. Once again Janet responds by asking, "Where is Shantel?" and again Shantel waits to be discovered behind the diaper. When Janet removes the diaper, Shantel's eyes are as big as her grin. Then Shantel looks away and tries to put her finger in her mouth. "I guess you have had enough peekaboo," says Janet. "Let's get you ready for lunch."

Many adults regard play as an activity of little value that children do to keep themselves busy or to have fun. Psychologists and educators have quite a different view of play. They agree with the popular notion that children are, indeed, busy and having fun when they play, but they regard play as vital to the healthy development of the child.

Through play, children learn about themselves, others, and the world around them. Shantel, for example, may have learned many things from the game of peekaboo. She may have learned that the adult is a caring, friendly person. She may have learned that she can influence the adult (when she stopped enjoying the game, the caregiver stopped playing). She may have been learning that people exist even when she can't see them. Play and learning, then, cannot be separated.

In spite of its importance, we do not have a clear definition of play. The professional literature reflects a wide range of theoretical approaches as to why children play, how play develops, what influences play, and what the role of the adult should be in the child's play (Rubin et al., 1983). The issues are many, and a full discussion of them is beyond the scope of this book. However, we will try to draw from available knowledge some understanding about play that can help us plan for, support, and enrich the play life of the infants and toddlers in our centers.

The Roots of Play

Healthy newborns come into this world with an amazing array of skills and capacities that enable them to begin to function in this world. They are able to look, listen, and relate to others. Part of the great design of these little human beings is that they seem to be programmed to use these skills to be active and to respond to the things and people in their environment. From the first days they are ready and motivated to begin to learn and adapt to the world. Within a few short weeks they can discriminate faces, smile, and begin short social interchanges with their loving parents. Parents, in turn, are delighted to respond to babies and include them in many social interchanges. Once this has happened, babies have taken the first steps in social play — a kind of play that will change and develop over the years and will affect their social relations through adulthood.

Infants and young toddlers learn mostly through direct active experience as they move, look, smell, taste, and listen.

At the same time, each baby is searching for, listening to, and feeling objects in the environment. Slowly, the infant matures and becomes fascinated by these objects and, by four months, begins to look at them and hold them. The baby has, literally, grasped an important part of the world in his or her hands. This is the beginning of exploratory object play, a form of play that will be the focus of attention for the next two years and that will lay the foundation for understanding and thinking skills that the child will need throughout life.

Clearly, the roots of play are established within the first months. Over the next two years both social and object play will change and become more elaborate as the child's new abilities emerge. However, the complexity of play will progress only if parents and other significant adults continue to respond and interact with the child and if the child is given the physical space, time, and objects to explore.

Understanding Play

The definitions of play that exist in the early childhood literature are mostly derived from studying the play of preschool children, rather than infants and toddlers. While differences appear in the way play is defined, there do seem to be some characteristics that are generally agreed upon (Rubin et al., 1985; Rogers & Sawyers, 1988):

❑   First, the motivation for playing should come from within the child. It should be something that the child herself wants to do. If the child fills a bucket with small blocks because the caregiver asks her to, and she anticipates a reward, this is thought to be less genuine play than if the child simply wants to fill the bucket. Thus, genuine play involves free choice. The same activity can be thought of as play or not play, depending on whether the child chose it.

❑   Second, in play, the focus is on the actual activity, rather than on the end result. For example, it is the actual filling and dumping of sand that is more important than a vision of a final product, such as a sand cake.

❏   Third, play is non-literal. That is, objects are used in a way that is not necessarily the way they were intended to be used. A pot and a spoon, for example, will be used for banging and noise making in play, rather than for cooking.

❏   Fourth, in play the children are actively involved. Watching or listening to someone else is generally not thought of as play.

❏   Finally, play is usually accompanied by signs of pleasure. Children usually look as if they are enjoying themselves when they play.

Not all play activities fit all of these criteria absolutely. For example, often toddlers' facial expressions are intently serious, rather than lit up with pleasure, when they are engaged in play. However, these criteria do provide a guide for determining to what extent children have the opportunity to play in group care.

The Development of Play

The development of play, like most aspects of a child's development, evolves in fairly predictable stages. For example, if we look at how babies and toddlers in different stages of development would likely play with a large block, we would see the young baby swiping at it. At the next stage the baby would likely attempt different ways of manipulating the block, such as hitting, dropping, or shaking it. The young toddler tends to repeat activities with objects in a seemingly endless fashion — for example, pushing a block back and forth, filling a box, dumping its contents, and filling it again. The next stage involves constructing — building or making things with blocks, for instance — and the most advanced stage of play for this age group involves playing "as if" — as when a block becomes a car in play. While a baby is not as capable as a two-year-old of playing "as if," the toddler can and does enjoy the simpler manipulations of younger babies, and often incorporates them into his play (Seedfelt & Barbour, 1987). The simpler manipulations in which the baby seems to be attempting to find out what objects are like are usually referred to as exploration, while discovering what he can do with the object is referred to as play

(Hutt, 1976). However, exploration and play are so closely linked that experts are far from unanimous about the distinction between them (Rogers & Sawyers, 1988).

The development of social play of toddlers has been the subject of much debate. Traditionally it has been thought that, until the age of two and a half, children engage in solitary play (by themselves) or in parallel play (when they play in the same area but do not relate to one another — playing beside, but not with, each other). Today there is more evidence that children below the age of two do engage in mutual play and can be quite skilled at soliciting a play partner by smiling, offering a toy, and so forth.

Although play develops in a fairly predictable sequence, there are wide individual differences in the way children play. Some babies are very active and in constant motion, others move more slowly and prefer to concentrate on one object for a long time. Some young toddlers will venture to climb anything, while others are more cautious. Some children eagerly initiate social contact, while others tend to wait until they are approached.

As all areas of a child's development are interrelated, any type of play activity is usually related to more than one area of development. Any play activity, then, may influence the "whole" child. For example, a toddler's feeling of success when she manages to place a small stacking cup in a large one relates not only to her fine motor skills but also to her developing understanding of concepts such as in and out or smaller and larger, and to her good feelings about herself.

The Role of the Adult in Promoting Play

The adults who care for babies and toddlers have a significant role in their play. The presence, support, and participation of adults (when necessary) contribute to the quality of the child's experience. As Willis and Ricciuti (1975) point out, giving just the right kind of help in just the right amount at the right time is superlative caregiving, and is a goal to be worked towards constantly.

What is the right amount of help? It might be useful to consider roles of adult involvement in play. The first role is to ensure that the children have the time to play, the space to play, and the

Caregivers can initiate play with activities such as action rhymes and finger play.

equipment to play with. When we think of play in a preschool setting, we understand the importance of having large blocks of time available for children for free play. When we talk about providing time for infants and toddlers to play, the implication is slightly different. Certainly babies need time in between routines for exploring and playing. But providing time to play also means recognizing that play happens at all times of day — during diaper changing, or mealtime, or as children arrive in the morning, or while they are on a walk. Ensuring time to play sometimes means being flexible enough, and observant enough, to let the play that happens continue to happen, whether or not it is officially play time. Caregivers should attempt not to disturb children who are involved in playing unless it is absolutely necessary. For the adult, waiting an extra minute usually is not difficult. For the infant or toddler, that extra minute may well mean feeling satisfaction at having completed the exploration or play rather than frustration at being interrupted.

A quality program provides many opportunities for a child to choose how to play.

Infants and toddlers under the age of two are in what Piaget (1972) termed the sensorimotor period of development. Much of what they learn happens through direct active experience as they move, look at, smell, feel, taste, and listen to the people and things in their immediate environment. Their exploration and play are with the here and now. For the active and curious infant or toddler, each day is a day of discovery — discovery of the new and rediscovery of the familiar. Clearly, the variety and quality of the objects that we provide, as well as the way we arrange the space in which the children move and play, determine whether the children are able to choose what interests them, what they can do, and how they can explore or play.

While providing equipment, space, and time is absolutely essential, caregivers themselves are most important in facilitating the play of infants and toddlers. Their involvement and verbal and non-verbal responsiveness to the children determine the quality of the play experiences. Sometimes just having an adult close by gives children the security they require to focus their attention on their play. Then the adult can, at times, enter into the play situation that the child has initiated (as with Shantel, at the beginning of the chapter), and can become a responsive partner. This means following the child's lead, and playing along with whatever the child is involved in.

The very special developmental needs of infants and young toddlers require that the adult sometimes initiates play. The young child in day care needs an adult who knows when and how to initiate many one-to-one playful interactions during the day. There are some babies and toddlers who are slow starters and need the help of a caregiver to become involved, there are babies who have periods of stress, and there are children with special needs for whom it is more difficult to initiate play on their own. An adult who initiates a playful interaction with the baby or toddler must watch very carefully to ensure that the child is interested in and enjoying the play, and once the child has joined in, the adult should follow the child's leads where possible.

In group settings the caregiver often initiates playful activities with small groups of two or three children. If the meal cart is unexpectedly delayed and children are all ready to be seated at the table, the caregiver may initiate a finger play to make the waiting easier. Often, the caregiver will initiate activities to make the day go more smoothly. These activities and games are an important part of group life with infants and toddlers, and are perfectly appropriate as long as the children are not bombarded with too many activities, and as long as children are not pressured to participate. However, these adult-directed activities are not to be confused with play, or thought of as a substitute for play.

There is growing educational research support (Caruso, 1988) that play that is spontaneous and initiated and directed by the child is significantly related to infant learning and development. The National Association for the Education of Young Children states that play initiated and directed by the child and supported by the adult is the cornerstone of developmentally appropriate practice. That is, a quality program provides many opportunities for a child to choose how to play, with what and with whom to play, and when to play, and then the child is free to end the activity when he or she is satisfied. Willis and Ricciuti (1975) suggest that we look at play within all areas of development, such as social interaction, language activities, perceptual and cognitive activities, large motor activities, and small motor activities. This approach helps us ensure that the kinds of activities we provide for children relate to all areas of development.

The Role of the Caregiver: Play Times, Other Times

To Protect

❑ From overstimulation and from understimulation.
❑ From health and safety hazards.
❑ From other children (sometimes).
❑ From stress.

To Support

❑ By nurturing with affectionate, responsive care.
❑ By providing the security of her presence.
❑ By withdrawing when not needed.
❑ By participating in play.
❑ By reading the babies' and toddlers' cues and responding.
❑ By providing time, space, and things to play with.

To Enrich

❑ By taking advantage of "teachable moments."
❑ By offering challenges.
❑ By expanding language.
❑ By modeling behaviors.
❑ By providing challenging toys.

To Observe

❑ Individual differences in feelings, emotions, and temperament.
❑ Differences in developmental abilities.
❑ Differences in interest and enjoyment.
❑ Differences in the use of equipment.
❑ The whole playroom.

PRACTICAL APPLICATION

1. Observe an infant and then a toddler for twenty minutes during the day. List all the examples of play that you observed. How did the caregiver promote play? How were equipment, toys and materials used?

2. Observe several different children playing with the same kinds of toys (e.g., rattles or soft toys). Note how their play is similar and how it differs.

3. Ask three parents or grandparents from different cultures to describe the games that they often play with babies (such as peekaboo or finger plays). If you have a chance to observe such interactions, do so. In what ways are the games similar, and in what ways are they different? In each case, what do you think the baby might be learning from participation in these games?

Emotional Well-Being

Objectives

- ❖ To describe the emotional development of infants and young toddlers.
- ❖ To discuss the role of caregivers in promoting the emotional well-being of all the children in their care.

Opening Thoughts

What do you mean when you say that someone is well adjusted or a "together" person? Think of someone you know who is well adjusted. What do you think contributed to the fact that this person is well adjusted?

Comments on Opening Thoughts

- ❖ The foundations of emotional well-being begin in early infancy.
- ❖ The family is the primary source of a child's emotional well-being.
- ❖ Relationships with people outside the family can influence the child's emotional well-being.
- ❖ A primary task of all caregivers is to promote the emotional well-being of the children in their care. ❐

A n eleven-month-old baby named Josh was seated in a highchair in a family restaurant. At the table beside him sat his parents and five-year-old sister. After finishing most of his dinner he started banging his spoon on the table. Tap, tap, tap. His mother looked up at him, smiled, and responded by imitating his gestures. Tap, tap, tap. The baby's face broke out in a broad grin, and a game of Follow the Leader began. Before long, the baby had the diners at the table next to his family looking at him, smiling, and playing along — tapping their spoons on the table as well.

In those few moments Josh must have felt an incredible sense of well-being. He had orchestrated an entire restaurant: "Look what I can make happen!" One can venture to predict that Josh was on the way to developing a sense of positive self esteem. People who feel good about themselves, and confident in themselves, are described as emotionally healthy. And emotional well-being seems to be at the root of success in most aspects of life.

The foundations of a healthy personality and healthy emotional development are generally laid within the framework of a child's earliest experiences within the family. Through the loving interactions that occur between infants and the key adults in their lives, a sense of basic trust and feelings of self worth are formed. Though the process of developing positive self esteem continues throughout life, the "emotional root system" (National Center for Clinical Infant Programs, 1988) for future growth and development has its foundations in the earliest year.

"Bonding" is the term often used to describe the developing relationship between parents and children that begins immediately after birth (Craig, 1989). The touching, kissing, cuddling, and eye contact that we see parents and infants engaging in are the outward expressions of bonding. Inwardly, bonding is felt by a strong pull toward and fascination with the other (Craig, 1989). How many times does the new parent pop in to the nursery to "check" on the baby? While bonding has been described as the mother's domain, in recent years fathers' active participation in delivery and care of newborns has brought them into the bonding picture as well.

Today we think of bonding as the beginning of an ongoing process of attachment that is fostered by interaction with the child in the early months (Bee, 1989). Attachment is defined as "an affectional tie that one person forms to another special person in his life" (Ainsworth et al., 1978). Signals of the baby's attachment, usually to the mother, include behaviors such as crying when the mother leaves, smiling when she returns, and — when the baby is mobile (at about six or seven months) — crawling after her to stay near. Many experts in child development (Honig, 1975; Thoman & Browder, 1987) describe the process of attachment as a dance. "The process of attachment seems to be the opportunity to develop real mutuality — to practice the dance until the partners follow one another's lead smoothly and with pleasure" (Bee, 1989). This takes time and practice. Greenspan (1990: 16) describes how babies need to "be wooed into a loving relationship." But babies need to give love as well. They are not just passive recipients. They come equipped with, and use, wooing skills to "hook" the adult. They smile, they coo, they nestle into a cuddle. If the adult is receptive to these cues, the dance is set in motion. The importance of understanding attachment lies in the recognition that loving relationships form not just on the basis of doing things to the baby or for the baby, but on doing things *with* the baby. Attachment is a partnership, where each partner's actions are activated and modified by the other's.

The acquisition of trust in people and the world was described by Erikson (1963) as the first emotional task of infancy. Infants need to establish a trust in the people caring for them and in the environment around them. This trust is built when warm, loving attention is available and prompt responses to their needs are given.

Historically, there has been a great fear of overindulging or spoiling babies with too much attention, or by picking them up each time they cry. However, if healthy attachments occur through sensitive responding — and trust is acquired through having needs met — we must seriously reconsider this fear of spoiling. It has been demonstrated that babies whose mothers respond quickly to their crying cry less in the long run than do babies who are left to cry (Bee, 1990).

If strong attachments in infancy are a prerequisite for healthy development (Grusec & Lytton, 1988), and healthy attachments require that adults consistently and sensitively respond to babies' cues, an important question arises. Can caregivers, who have more than one baby to respond to at a time, provide secure attachment relationships with the infants in their care? One study by Goosens and van IJzendoorn (1990) suggests that caregivers appear to be able to compensate for spending less time with each infant by providing quality time. Babies seem to demonstrate secure attachments when they are cared for by caregivers who get to know them very well; who are trained to understand the needs of infants; and who are sensitive to these needs. Nevertheless, it is clear that building such an attachment will be difficult when a caregiver has many babies to care for.

We are likely to see the baby anywhere from six to twelve months protest vehemently at separation from mother and show signs of fear and anxiety when in the presence of strangers. While listening to a baby cry is upsetting, this response to separation and fear of strangers marks an important milestone. The baby's intellectual development has progressed to the stage where he or she can make the distinction between familiar and unfamiliar people. The degree to which different infants respond in this way varies considerably, and it is not known why these differences occur. It may be related to the baby's temperament, or to events or stress in the child's life. Having many caregivers does not reduce the baby's fear of strangers, contrary to what might be expected.

Once the child has developed clear attachments to special people, we are able to see the emergence of behaviors that are related to attachment. First, we see "social referencing" (Bee, 1989). This means that the baby uses mother (or another person to whom he or she is attached) as a safe base, and as a way of getting clues about new situations. We have all seen how a baby looks at mother when a stranger offers a new toy. Feeling safe in the presence of an attachment figure allows the baby to explore the environment more freely.

During this period, some babies latch on to objects such as stuffed animals, blankets or pillows, favorite toys, or pacifiers. These objects provide them with a sense of security at a time of life when there are so many pulls in so many directions. While these objects do become worn and soiled, we must understand that they are very important to the child — and find a way, together with the parents, to ensure that they are sanitary!

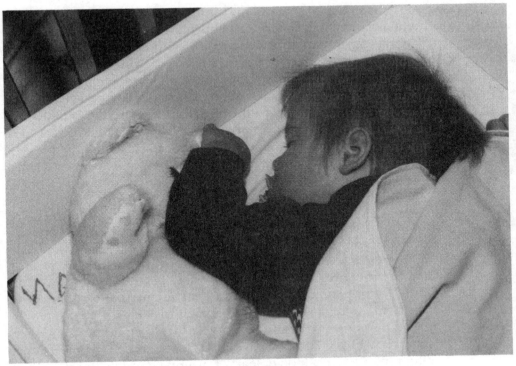

Some babies latch on to objects that provide them with a sense of security.

Babies and toddlers should be able to have their favorite objects with them as they are needed. Some adults worry that the child will not be able to separate from a favorite object. This is rarely the case; dependence on an object usually wanes as the toddler grows up and does not need the added security.

As babies move into toddlerhood, the major milestone of emotional development is the development of autonomy, or independence (Erikson, 1963). Infants who feel secure in their attachment to significant others are now becoming aware that they are separate beings and they want to do things for themselves. They are gaining a sense of who they are, what power they have in the world (remember Josh at the beginning of this chapter) and what they are allowed and not allowed to do. Expressions of autonomy are seen in "Mine," "Me do" and "No, no, no." Toddlers have a reputation for being tiresome and difficult, but some of this difficulty arises from not being understood. Lieberman explains the need, with toddlers, to "negotiate a mutually satisfying balance between the safety of closeness (attachment) and the excitement of exploration and discovery" (Lieberman, 1991: 6). The caregiver, then, needs to provide security and physical closeness sometimes and then to "let go," when appropriate — to allow the child to set forth on independent explorations and discoveries.

Toddlers need to experiment with the boundaries of what is acceptable behavior (Anselmo, 1987). They try to make sense of the rules (sometimes too many of them) that adults try to enforce. One toddler, having dropped his toy truck into the toilet, received a firm "no" from his mother. The next day, he returned to the "scene of the crime," repeated the action, then tugged his mother in to see what he had done. This time, he did not wait for her to react. He looked at her seriously and said, "No." This young chap was not intending to test his mother's patience. He was trying to make sure he understood the rules.

We mentioned that many infants react with fear to strangers. In toddlerhood, the child's developing imagination can result in different kinds of fears. Both real and imaginary objects, animals, and people can become objects of fear. It is important never to laugh at fears, or to use fears to influence a child. Reassurances, patience, and imaginary or real solutions — such as a teddy bear on guard duty or a night light — can be helpful to the child (Anselmo, 1987).

Many descriptions of toddlers begin with the term "self-centered." Toddlers' interests are in themselves, and their world consists of the immediate, the here and the now. Their moods change quickly, from glee to frustration. Often they strive to be fiercely independent. While self-centeredness is not generally thought of as a desirable trait in adults, toddlers have to be self-centered. An understanding of why toddlers behave as they do, and of the fact that it is important for them to go through these struggles for independence and autonomy, can make the difference between simply tolerating this age group and genuinely enjoying it (Gonzalez-Mena, 1986).

The Role of the Caregiver

Ensuring that the emotional needs of infants and young toddlers are met while in group care is a heavy responsibility for caregivers. The complexity of attachment and the need to respond to infants on a very personal level and to foster a healthy sense of autonomy in toddlers requires the caregivers' full attention.

To Protect

The caregivers need to protect the children from emotional harm by respecting their individuality, fostering the development of trust, and encouraging the struggle for autonomy. Below are some ways we can achieve these goals:

❏ Limit the number of children in groups.

❏ Ensure stability by providing a primary caregiver, and when a change in caregivers is necessary, make the transition gradual.

❏ Provide consistency in routines such as feeding and napping so that babies and toddlers feel secure.

❏ Ensure that the environment is not too overwhelming: too much noise or too many toys make it difficult for young ones to gain a sense of competence.

❏ Allow babies a chance to calm themselves when distressed, but never ignore crying or other signs of distress.

❏ Ensure that babies and toddlers are never ridiculed and that sarcasm or other forms of disrespect are never used.

❏ Provide extra support through difficult, stressful times (e.g., teething, illness, new environments, or new people).

To Support

The emotional well-being of babies and toddlers is supported when the primary bond between baby and parents is acknowledged and supported. In addition, attentive, responsive caregivers can do much to support the emotional development of the child. For example:

- ❑ Watch for and respond to babies' body language.
- ❑ Address the baby or toddler by name.
- ❑ Ensure that each child receives special time with the caregiver each day.
- ❑ Help the child express his or her feelings.
- ❑ Accept the child's feelings (of frustration or separation anxiety) as legitimate.
- ❑ Provide warm, responsive physical contact.
- ❑ Maximize the opportunities for infants and toddlers to "feel free" to explore in a safe setting.
- ❑ Provide responsive toys so the child feels some control.
- ❑ Ensure that the surroundings are familiar so that babies and toddlers feel secure. (Changes make life interesting, but do not provide too many at a time.)
- ❑ Ensure that parents feel welcome in the center.
- ❑ Continually communicate with parents.
- ❑ Provide pictures and other symbols of the children's family and culture.

To Enrich

Caregivers can do much to enhance and enrich the young child's positive sense of self. They should aim to maximize the child's opportunities for success, for having an impact on surroundings, and for feeling very special. Caregivers can enrich the emotional experiences of young children with the ideas below:

- ❑ Imitate the baby's gestures, movements, and sounds.
- ❑ Play games such as Catch Me and Hug Me, which are good because children are developing attachments but also want to explore.
- ❑ Unobtrusively ensure success (an untied or opened shoe is easier to take off; a container with a loosened lid is easier to open).

To Observe

In order to protect, support, and enrich infants' and toddlers' emotional development, the caregiver must constantly observe them, looking for individual differences in the way that they respond. Observing includes using all of your senses to gain information. Below are some questions that may guide your observations:

1. How does the baby respond to different types of hugs or cuddles?
   - By tensing up?
   - By snuggling in?

2. What seems to work to calm the baby?
   - Rocking?
   - Humming or singing?
   - Fast, jerky movements?
   - Walking?

3. What situations cause the toddler frustration?
   - Too much noise? Activity?
   - Times before nap and meals?
   - Playtime with other children?
   - Transition between activities?

4. What signs do the babies or toddlers give to show that they are pleased with themselves?

5. What are the different ways different children show the caregiver that they need some attention?

6. How do the babies or toddlers respond when the adult they are attached to leaves the room? What steps ease the transition?

Children with Special Needs

All of the above information on observation is relevant to children with special needs. However, additional notes may be relevant. Some children with special needs may react negatively or have inconsistent responses to being touched. To infants who have been hospitalized, touching may be a reminder of the pokes and prods experienced at that time. Infants with limp muscle tone may need more stimulation and touch before they respond. Visually impaired infants may startle or appear frightened when they are picked up because they do not see the adult approaching. Hearing impaired children may react in a similar way because they do not hear the caregiver coming. Very gentle approaches while speaking softly to the infant may be helpful. Try different approaches, touches, ways of holding the child. Try and try again. The biggest mistake that caregivers and parents make is to assume that the child does not like to be held or doesn't understand (i.e., the child is just as happy lying alone) so they give up. All babies will benefit from physical contact; caregivers may simply need to learn how best to provide it.

Children with special needs will react in typical ways while developing autonomy and independence.

Children with special needs will react in typical ways ("No, no," "mine," and temper tantrums) while developing autonomy and independence. As children develop, these reactions to situations should subside. For example, once the child learns to ask for the bottle, tantrums arising from not having it usually decrease. If this type of response is not occurring with special-needs children, language development may be a concern. Provide the children with simple language or cues and lots of opportunities to practice. Often, when a child has a visible disability, we tend to think of his or her needs in terms of that disability, and sometimes ignore other aspects of development. The most important thing to remember is that children with special needs have the same needs as all children for loving responsive care and for the opportunity to develop security, attachment, and autonomy. They may need a bit of extra help and attention in the process.

TIPS FOR TOYS AND EQUIPMENT

- Privacy corners arranged within the larger setting.
- Comfortable areas for hugs and cuddles.
- Lots of soft pillows and stuffed animals.
- Large mirrors at infants' eye level.
- Responsive toys: squeeze toys, jack-in-the-boxes, musical toys.
- Comfortable areas for staff to rest.
- Comfortable arrangements for parents to breastfeed or spend time with baby.

✔ *Caregiver Checklist*

DOES THE CAREGIVER:

1. Respond promptly to babies' signals of distress?

2. Provide warm, physical contact as required by all children?

3. Relate to the children respectfully at all times?

4. Empathize with children who are feeling sad or distressed?

5. Interpret and label toddlers' feelings?

6. Offer children appropriate choices throughout the day?

7. Ensure predictability during the day?

8. Personalize the environment by allowing articles from home?

9. Provide small spaces for the children and other areas where children can be away from the group?

10. Ensure that toys and equipment provided allow children to feel successful?

11. Support parents and make them feel welcome and comfortable?

PRACTICAL APPLICATION

1. Think of your home. What aspects of your home setting contribute to a sense of warmth, security, and well-being? Now observe a center. What aspects of the center do you think provide the children with a sense of warmth, security, and well-being? What recommendations would you make to the center based on that comparison?

2. Observe the interactions between a mother and child at home. What were the interactions that you felt contributed to the emotional well-being of the child? In what physical context did these interactions occur (e.g., in her arms sitting on a sofa, tucking into bed, etc.)? Compare these interactions with the interactions between the child and caregiver. What were the similarities and differences?

3. After the children leave the center at the end of the day, think about all the opportunities available during that day to promote emotional development. In what ways were security and attachment promoted for infants? In what ways were autonomy and independence promoted?

4. Observe an infant and then a toddler for twenty minutes during the day. List all examples you saw of the caregiver promoting emotional well-being. How were toys, equipment, and materials used?

5. What recommendations would you make to promote emotional well-being in this setting? What room arrangements would you recommend? What interactions would you try to encourage?

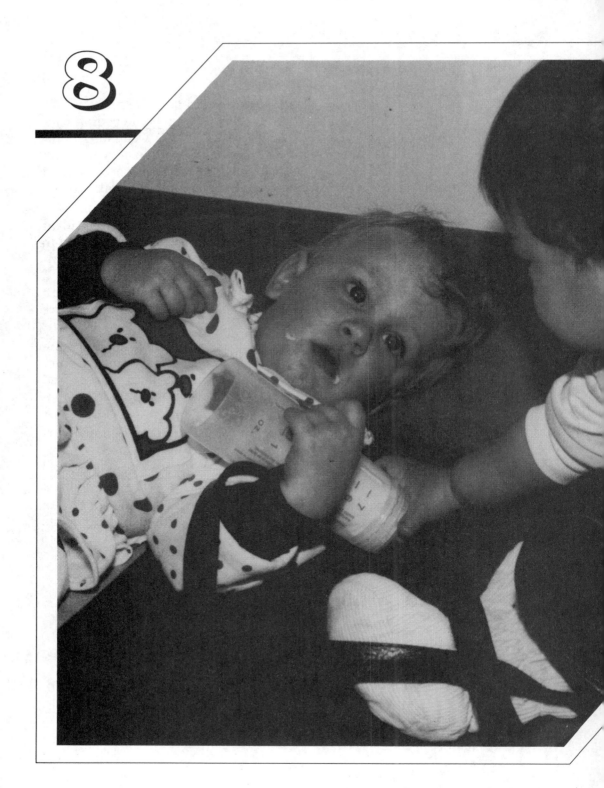

Social Development

Objectives

- ❖ To understand the infant, from birth, as a social being.
- ❖ To discuss the ways in which the caregiver can foster positive social interactions.
- ❖ To stress the importance of paying attention to the social development of children with special needs.

Opening Thoughts

Think about all you did yesterday and the social interactions in which you were involved. Were they positive or negative? What factors (e.g., the setting, the people involved, the occasion) influenced the type of interaction? How did you know how to behave — did you follow social convention or did someone tell you what to do? Did difficulties arise because you didn't know what was expected?

Comments on Opening Thoughts

- ❖ Social interactions form the basis of much of our personal, professional, and leisure activities.
- ❖ Learning about social interactions begins early in life.
- ❖ The conventions that guide our social interactions are complex and change from situation to situation.
- ❖ Understanding the social development of infants and toddlers can help guide caregivers as they support the social interactions of infants and toddlers. ❐

J ean, a young mother, went to observe an infant room in a center, to see if it would suit her baby. One baby was having her diaper changed, two were on the floor playing, two were sitting in their highchairs while a caregiver was feeding them. Suddenly, one of the babies on the floor broke out in a loud wail when his companion snatched the toy away. In what seemed like less than a second, most of the babies in the room were crying. When the caregivers finished restoring the calm, they smiled and remarked to Jean, "That crying is sometimes contagious."

Observing and listening to this not unusual occurrence should be enough to convince anyone that infants, even from the earliest age, are affected by each other. From infancy through toddlerhood, the children in group care live together for many hours of each day. How they influence each other and relate to each other is affected by their developmental abilities, the environment in which they spend their time, and the care and guidance of the adults who are responsible for them.

The roots of social development are found in the early interactions between infants and their parents. Through the process of bonding and attachment, children develop a sense of trust in the people around them, and learn about themselves. Young children who have close and secure attachments to the significant adults in their lives will be more likely to develop positive social skills and interests later on (Hughes et al., 1988). The interactions between parents and infants that lead to bonding and attachment are usually the first social contacts of the baby. It is, therefore, difficult to differentiate between emotional and social development. Indeed, many textbooks combine the two areas as psycho-social development. However, because group care of infants and toddlers involves so much interaction among very young children, we will review here some highlights of social interaction. They include understanding how infants and toddlers relate to and affect each other, how they develop empathy, and how they begin to learn about the kinds of behaviors that are expected of them.

Infant and toddlers have often been described as self-centered, and therefore incapable of understanding or caring about their peers. Yet from an early age infants show a keen interest in other children. We have all seen babies watch one another with delight, smile at each other, vocalize to each other, and gesture to each other. Babies, if given the opportunity, will explore one another much the same way as they would a toy or object — with pokes, prods, and other means of investigation. One seven-month-old baby named Sarah, who was placed on the floor with two other babies and a few toys, was attracted by the red booties of the baby beside her. Within moments the red bootie became a fascinating object of exploration, and Sarah looked quite con-fused when her playmate protested with a loud wail as the bootie and the foot inside it went into Sarah's mouth! Sarah did not understand that her actions could cause discomfort to another child, and was dependent on the caregiver to substitute the red bootie with another interesting object to explore.

By the age of approximately one year, babies can be seen enjoying each other's company in a playful way, such as chasing each other or laughing together (Willis & Ricciuti, 1975). Just

From an early age, infants show a keen interest in other children.

after a year, we often see one child join another who is playing with a toy, and the two will look at the toy together, gesture to each other, and laugh (Fogel, 1991). In early toddlerhood we often see clustering (Jones, 1979) — that is, when one child is involved with a toy or activity, other children cluster around, wanting to do the same thing. A toy that is being played with is more interesting than one that is on a shelf or on the floor.

Between eighteen and twenty-four months of age we see toddlers playing together frequently, inventing games (such as throwing the sand out of the sandbox), imitating each other, offering each other toys, and talking to each other. While young children enjoy each other's company, they are not yet ready to be cooperative or collaborative. Usually one child influences another and, as long as one is content to lead and the other to follow, the interactions are enjoyable.

The interactions of toddlers are affected by the kinds of toys and equipment that are available to play with. Low ladders and slides, big boxes, and other large, immovable play equipment seem to promote positive interactions. More fighting and struggling seems to occur with smaller, more portable toys (Fogel, 1991).

Clearly then, infants and toddlers are attracted to each other and enjoy the company of each other. But do they "care" about each other? Being affected by what another is feeling, and desiring to help another person, is what is often referred to as empathy. Are infants and toddlers capable of empathy?

The description of the choir of crying babies at the beginning of this chapter would be referred to by some experts as the beginning of empathy (Kaplan, 1991). Babies somehow respond to signals of distress, mostly by becoming distressed themselves. Some time in their second year of life, babies begin to try to act on these feelings. A fourteen-month-old may bring his blanket or bottle to another child who is crying or to an adult who seems upset. While toddlers cannot be expected to understand that others are very different from themselves (adults are unlikely to be soothed by a bottle), these attempts to help out are important milestones of development that should be encouraged and fostered.

Infants and toddlers, then, are probably much more socially competent than they are usually given credit for. Not only do they want to be with other children, they are affected by them, and often show caring behavior by trying to comfort another child in distress. However, social relations between toddlers are often not trouble free. Several developmental factors prevent smooth positive interactions. This means close supervision is necessary, along with a fair amount of assistance from the adults who care for them.

Toddlers are struggling to understand who they are and what control they have on the world. Their struggle for autonomy requires that they focus on themselves, their needs, and their world. It is difficult for them to consider the needs of others at this point. Sharing and taking turns are abilities that are only beginning to emerge in toddlerhood (Miller, 1984). It is not advisable to force a toddler to give up a toy that she is involved with in the name of being a good sport. "It takes a long time and many gently guided experiences to learn to share" (Miller, 1984). Usually, if the child is not pressured and is allowed to feel "ownership," she soon moves on to another activity. It makes life so much easier for caregivers and children if duplicates of favorite toys are available.

Part of autonomy also involves exerting power and authority, as in the common assertion, "Me do it." The power struggles often occur between adults and children, but are part of toddlers' interactions as well. And often, because toddlers lack the language skills required to voice displeasure or frustration, messages are made clear by hitting, throwing, screaming, or biting. Caregivers have to be very observant, and often they have to move in quite quickly to redirect or to intervene in a struggle to prevent physical harm.

An important aspect of the social development of infants and toddlers is learning what is acceptable and unacceptable behavior. Learning to control one's impulses and behave in a socially acceptable fashion begins in infancy when the baby, about to embark on an activity that is out of bounds, responds to a firm "no." The child is helped to develop socially appropriate behavior by a combination of various factors: an environment with limited restrictions, clear and consistent limits, and lots of reinforcement and modeling of acceptable behaviors (e.g., allowing the child to touch others gently and showing the child how to interact with others by gentle touches or strokes rather than hitting). Most important, however, is that caregivers should set expectations and limitations that are realistic in terms of the child's development. A lot of patience, repeated reinforcement of positive behaviors, and repeated discouragement of negative behaviors is essential.

When children have physical or mental disabilities, their developing social skills are often neglected. For example, if a toddler is unable to see or to walk, we tend to promote activities that are specifically related to helping overcome these disabilities, and sometimes overlook the child's need to develop skills in interacting with other children. Participating in an integrated setting offers a wonderful opportunity for children with disabilities to learn to interact with others, provided that care is taken to ensure that they have the opportunity to play with and learn about the children with whom they are in contact.

While toddlers enjoy each others' company, they are not ready to be cooperative.

The Role of the Caregiver

It is important to remember that social behaviors are constantly being learned. Unlike other skills such as crawling or walking, being friendly and sociable is not something children will learn unless they are helped. A prime factor in the socialization of very young children is the caregiver who shows the baby how to stroke gently instead of hitting, who makes it clear to toddlers that they must not hurt another child, and who constantly models caring behaviors by responding to the needs of the children. Social contacts between the caregiver and the child and among the children themselves occur naturally and spontaneously all day long. Caregivers can foster the social development of infants and toddlers in a variety of ways.

To Protect

As babies and toddlers learn how to interact, they will need protection from one another. They will need to be protected, too, from being overstimulated by many other children who are also developing social skills. Some suggestions for protecting infants and toddlers in this area are listed below:

❑ Limit the number of children in a group.

❑ Minimize large group experiences.

❑ Guide babies while they are exploring other babies.

❑ Assist in conflicts or struggles between children when children are distressed or hurting each other.

❑ Provide sufficient toys or duplicates to prevent conflict.

❑ Never laugh at, tease, or shame children's efforts.

❑ Avoid making children feel guilty.

❑ Avoid forms of discipline that isolate the child.

❑ Remove breakable or unsafe objects so caregivers don't need to say "no" very often.

❑ Remind children of the limits before an activity, in a positive way.

❑ Remember that children are watching and learning from your own behavior — with them, with parents, and with staff members.

To Support

During all activities, the caregiver must be available to support social development by trying to:

❑ Provide opportunities for babies to be in contact with other children so they can watch and touch them.

❑ Provide opportunities for toddlers to interact in small groups of two or three.

❑ Respond to children's difficulties and struggles calmly and in a matter of fact manner (e.g., "You don't hit Sally; it hurts her").

❑ Use distraction or gentle redirection to avoid conflict.

❑ Provide choices instead of rules. If it is a quiet time, instead of saying, "You must be quiet," offer a choice of looking at pictures or snuggling up with a favorite stuffed animal.

❑ Be consistent and keep your word so that children develop trust in adults.

❑ Repeat rules simply, clearly, and many times.

❑ Attempt to focus on the "do's" not the "don't's."

To Enrich

Social interactions occur continuously during the day, so social development can be enriched by ensuring that caregivers:

❑ Model positive social behaviors such as sharing.

❑ Initiate turn-taking by introducing games such as rolling a ball or toy truck back and forth, or using words such as "It's Sarah's turn."

❑ Model empathy and concern for others, and praise children's attempts to do the same.

❑ Give children the words to describe their feelings (e.g., "You are angry," "You are hurt").

❑ Offer alternatives to undesirable behavior (e.g., stroking instead of hitting).

❑ Praise and encourage children's positive social behaviors.

❑ Help children to see how their behavior affects others (e.g., "It hurts when you pull his hair").

To Observe

Social skills such as how to interact, to be interested in people or to have empathy are almost impossible to teach except as they are happening or about to happen. It is crucial that caregivers be there actively observing and seize the opportunity to foster a social skill as it happens. Observation is critical to fostering social development and identifying problems. Caregivers can observe the following:

1. Are the baby's interests and exploration directed to objects only? Or is the baby becoming aware of and developing interests in other people, in other children?

2. Does the baby attempt to reach out or initiate contact with the caregiver? With other babies? If so, how?
   – Does he smile?
   – Does he cry?
   – Does he extend his arms or lean over?

3. How does the toddler initiate social contact with others?
   – Does she use sounds or words?
   – Does she poke or pull?

4. Is the toddler beginning to realize his effect on others?
   – Does he see that he can hurt or make a child stop crying?
   – How does he show that he realizes this?

5. What toys seem to be most difficult for toddlers to share?

6. What toys and equipment seem to promote positive interactions between children?

7. What activities do children spontaneously "cluster" around?

8. Are there times of the day when different children seem to play together best with other children ?
   – Mornings?
   – After nap?

9. Are there times of the day that seem more difficult for most of the children?

Children with Special Needs

Because social skills are very complex in nature, they are often not promoted with special-needs children. It is often assumed that children with special needs do not learn very well by observation and imitation. However, the importance of enhancing social development cannot be overstated, especially if integration is the goal. Children with special needs must be helped to interact successfully and to be included in activities with other children. Caregivers can help if they know how social skills develop and are prepared to promote them actively. Although this should be the case when caring for all infants and toddlers, it may be necessary for caregivers to be more involved with the special-needs child.

Opportunities for social interactions with adults and peers must be planned (Guralnick, 1976). Simply having children with special needs in settings with non-disabled children does not mean that social interactions will occur or that children with special needs will develop social skills. Generally, the literature suggests that non-disabled children do not actively reject children with special needs at this age (Guralnick, 1981; Bailey & Wolery, 1984); however, caregivers should be available to plan and encourage interactions between non-disabled children and their disabled peers, and to praise children when interactions do occur. Caregivers should allow children with special needs to solve their own problems with other children, but should assist when a child is distressed. Other support and guidance may be necessary.

Children with visual impairments have several common difficulties in social situations. Lack of vision means they miss a lot of non-verbal information and cues that are so relevant to social situations for very young children. For example, a facial expression or the position of the arms can tell much more than words. The child with visual disabilities needs someone to describe and interpret this information for him (e.g., "You hurt Tammy. She is crying. Listen. Feel where it hurts. That's where Tammy hurts"). Children with visual impairments often do not smile (Bailey & Wolery, 1984). They will need to be praised when they do.

Raver (1991) suggests that infants and toddlers with hearing impairments usually do not experience delays in social development. Difficulties will ensue, however, as the other children begin to develop language skills and the hearing impaired child does not. Encouraging non-disabled children to join in and learn an alternative communication system (e.g., at least a few signs) may help promote interactions.

Children with physical disabilities may lack motor movements to initiate interactions with other children and they, too, may not have the ability to smile (Bailey & Wolery, 1984). Setting up situations around the physically impaired child, so that other children are close by, may encourage interactions to occur.

Children with developmental delays may experience difficulties similar to those noted above. It is important to remember that they need to be included and encouraged to interact. They need opportunities in which they can be shown to interact with others. These children do not have to be labeled as having "behavioral problems" if care is taken to develop social skills from infancy and toddlerhood.

TIPS FOR TOYS AND EQUIPMENT

- Low climbing equipment.

- Large boxes.

- Play houses.

- Large peekaboo boards (boards with holes big enough to stick heads through).

- Rocking boats that sit two to four children.

- Mirrors.

- Large laundry baskets, towels, small brooms.

- Dolls of both sexes and different ethnic groups.

- Unbreakable dishes, utensils, pots, and pans.

- Simple dress-up clothes (low-heeled women's and men's shoes, hats, etc.).

✔ Caregiver Checklist

DOES THE CAREGIVER:

1. Model positive social behaviors such as smiling, gentle touches, talking in pleasant tones?

2. Demonstrate alternative ways of interacting when infants or toddlers are hurting each other?

3. Model caring behaviors such as helping, offering sympathy, etc.?

4. Use redirection and distraction to avoid conflicts?

5. Avoid expressions of disapproval, comparing some children to others, or labeling children?

6. Arrange the setting so that toddlers are encouraged to congregate in groups of two and three rather than in large groups?

7. Recognize when children are frustrated by being with other children and offer time away from the group?

8. Provide enough toys to minimize conflict?

9. Demonstrate realistic expectations, not expecting children to share all the time, take turns, or wait for long periods?

10. Interact with parents and other staff members in a manner that models respect and empathy?

PRACTICAL APPLICATION

1. After the children leave at the end of the day, list all the toys, equipment, and materials available in the room that could encourage social interaction among the children.

2. Observe two toddlers as they play together with a toy or piece of equipment in the center. Then describe how the children interacted with each other. How long did they play together? Was the caregiver involved?

3. Observe an infant, and then a toddler, for a twenty-minute period at some point during the day. List all of the social interactions in which they were involved. What did the caregiver do to enhance social skills? What differences were there in the ways the caregiver interacted with infants and with toddlers?

4. What recommendations would you make to promote social development in this setting? What toys or equipment would you advise? What could the caregiver do?

9

Sensory Experiences

Objectives

❖ To review the importance of sensory exploration for infants and toddlers.

❖ To discuss the role of the caregiver in providing the infants and toddlers with a rich variety of sensory experiences.

❖ To consider the ways in which sensory experiences can be provided for children with special needs.

Opening Thoughts

Try to recall what information about the world you received in the last hour through your senses of touch, taste, smell, hearing, and sight. What was the impact of this information on your mood and feelings, and on your understanding of the situation?

What are the differences between adults and young children in the ways they experience the world through their senses?

Comments on Opening Thoughts

❖ We often take for granted the amount of information we take in through our senses.

❖ Infants' and toddlers' abilities to take in information through their senses is well developed. The ability to make sense of this information and to process it develops over time.

❖ Infants and toddlers are dependent on adults to arrange, interpret, and help them learn from sensory experiences. ❐

One warm morning Sandra, the caregiver, put a low table outside, covered it with paper, and placed a blob of fingerpaint on it. Twenty-two-month-old Ahmad rushed over in anticipation, succumbed to Sandra's efforts to put an apron on him, and eagerly plunged his hands in the paint and began to smear. Twelve-month-old Mira toddled up to the table and watched intently for a long time. She cautiously touched the paint with the tip of her finger, looked at it, and began to cry.

Ahmad and Mira were responding to a sensation in very different ways. They both could see, touch, and feel the wet finger paint, but their understanding of its purpose and the emotional response it evoked were very different indeed.

Babies are amazing. Most babies arrive in this world with the ability to see, hear, taste, smell, feel, and touch. From the time that they are born, they actively seek out experiences and sensations that provide them with information about themselves, and the people and the world around them. The first sensations of being well-fed, warm, and in contact with a loving adult are the beginnings of the development of a sense of trust and security. The satisfaction of these basic needs enables the baby to seek out sensations from the world. This reaching out to people and things around is essential to the healthy growth and development of the baby.

Response to sound is one of the most highly developed abilities in the newborn infant (Bayless & Ramsey, 1982). In fact, many mothers have reported that their unborn babies become more lively when music is played. By three months of age babies can differentiate the voice of their mothers, and show that they are excited by the sounds of familiar rattles or bells. Familiar sounds are reassuring to most babies. By eight or nine months, babies not only differentiate different tones and pitches, they also try to reproduce them (Bayless & Ramsey, 1982).

While it was once thought that new babies do not see, we now know that babies can see shapes and contours from birth. By one month babies relate to the sight of human faces; by two months they can differentiate between pictures of "normal" faces and those that have the features in the wrong places; and by three months of age most infants can distinguish between different faces. In addition, we know that, of all the possible things to look at, most infants find the human face "particularly appealing" (Hughes et al., 1988).

Babies' senses of smell and taste are so highly developed that they can differentiate between the smell of their own mother's breastmilk and that of another mother at one week of age, and between the taste of breastmilk and formula at the early age of ten days (Brazelton, 1977). They turn away from unpleasant smells and spit out liquids that have a taste that is unfamiliar or unpleasant to them.

Similarly, the newborn baby responds to touch. Tactile stimulation — that is, being touched — is as vital to the healthy development of infants as is food and water. The importance of tactile stimulation has been recognized by pediatricians working with premature babies who spend most of their hours in incubators. Many hospitals line the incubators with furry blankets and organize parents and volunteers to stroke the babies to help compensate for the lack of tactile stimulation that full-term babies normally receive.

These examples of the ways in which very young babies use their senses are particularly exciting if we consider that not long ago babies were considered underdeveloped and uninterested in their world. In light of present research trends, it is highly likely that in a few years' time we may have new knowledge about even more capabilities of babies at even younger ages. Babies are, indeed, amazing.

Unlike all other aspects of development, which unfold gradually through life, the ability of the senses to absorb information is well developed within the first few months of life. Not only do young babies have this ability; most of them are naturally highly motivated to use their senses. We don't have to stimulate babies artificially. Our responsibility is, essentially, to ensure that their basic emotional and physical needs are satisfied and to provide an interesting environment with the opportunity to interact and explore.

Through their senses, babies and toddlers receive and collect information. The ability to use these developed senses to learn about themselves and the world around them depends on maturation, health factors, emotional state, and the quality of the environment. The young baby is much more dependent on adults to bring sensory experiences to him or her than is the crawler or walker. A baby or toddler who is in distress will be less likely to notice or enjoy the variety of sensory experiences in the environment. And certainly, the richness of sensory stimuli in the environment will affect the baby's motivation to seek out and enjoy sounds, smells, and sights. An environment that is uninteresting can deter the baby's motivation to explore. One that is too stimulating (too noisy or with too many visual stimuli) can cause the baby to withdraw. Many adults have learned how to listen, or watch, selectively. A father engrossed in a hockey game on television may be quite oblivious to the children who are playing beside him. Most babies and toddlers do not have that ability, and too much noise, or too many things to look at at once, can cause the baby to "tune out" or feel distressed.

There are very noticeable individual differences in how babies absorb and respond to sensory input. The toddler who fusses when being zipped into a coat is likely a baby who was sensitive to tactile stimulation and did not enjoy being swaddled. Some babies cry when the room is too noisy; others seem not to notice noise. Some of these differences are related to temperament. Other differences in the way infants and toddlers respond to sights, sounds, smells, and things to touch are a result of previous experiences. Babies coming into day care will have preferences based on the practices of their families. In some cultures babies are swaddled tightly or carried around for much of the day on parents' fronts, sides, or backs. A baby used to these sensations of close contact may feel insecure when the amount of contact is reduced. Similarly, the smells in homes from different kinds of cooking may be quite different from those in the day-care center. Different babies, taken for a walk around the room, will focus their gaze on different objects. What is of interest to one baby may not be noticed by the other. As infants mature, differences in the way they respond to stimuli become more and more apparent. As we saw in the example of finger painting at the start of this chapter, some children love the feeling of mud oozing between their fingers while others find the experience unpleasant. Some children like to walk barefoot or run around in a diaper. Other children are uncomfortable without their pants, shoes, and socks on. Forcing a child to try new sensory experi-

An environment that provides a rich variety of sensory experiences is a prerequisite for good health, emotional well-being, and learning.

ences is disrespectful and often backfires. Being sensitive to, and respectful of, individual preferences and choices helps the child develop a sense of identity — a sense of individual style and aesthetic preference.

We often think of the sensory environment as being made up of "things." But we should remember that, for infants especially and toddlers as well, many pleasant and meaningful sights, sounds, smells, and touches come from people. The sounds babies make with their own bodies when they clap, or pound, or "cluck" with their mouths; the smell of the caregiver's face cream or the feel of her hair; and the warmth of the caregiver's body are among the most enjoyable sensations.

An environment that provides infants and toddlers with a rich variety of sensory experiences, that stimulates their curiosity, enriches their understanding, develops their interests, and provides them with pleasure is a prerequisite for good health, emotional well-being, and learning.

Role of the Caregiver

The caregiver's role is to ensure that infants and toddlers have ample opportunities for rich sensory exploration. The caregiver has to respect individual differences in children's preferences, and to ensure that the sensory experiences of the child will be pleasant, interesting, reassuring, and meaningful.

To Protect

The caregiver must protect the children from over- and understimulation, and must ensure that the environment is safe. Below are some ideas for accomplishing these aims:

❑ Avoid visual overstimulation (e.g., too many pictures, pictures hung on patterned wallpaper).

❑ Avoid overstimulating the child with sound (e.g., minimize competing background sounds, use television or radio sparingly).

❑ Avoid overloading more than one sense (e.g., do not combine too much visual and tactile stimulation with talking; the child may not be able to sort out all the stimuli).

❑ Ensure that the objects explored are non-toxic, washable, large enough so as not to be swallowed, and that parts (e.g., eyes of stuffed animals) will not break off.

❑ Avoid sand play or play-dough for young babies who put things in their mouths (homemade play-dough contains large quantities of salt that can be unhealthy).

❑ Provide comfortable quiet corners as "shelters" from stimulation.

To Support

Caregivers should set up the environment to provide a balance of sensory stimulation, and should help the child learn from sensory experiences. They can support the child in the following ways:

❑   Provide a setting full of varied experiences. Think about the setting in terms of available sights, sounds, smells, tastes, and touches that would appeal to or interest young children.

❑   Take time to experience new things while on a walk or in the yard.

❑   Provide many opportunities for water play activities throughout the day (in individual basins or while washing or bathing).

❑   Provide sand tables for toddlers over eighteen months.

❑   Allow enough time for exploring; try not to distract or disturb a child who is enjoying an experience.

❑   Provide props (e.g., sticks, spoons, brushes) for children who do not enjoy certain sensations directly.

To Enrich

A good infant and toddler center will have an interesting environment that fosters curiosity and exploration. There are some special activities that caregivers can engage in to enrich children's sensory experiences:

❑   Allow toddlers to participate in food preparation (e.g., feel the cookie dough, smear margarine on the cookie sheet).

❑   Provide children with boxes of materials that relate to specific categories of sensory experience (e.g., feely boxes, boxes of bells and rattles).

❑   Provide for different smelling experiences (take children over to flowers, bring spices such as cinnamon or vanilla, etc.).

❑   Provide sensory experiences with objects from the outside world (e.g., wood, stones, snow, leaves).

❑   Give children words to make their sensory experiences meaningful (e.g., "That's hot," "That's soft").

❑   Think about smelling, touching, and feeling during daily activities (e.g., smell the diaper cream, smear mud).

❑   Sing to children.

❑   Provide opportunities to hear music from different cultures.

Special Note

There is much controversy about using food products for sensory experiences. Painting with pudding or using cornmeal as sand are two examples. Many adults find playing with food offensive for ideological reasons, and this view needs to be respected. The approach we support here is that children can be given an opportunity to explore food products as a natural part of food preparation and eating. This will enhance sensory development without causing confusion between toys and food. Many rich sensory experiences take place in a home setting during food preparation — for example, dipping hands in a bag of flour, grasping a handful of oatmeal, or poking fingers into bread dough. These can be integrated into group care activities. Nevertheless, there may be special circumstances that make the use of food for sensory exploration important. Many physiotherapists use food substances for their work with children with special needs, and follow-up activities with the same substances may be important for the child.

To Observe

With infants and toddlers generally, and particularly those with special needs, it is important to attend to the way in which they respond to sensory stimulation. Many young children have sensory impairments; for example, they do not hear well or are visually impaired, and these problems are sometimes not detected in the early years. Careful observation of and attention to sensory development may provide caregivers with information that can prevent many problems later on.

1. Does the baby attempt to look for objects?
   - What kind of objects?
   - Where are the objects relative to the baby when she looks for them?

2. Which babies seem to focus more on which objects?

3. When toys are presented to different children, how do they respond?
   - Do they try to take the toys?
   - Do they show excitement?

4. How do different babies and toddlers examine different objects? What senses do they use?

5. How do babies and toddlers of different ages respond to sounds?
   – Turn their heads?
   – Startle?
   – Show interest, excitement, or enjoyment?

6. How do the voices of different people (mothers, caregivers, etc.) affect the babies and toddlers?

7. What types of touching does each child enjoy?
   – Soft, gentle caresses?
   – Tickles?

8. Does the baby tolerate touching on different parts of his body?
   – On hands and fingers?
   – On arms, tummy, back, legs, or feet?

9. Does the child like to touch and feel new things?

10. Which children seem to "rush in" to enjoy feeling different sensations?

11. Which children take their time, and are more cautious?

12. Which children indicate that they do not enjoy these sensations?
    – How do they show their displeasure?

Children with Special Needs

Children with special needs may require extra care and attention to develop sensory skills, since these skills are so important in all later learning. Caregivers should be sure to label and explain what the child is seeing, feeling, tasting, or hearing (e.g., "That's a cat. It's warm, it's soft, it's cuddly"). Providing sensory information in many different ways (e.g., "Look at the cat; feel its soft fur;

smell the cat; listen to it purr) may help the child to develop a clearer idea of what an object (such as a cat) is.

It may be necessary to teach a child with special needs to attend to sensory input. A child who hears or sees things but does not find them meaningful in any way may have learned to ignore sounds or visual inputs. Try, as much as possible throughout the day, to keep the child engaged. Have the child participate, talk about, describe, and explain objects and sensations. Other children may also assist in keeping the child engaged. If there is enough going on that is interesting, the child will not want to tune out. Watch carefully, though, for signs that the child may be getting too much stimulation. Does the child pull away, withdraw, cover eyes or ears? If so, step back and slow down. Children with special needs will also use quiet corners when they feel that they've had enough. Plan an area close by so that they can use it when they want.

Young children with visual impairments often use touch and hearing to get information. These babies are often very quiet, and adults may interpret this as unresponsive behavior. However, they are indeed responding: they are focusing to hear what is happening in their world. Talk to the child softly as you approach, so as to provide advance warning and avoid startling the baby. Identify sounds for the child (e.g., "That's the doorbell," "That's my watch"). Be sure to describe what you see as the child explores. Providing the visual information may help the child develop a total concept, especially of things she cannot feel or touch (e.g., the cars on the road). Tie together all the information the child requires — touch, sound, smell, and sight (Raver, 1991).

Children with hearing impairments need to have the auditory world described for them, in order to develop an understanding of how it works. Why did the caregiver walk over to the door and open it? How did she know when to pick up the telephone? Give the child this information. Children with some degree of hearing loss (e.g., those with ear infections) may react with fear to loud sounds (e.g., trucks, vacuum cleaners) since the noise hurts their ears. Watch for children's reactions to all sounds.

With special-needs children, as with all children, interpreting and tying information together will be a primary goal for caregivers.

Tips for Toys and Equipment

- Lots of pillows — hard, soft, big, and small — covered with different fabrics and textures.
- Texture mat for crawlers.
- Blocks or tin cans covered with different textures.
- Tin cans covered with different textures.
- Patches and pieces of fabric.
- Bean bags filled with socks, fabric, etc.
- Scarves, hats, shoes.
- Feely boxes (cardboard boxes lined with different materials to touch).
- An assortment of rattles of different sizes, shapes, and sounds.
- Squeaky toys.
- Different kinds of bells.
- Noise makers. Many everyday objects can be used for this (e.g., spoon and cup or bowl, pot lids).
- Plastic bottles, cans, and containers filled with water or different objects (e.g., stones and beads large enough so they can't be swallowed) to make a variety of sounds .
- Pots, lids, spoons, bowls for making noise.
- Musical instruments — drums, cymbals, shakers, bells.
- Flashlights and a darkened area to play in.
- Sunglasses to give toddlers a different view of the world.
- Bright, colorful toys that attract attention.
- Bright, colorful dress-up clothes that will give children something interesting to look at.
- Texture books and books with clear, large pictures and little background stimuli. Babies and toddlers particularly enjoy pictures of animals and babies.
- Water play during routine care and bath time too.
- Sand tables for toddlers over eighteen months.

✔ *Caregiver Checklist*

DOES THE CAREGIVER:

1. Ensure that all objects for sensory exploration are clean and safe?

2. Present young infants with bright objects to see, to follow with their eyes, and to grasp?

3. Ensure that the toys offer a variety of sizes, shapes, textures, and weights?

4. Occasionally demonstrate to babies different ways in which objects can be manipulated (rolled, stroked, patted)?

5. Notice the different ways in which children respond to different sensations, and respond to individual children's interests?

6. Label and expand on the children's experiences by using simple concepts such as hot, cold, soft, hard without distracting, intruding, or interrupting individual exploration?

7. Appreciate, pick up on, label, and occasionally imitate body sounds that the child naturally makes (mouth noises, slapping, stomping)?

8. Sing to children varying the tone of voice?

9. Refrain from yelling?

10. Use herself or himself as a sensory stimulus — letting babies touch, stroke hair, feel clothing?

11. Protect children from overstimulation and watch for competing stimuli?

12. Allow children to manipulate natural objects?

PRACTICAL APPLICATION

1. Examine the toys and equipment that are present in your playroom. List and describe what sensory experiences these would provide for the child.

   a) Do you feel that these objects provide a balance between noisy and quiet, soft and hard, busy and calm?

   b) What changes or recommendations would you make based on that observation?

   c) Observe an infant and a toddler as they play with these toys and materials. Then describe how they interacted with them. Compare the responses of the caregiver in these interactions.

2. Observe a small group of infants and then toddlers for a twenty-minute period during the day. List all of the sensory activities in the observation period. How was the caregiver involved in promoting sensory experiences?

3. What changes might you recommend to enhance sensory development? How could the setting or toys and materials be improved? How might the role of the caregiver change?

10

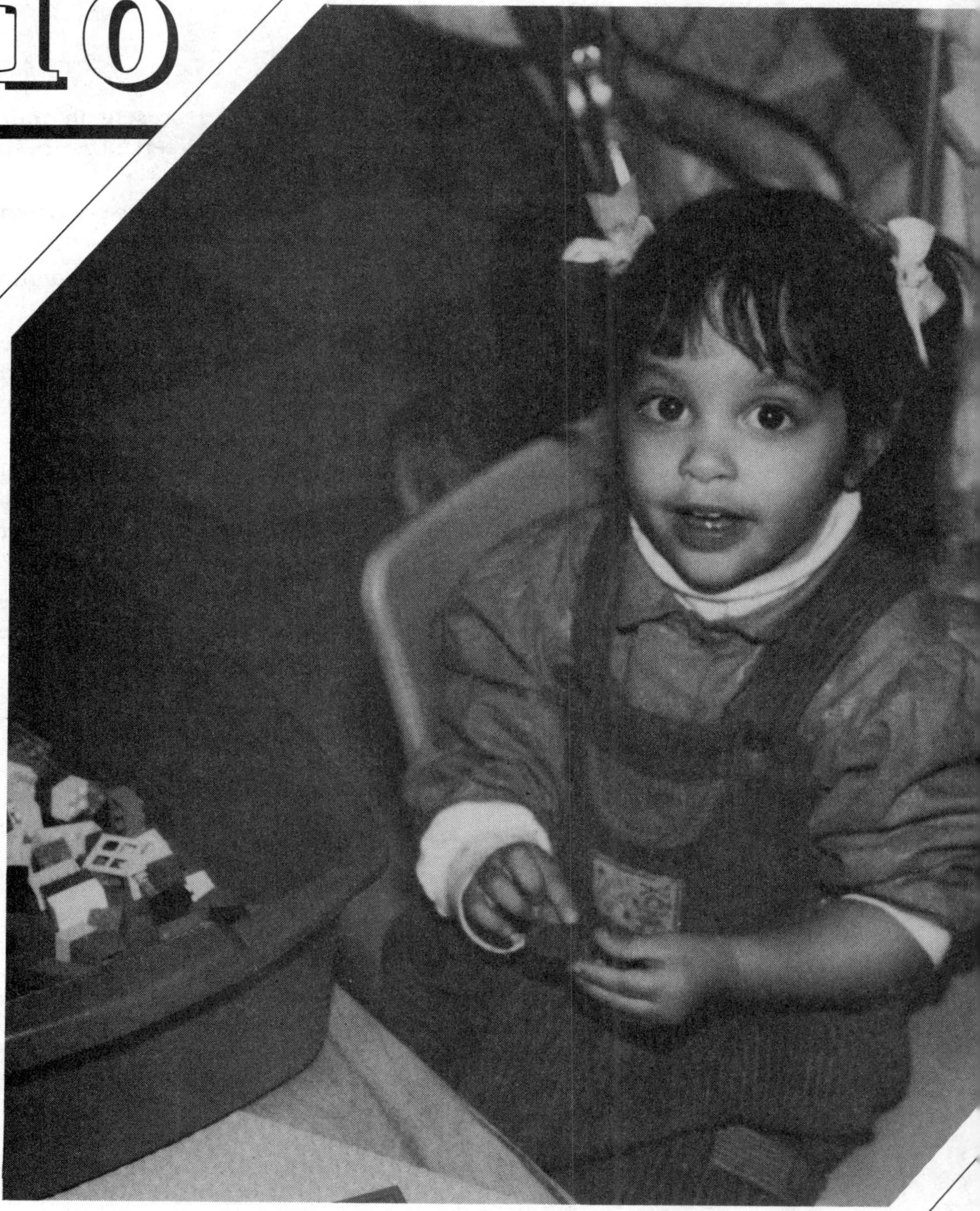

Fine Motor Development

Objectives

❖ To review the sequence of fine motor development in infants and toddlers.

❖ To discuss the role of the caregiver in facilitating fine motor development of infants and toddlers.

❖ To determine how the child with special needs benefits from fine motor experiences and how these can be included in group-care settings.

Opening Thoughts

Take a few moments to reflect on what life would be like if you could not use your hands. How would your development have been affected?

Comments on Opening Thoughts

❖ Emerging fine motor skills enable infants and toddlers to explore their world actively.

❖ Non-mobile infants are dependent upon adults to provide manipulative toys and materials.

❖ Fine motor skills are related to cognitive abilities — the head and the hands work together. ❐

Eight-month-old Carissa is sitting in her highchair waiting for lunch. The caregiver has set out several toys to amuse her while her lunch is prepared. She takes the soft rubber caterpillar in her left hand and squeezes it over and over. She picks up a set of keys on a ring with the other hand. Carissa looks at the keys, then at the caterpillar. She shakes the ring and listens to the noise it creates. She stops and shakes the caterpillar. No noise. She looks at the keys and bangs them against the table. Her eyes widen at the sound they make. Her attention is caught by a string of very large beads. She drops the caterpillar, looks to see where it lands and picks up the chain. As she picks it up, she watches closely. Some of the beads trail out of her hand. As she shakes them, the bottom ones bang on the tray. She stops, listens, and shakes again. After the third try she looks at the tray while shaking the beads and realizes that she is producing the noise all by herself!

This young baby delights in her hands. What power! They bring things to her, they make wonderful noises, and create interesting spectacles. Carissa has just spent time exploring and manipulating the objects in her world. She has used her hands in a variety of ways and picked up information about how things work. Her hand skills enabled her to engage in enjoyable sensory experiences, which, in turn, encouraged her to try other ways of manipulating objects. These hand skills are referred to as fine motor skills. Fine motor skills develop in a predictable sequence, although the timing differs from baby to baby.

When a parent puts a finger into the newborn's hand, the baby will squeeze it tightly. Although this is a reflexive action (the baby is born with the capacity to do this), this fine motor skill is exciting for parents and marks the starting point in the use of hands and fingers to do things. Fine motor development lays the foundation for a variety of other abilities. Children will learn to use their hands to eat, to dress, to explore, and to play with toys. In infancy and toddlerhood, heads and hands work together to understand the world. Doing with the hands enables the child to develop understanding of the object. Young children need to learn to use their hands, eyes, and mouths together. Hand skills are related to the child's developing a positive self image ("I can do it") and positive emotional growth.

After spending the first two months with their fingers tightly clenched most of the time, infants will begin to grasp objects placed in their palms with the whole hand. Fogel (1991) suggests that infants who are given objects that can be easily held, such as a ring with a hole in the middle, will master the task more quickly than children given objects that cannot be easily grasped. At this point, babies do not yet fully realize that when they loosen their grip, the toy will fall. It takes almost a year for a baby to learn to grasp and let go on purpose.

Since young infants do not possess the ability to reach or move to obtain objects, the caregiver will need to provide enough toys close enough to the babies so that they can learn to reach and bat or swipe. By four months, infants are able to grasp small objects, grasp and shake a rattle, and look at their fingers and hands (Allen & Marotz, 1989). They are beginning to bring things to their mouths and some have found a thumb to suck. Eye-hand coordination is beginning as they use eyes in combination with

Infants usually reach for objects with two hands, and delight in mouthing everything in sight.

hands to do things. Infants will progress from holding objects in one hand to switching an object from one hand to the other while continuing to take delight in mouthing everything in sight. Babies will usually reach for objects with two hands. Providing them with objects large enough to be held in two hands is helpful.

According to Thelan and Fogel (1989), this skill of reaching, along with the ability to put a hand into the mouth and keep it there, contributes to the child's emotional well-being. After four months of age, with these developments, babies are able to calm themselves by thumb sucking.

Over the next four months, from five to eight months, babies develop a number of interesting hand skills that allow them to explore their environment more thoroughly. Babies now attempt to pick up small objects by raking their hands along the table or floor. This involves the baby putting a hand over a chosen object and then closing the hand into a fist over it. The object is raked or captured by the movement. The child will reach out with one hand for a desired object now and will transfer items from one hand to the other (Karnes, 1982). The baby has developed new ways to manipulate objects including shaking, pounding, and dropping them. A cup and a table top make marvelous music to the infant at this stage: he or she can now bang and sing along and then drop the cup over and over again. These simple, repetitive activities provide the infant with the opportunity to practice and refine emerging motor abilities and to feel successful.

Throughout these initial stages of fine motor development, the adult plays an important role, not only in providing objects to manipulate but in positioning babies to explore and use their hands. Infants who are held in a sitting or upright position (preferably on the caregiver's lap), have both hands free to reach and grasp. Research indicates that babies held in an upright position are more attentive to their physical environment than infants lying on their backs (Fogel, 1991). However, infants who are not able to sit on their own should not be left sitting unsupported or propped up for more than a few minutes at a time.

Once the baby is more mobile and can sit alone, new avenues of exploration open up. Until now, manipulation of objects seemed to be an end in itself. A transition is now occurring as the baby begins to use hands purposely to examine toys. This new behavior is an excellent sign of intellectually curious explorations that are directed by the baby's growing intelligence (Honig, 1990). This is just the kind of behavior Carissa exhibited as she played with the beads and the caterpillar in the description at the opening of this chapter.

The infant has now progressed from raking objects to using the thumb and pointer finger together (Karnes, 1982; Allen & Marotz, 1989). This action is known as the pincer grasp. The use of thumb and forefinger is particularly useful in self feeding, when the child is quite content to pick up small pieces of food and feels very successful at being able to get them into his or her mouth.

Toward the end of the first year, infants start to coordinate more of their abilities. They place things into containers, and can use their arms and hands to make gestures such as waving bye-bye. They develop new ways to explore objects, by poking, feeling, dropping, and throwing. They are able to imitate simple actions such as playing pat-a-cake, pushing a button, or opening a box.

Sometime around the first birthday, babies become toddlers. They move around and seek new objects to explore and manipulate. Toddlers scribble with crayons, turn pages in books, throw and roll balls, and stack objects. They love to fill containers with anything, then dump it out, and fill and dump, and fill and dump! Water play and pouring from a cup becomes a favorite

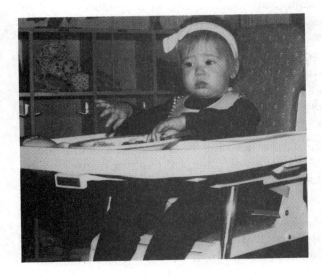

The pincer grasp is particularly useful in self feeding.

activity. Toddlers play with their first puzzles (simple ones with two or three pieces, usually) and strings of very large beads. Through all this manipulation, they are learning that their actions cause interesting things to happen. Again, head and hands are working together.

By two, toddlers have come a long way from that first reflexive grasp of a parent's finger. However, unlike sensory development, their fine motor skills still have a long way to go before they are fully developed. We have to remember that many of the tasks we sometimes expect children to do, such as puzzles and sorting shapes, require that fine motor skills be fairly refined. If children are frustrated repeatedly by unsuccessful attempts, their motivation to continue trying may well be hampered. If we are careful to provide opportunities for manipulation that are appropriate, children will enjoy that "I can do it" feeling that contributes to a positive self image and helps them on their way to mastering the challenges that lie ahead.

Role of the Caregiver

To Protect

Infants and toddlers are in a constant state of doing something, usually involving their hands. As young children actively explore their world, they will need to be protected from harm. This is especially relevant for babies who are putting anything and everything into their mouths. Caregivers will need to be vigilant in checking toys, equipment, materials, and the general setting to ensure that all is safe. Below are some ideas for protecting children as they develop fine motor skills:

❑ Check that toys and all other objects do not have small parts or parts that can be broken or taken off (e.g., buttons, snaps, small wheels on cars).

❑ Ensure that all toys are non-toxic and washable, and that they are washed regularly.

❑ Ensure that the floor is cleaned regularly and that it is free of objects that should not be mouthed.

❑ Ensure that toddlers can play with beads or other small toys in an area removed from the reach of mobile babies who are still mouthing.

❑ Avoid unnecessary frustration caused by toys that are well beyond the skill level of the child.

❑ Prevent unnecessary disruptions when children are concentrating.

To Support

Caregivers need to be aware of hand skills and how they develop so that they may actively promote progress in this area. They can support fine motor development in the following ways:

❑ Provide toys that respond to whatever motion the child makes (e.g., toys that do something when swiped at).

❑ Provide opportunities for the child to use both hands; offer toys to both hands.

❑ Provide opportunities to use two hands together (e.g., use a large ball that is easy to hold onto with two hands).

❑ Provide opportunities to repeat, repeat, and repeat again a particular motion.

❑ Provide toys that can be used in different ways at different skill levels (e.g., balls, blocks, stacking cups).

❑ Provide toys of different textures and shapes to manipulate.

❑ Provide objects that will be easy and safe for toddlers to carry.

❑ Have toys available on low shelves for easier access and choice.

❑ Pick up and tidy toys frequently to maintain order and establish predictability (so that children will know where to find toys and will be encouraged to explore independently).

❑ Offer assistance and reassurance to infants and toddlers who are concentrating on a new task.

❑ Ensure that toddlers who are "on the go" also have opportunities to practice fine motor skills.

❑ Provide opportunities for self feeding (with fingers, spoons, and cups) and dressing (e.g., pulling off socks).

To Enrich

The world of infants and toddlers grows and expands quickly as they develop new ways to manipulate and explore. We can enrich the development of fine motor skills by making use of the following activities:

❑ Imitate and follow babies' actions with their hands (the baby claps, you clap).

❑ Play action songs; this is a good way to develop interest in hands.

❑ Model fine motor movements (e.g., show how to activate a toy or how to string beads).

❑ Provide ever-challenging toys.

❑ Demonstrate different possibilities (e.g., rolling the ball, patting the stuffed animal).

To Observe

Hand skills form the foundations for much of the learning that occurs in infancy and toddlerhood. The following observations will help you watch this development as it occurs in each child.

1. What kind of hand movements are the babies making?

2. Is the baby coordinating hand movements?
   – With seeing?
   – With her mouth?
   – Two hands together?

3. Can the baby follow objects and reach for them?

4. Is the baby or toddler exploring objects in different ways?
   – Shaking?
   – Banging?
   – Dropping?
   – Throwing?

5. What does the baby do with two objects?
   – Hold only one?
   – Hold one in each hand?
   – Transfer from hand to hand?

6. How does an eight-month-old baby use his hands to play with a ball? How is this different from the way in which a year-old, eighteen-month-old, or two-year-old uses his hands?

7. For how long does the toddler stay with a task such as interlocking blocks?

8. Which fine motor activity does the toddler seem to enjoy most? How can you tell?

9. Does the toddler initiate fine motor activity on her own, or does she usually wait until the caregiver offers these toys?

Caregivers can model fine motor movements by showing how to activate toys.

Children with Special Needs

For some children with special needs, practice and repetition will be essential to the mastery of simple fine motor skills. Try to vary the objects used somewhat so that the child does not become bored but still has the chance to practice similar skills. For example, you could have a variety of toys with similar knobs to activate, so that the hand movement is the same but the end result is different. The variety will keep the baby's attention. Introduce new objects slowly so there is ample opportunity to explore each one.

Children with visual impairments may need special adaptations. If they do not know that the object is there, they won't reach out for it. If they don't reach, they won't develop more elaborate hand movements. Toys hanging on an A-frame or located

All children can be encouraged to develop fine motor skills in the course of routine activities such as eating.

close to the child, along with constant reminders that toys are there, will help. Children with hearing difficulties may require objects that are visually attractive rather than dependent on sound. Physically disabled children may require special adaptations and teaching to promote fine motor development. Finnie (1981) provides many ideas to promote the functional use of hands for children with cerebral palsy.

The caregiver can provide most help for the child with special needs by being aware of the child's requirements and providing sufficient opportunity for practice and exploration. Where ongoing difficulties or problems are noted, assistance from an occupational therapist should be sought.

TIPS FOR TOYS AND EQUIPMENT

- Rattles.
- Brightly colored objects the child will want to reach for.
- Mobiles.
- Toys hanging on an A-frame that can be swiped at, reached for, grabbed, and manipulated.
- Balls and beanbags to throw.
- Objects to stack (e.g., boxes, stacking cups and rings, measuring cups, bowls, containers).
- Objects to sort (e.g., bowls, shoes, cups, spoons).
- Large crayons.
- Dolls with clothing for undressing and dressing.
- Blocks.
- Pots and pans with lids.

✔ Caregiver Checklist

DOES THE CAREGIVER:

1. Provide a variety of materials and objects for manipulation that allow for a range of fine motor experiences?

2. Encourage fine motor development in the course of routine activities such as eating, dressing, and undressing?

3. Ensure that objects are washable, non-toxic, and safe to put into mouths?

4. Encourage exploration and manipulation of objects in the environment?

5. Encourage coordination of fine motor skills and other skills (e.g., sensory, gross motor, and cognitive skills)?

6. Minimize conflict by having sufficient toys and materials?

7. Model various fine motor movements (e.g., turning on a switch, turning a knob)?

8. Provide toys that can be worked repeatedly, over and over?

9. Provide toys with which infants and toddlers can be successful?

PRACTICAL APPLICATION

1. Before the start of the day, take account of all of the toys, materials, and equipment available to promote the development of fine motor skills for infants and toddlers.

2. Observe in the playroom while children are present on two different occasions. Which toys did the children play with? Were these toys that you thought would be used? Were some toys ignored by the children? If so, why do you think they were ignored?

3. Observe an infant or toddler for twenty minutes at some point during the day. List all of the fine motor activities that the child engaged in during this period of time. How did the caregiver encourage fine motor development?

4. What changes could be made to enhance fine motor development? What would you recommend for toys, materials, and equipment? What could the caregiver do?

Gross Motor Development

Objectives

- ❖ To review the gross motor development sequence for infants and toddlers.
- ❖ To discuss the ways in which the caregiver and the setting can facilitate gross motor development.
- ❖ To examine how gross motor development can be supported and enhanced for children with special needs.

Opening Thoughts

List several gross motor activities that you engaged in during the past week. Beside each, note the purpose or reason for the activity:

Example: I ran because I had to get to class in time.

               I played volleyball because it was a chance to see my friends.

               I swam to reduce my stress level.

Do gross motor activities serve the same functions for infants and toddlers? What are the differences? What are the similarities?

Comments on Opening Thoughts

- ❖ Emerging gross motor skills are necessary to enable infants and toddlers to explore their world actively: they need to move in order to learn.
- ❖ Adults may need to engage in physical activity for stress reduction because many of their movements are restricted most of the time. In contrast, children are in a state of motion most of their waking hours.
- ❖ Adults have the independence to choose the kinds of gross motor activities they wish to be involved in. Babies are often dependent upon adults to plan an environment that provides appropriate gross motor experiences. ❐

Eighteen-month-old Chelsea and her caregiver are going for a short walk through the park, waiting for Mom to pick Chelsea up. Chelsea walks along the cement path, first slowly, then trotting, and then she comes to a sudden stop. She takes three steps back and continues on. The path goes straight ahead but Chelsea decides to try climbing on the rocks. She climbs up the first and sits, slides off, and tries the second. On the third rock, she is brave and tries to take one giant step up to the top. But the rock is too high so she asks for assistance. The caregiver takes her arms and helps her to the top of the rock. After climbing the rocks, she walks over the grass. Each step is slow and the caregiver can see her feeling the soft grass below. She walks, she marches, she runs, and she stops at the top of a small incline. She points "da" and slowly saunters down the hill. Up and down the incline she goes over and over again. "Look at the butterfly," says the caregiver but Chelsea ignores her. She is much too busy conquering the hill.

This is a typical walk for a toddler: practicing gross motor skills over and over to the exclusion of all else. Movement becomes the toddler's primary activity. Walking is not just a matter of getting from point A to point B but is an experience in itself. Chelsea was so intent on what she was doing that she may not even have heard the caregiver. How does the baby get to this point? What are all the things that need to happen before babies can coordinate their movements to include all of the activities that Chelsea did in ten minutes?

Movement in the mother's womb is the first sign of life and is received by the mother with excitement and pleasure. Throughout the early years, movement continues to be met with excitement because gross motor milestones are the most visible signs of development that parents watch for. The gross motor skills emerge in a predictable sequence. They tend to unfold, regardless of the level of stimulation, in much the same order from child to child. However, the rate of development can vary vastly from child to child, even sibling to sibling. For example, children may take their first steps anywhere between nine and sixteen months, and will be considered normal.

Infants enter the world with a number of reflexive movements that begin to fade within the first month. They are replaced, as the child develops, with muscle control and voluntary movements. Newborns will kick up their legs in reaction to a loud noise. As the reflex fades, they will develop the muscle control needed to lift and kick up their legs voluntarily.

The infant's first milestone is head control. Head control develops gradually from momentarily lifting and holding the head to lifting and holding it for longer periods of time (Allen & Marotz, 1989). Development continues as infants gain control of their shoulders and upper back, which enables them to sit and roll.

Babies have usually gained enough trunk control to sit with support at around four months and can sit unsupported at around eight (Allen & Marotz, 1989). At around six months, many babies can remain sitting unsupported once they are placed in a sitting position. But often the baby falls forward, face to the floor, at the caregiver's mercy to be rescued. There is really no need to prop babies up before they can sit on their own, except for very short periods to play with the caregiver. If the environment is well planned and the baby has space, the world is just as interesting and challenging from stomach or back.

Sitting is a key event for young babies because now they are in an upright position and have a very different view of the world. When children can sit alone, their hands are free to explore, mouth, reach, or grasp objects at will.

At around half a year, the baby can begin to roll. Tummy to back usually occurs before back to tummy. The first rolls often end in tears of surprise as the baby discovers this new ability. With time and practice, rolling becomes more refined. Some babies begin to move by squirming on their stomachs, rolling onto it, or pivoting while sitting. Real crawling begins at about nine months of age, after much practice rocking back and forth on all fours and shifting weight. Now the child has a whole new world to touch, feel, see, and explore.

Somewhere between six and twelve months, babies will pull themselves to a standing position. It is not uncommon to see an infant howl in distress while standing because he or she does not know how to get down. It is important to have many firmly attached shelves and pieces of furniture so babies can practice pulling themselves up and sitting down again. Soon, the child

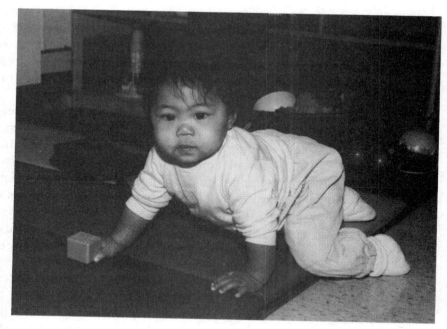

Once crawling begins, the child has a new world to explore.

begins to "cruise" by sidestepping while gripping onto something. As children get braver and develop more balance, they take small steps between pieces of furniture.

Somewhere around the age of a year, babies reach the most dramatic milestone. They begin to take their first unsupported steps. The transition from the first few wobbly steps to walking well alone seems to happen over a very short time. Soon babies are walking all of the time. Children love to walk and to move on different surfaces — on grass, over cracks in the sidewalk, up and down ramps. They seem to be compulsive carriers of all sorts of items and spend a great deal of time pushing and pulling objects. All of their waking hours are filled with movement — of themselves, toys, equipment, furniture: anything that can be moved will. Toddlers also begin to climb. They will clamber up equipment, furniture, and climbers. Children at this stage appear to be in a constant state of motion — up, down, forward, and back. Managing stairs is another feat of toddlerhood. Children initially will attempt stairs by crawling head first to see where they are going, whether they are crawling up or down. By the age of two or two-and-a-half, toddlers can walk up and down stairs by themselves. They will soon be trotting in preparation for running around the age of two and will be able to navigate "ride-'em" toys.

The development of motor skills is a fascinating process. But even more fascinating is the way in which the gross motor skills are interrelated with other aspects of development. We said in Chapter 10 that the hands and head work together as the child learns about the world. Now the feet and the head work together. For example, the child discovers that kicking the ball hard will make it move fast. All the gross motor movements involve sensory experiences that provide knowledge as well as pleasure (Fogel, 1991).

Caregivers should be aware of several points related to the development of movement. First, the sequence of development is quite consistent but the rate does vary enormously. Caregivers must observe children's progression from milestone to milestone carefully, taking individual differences into account. Some children may develop a little differently in some areas (Bee, 1989). For example, some children never crawl in the true sense of the word, but "bum scoot." Although this is not usual, it is useful for some children and they will likely learn to walk, climb, and run as other children do.

Second, research tells us that gross motor development will unfold no matter how much artificial stimulation the child receives (Weiser, 1991). The message here is that caregivers cannot push children. The stage must be set in terms of planning the environment and activities, but a baby will not sit up, crawl, or walk until mature enough to do so. The baby's desire to practice and try new things is influenced by the setting and people in that setting. The baby needs space, fresh air, few restrictions, good health, and nutrition. A stimulating, interesting, and challenging environment that is planned with different levels of motor ability in mind will promote opportunities for children to learn about themselves and what their bodies are capable of doing, and how good it is to feel "I can do it."

Toddlers enjoy navigating "ride'em" toys.

Role of the Caregiver

Each new gross motor skill takes practice, practice, and more practice. The child's motivation to continue needs the support and encouragement of a caregiver who recognizes and appreciates the child's efforts and enjoys gross motor experiences.

To Protect

Motor abilities develop at a very fast rate and babies do not yet fully understand all of the potential hazards in their world. For this reason, caregivers must protect infants and toddlers by considering the following:

❑ Prevent injuries by ensuring that furniture does not have sharp corners or edges and that shelves are securely fastened.

❑ Provide freedom to move but ensure that the setting is as hazard-free as possible (e.g., by picking toys up).

❑ Have a soft surface for babies who are learning how to walk so that falling is not traumatic.

❑ Ensure that the objects available for babies and toddlers to carry are safe and will not cause injury should the child fall (e.g., objects that are not sharp, pointed, or too heavy).

❑ Ensure that the equipment available is suited to the child's abilities (e.g., the baby just learning to walk will have difficulties getting on and off "ride 'em" toys or trikes; toddlers who are just beginning to climb should do so on objects that are small or have small steps or rungs).

❑ Set reasonable limits (e.g., "You cannot run in the kitchen area. Let's go into the play area to run").

❑ Always be available and on guard for falls and injuries. Caregivers must plan to be in strategic positions at all times.

❑ Limit access to stairs. Until the child is crawling comfortably, stairs may present a hazard.

❑ Don't "push" babies and toddlers; wait until they are ready.

❑ Avoid equipment that leaves the baby at the adult's mercy to be moved (e.g., jolly jumpers and walkers).

❑ Be aware of regulations regarding the type of equipment that may be used (e.g., walkers, jolly jumpers and rebounders are considered hazardous and banned in day-care settings in some places).

To Support

Caregivers will assume a role in helping infants and toddlers at all stages to develop gross motor skills, from the very immobile baby to the very active toddler. Caregivers can support development by providing a rich and varied environment where the children will want to move and explore and by being with them for reassurance. Support can also be provided through the strategies below:

❑ Provide a variety of interesting hanging objects or mobiles so that the babies can extend their arms and reach for, grasp, and kick them. Objects should be placed on both sides of baby at different distances to encourage her to roll over and to reach out.

❑ Young babies who are not yet mobile will need to be moved often to provide new and different things to see and experience.

❑ Young babies will need to be placed in different positions so that they can use their hands, find their feet, kick their legs, etc.

❑ Encourage babies to hold their heads up by presenting interesting objects (including yourself) or presenting objects in such a way that babies have to lift their heads to see.

❑ Encourage crawling by having soft, covered, and inviting spaces.

❑ Encourage standing by having child-size objects for the children to pull themselves up on (e.g., furniture, small tables, shelves that have attractive objects on them).

❑ Encourage the baby to walk by providing lots of praise and hugs when he reaches the final goal — you.

❑ Provide lots of opportunities for the baby to walk, climb, and run on different surfaces (e.g., carpet, grass, dirt, puddles, mud).

❑ Provide large objects of different shapes and sizes for the child to kick.

❑ Recognize little gains that the child makes. Caregivers should be available to praise children but should avoid constant praise. Commenting on what the child has done or describing the feat to others can be just as rewarding (e.g., "Look! Mary crawled up the ramp.").

❑ Demonstrate enjoyment in what the babies are doing. Have fun with them.

To Enrich

Although children will find almost anything to practice gross motor abilities on, the caregiver can enrich development with the following:

❑ Make a texture mat with different pieces of carpet, cloth, and fabric for the baby to crawl on.

❏ Encourage developing trunk control by propping the baby over a small wedge or pillow or over your thigh so he has to use shoulder and back muscles to hold himself up.

❏ Encourage sitting by putting interesting objects around the child that she can easily reach while sitting.

❏ Encourage rolling by slowly moving objects away from baby's immediate grasp so that he has to roll to get it.

❏ Plan environments that include equipment or toys for the next stage of development. For example, when the child is just learning to walk, provide sturdy, weighted, movable toys that do not move too quickly (e.g., children often push full laundry baskets).

❏ Create obstacle courses within the setting using chairs to go under, pillows to go over, tunnels to go through, places for climbing on, etc.

❏ Occasionally demonstrate new but safe ways for the child to use equipment or her own body (e.g., swinging on a low bar, making a bridge with her body).

To Observe

In order to support the infant or toddler through the development of movement abilities, caregivers should observe how the child progresses from milestone to milestone:

1. Is the baby beginning to develop head control?
   - For brief moments?
   - Is the length of time increasing?
   - In what position does the child best support her head? In your arms? Held up on your shoulder?

2. Is the infant developing trunk control?
   - Can he lift his chest off the floor when on his tummy?
   - How long can he hold it?
   - Can he support his head while over a pillow?

3. Is the baby developing the ability to sit?
- Can she sit unsupported?
- Can she get into and out of sitting position?
- Can she reach for toys while sitting?

4. Is the baby beginning to roll?
- From front to back?
- From back to front?
- Is the movement accidental or purposeful?

5. Is the baby beginning to walk?
- Will he stand holding onto something?
- Can he get up and down on his own?
- Will he move sideways while holding on?
- Is he beginning to take small steps from one spot to another?
- Can he walk alone?
- Can he maneuver on different surfaces?

6. How does the infant or toddler manage stairs?
- Head first?
- Crawling up and down?
- Standing and walking up and down?
- Walking up and down without holding on?

7. What other gross motor capabilities does the child have?
- Climbing?
- Trotting?
- Running?

8 Does the toddler seem to be in constant movement? Is she fairly active but not all the time, or does she seem to prefer quiet activities?

9. Does the toddler try new challenges on his own? Does he do so when you are nearby or usually only when you encourage him?

Children with Special Needs

Children with special needs, for the most part, will develop gross motor abilities in much the same sequence as all children, but the rate may be slower. Caregivers often do things for a child with special needs because it is faster or safer (e.g., carrying lunch to the table). If all of the child's needs and wants are met, the child will have no purpose for moving and exploring. An interesting, challenging environment will motivate the child to move and practice large muscle skills.

Hearing impaired children do not usually have difficulties in developing motor skills. In contrast, children with visual impairments often have difficulties in moving, especially when they initiate the movement. Walk with these children so they develop confidence in themselves. Have them push toys like strollers or carts that will hit objects before they do, and will act as a warning. Keeping the environment as consistent as possible will provide the security children need to be mobile. Encourage the children to walk independently even though it is faster to lead or take them. Especially in familiar surroundings, let them find their own way to the water table, the table for lunch, and outside. Although playpens allow children to explore by keeping the toys in a closed area, do not protect children with visual impairments in playpens unnecessarily. Sometimes adults feel that a visually impaired child will be hurt or stepped on in the middle of action with a group of toddlers. It should be sufficient, however, to ensure that the child is protected by not being in the middle of the floor, and to keep close watch. When children with visual impairments feel safe and comfortable in their surroundings, they will feel freer to move and explore.

Children with physical impairments will likely present the most difficulties in developing gross motor abilities. For example, as a result of brain damage, children with cerebral palsy will have an extremely difficult time in learning to control and coordinate muscle movements. Babies and toddlers with physical disabilities often look very different from other babies. They may be very limp and floppy or they may be tense and have jerky movements. Because these physical characteristics are so different from those caregivers usually encounter, they can be considered

Children require lots of opportunities to develop and practice gross motor skills.

frightening or too difficult to deal with. The child's parents will likely be the best ally in giving the caregiver ideas on how to best hold and position the child. Once the caregiver is comfortable with the child, then she will feel more comfortable in trying new ways of moving the child herself. For example, if the child tenses up when he is laid on his back, turning him or his head slightly to one side may be enough to let him lie while being changed. A physiotherapist may be consulted for further information. Finnie's (1981) book provides an easy-to-follow guide to positioning and handling.

Children with developmental delays will need lots of opportunities to develop and practice gross motor skills since their progress is often slower. These children will develop skills in much the same order, but will require extra help and practice.

TIPS FOR TOYS AND EQUIPMENT

Toys and equipment that encourage gross motor activities needn't be expensive. A box is just as much fun to move about as a fancy push toy. All of this material should be made available outdoors as well as indoors. Remember that the best piece of equipment is the caregiver! Babies can use the caregiver's body to crawl over and to hang on to, and many enjoy being swung into motion.

Precrawling Babies:

- Mats, blankets, soft surfaces to lie and move on.
- Mobiles or suspended objects to reach and grab for, or to kick at.
- Portable A-frames from which to hang interesting objects.
- Mirrors.
- Balls, squeaky toys, and rattles that the baby will reach for or roll over to try to get.
- Pillows for supporting or moving around on.
- Small wedges or hard pillows so that children can learn to hold themselves up.

Crawling Babies:

- A variety of surfaces and textures. Create these by adding pillows, mattresses, and cushions to climb over.
- Tunnels to crawl through. These may be as simple as a large cardboard box with two holes for crawling in and out of.
- Inner tubes or tires to crawl through, tubes or tires covered with sturdy fabric to crawl on, or inflatable wading pools to crawl into.
- Wide ramps or wedges.
- Large pillows or bean-bag chairs to crawl over and climb on.
- Objects that roll (e.g., large balls, weighted balls, large plastic bottles filled with water).
- Low shelves or furniture to encourage infants to pull themselves up.

Walking Babies:

- Push-and-pull toys of different sizes, shapes, and weights. A variety of objects to load and unload (e.g., purses, baskets, pails with handles, strollers, little shopping carts, or suitcases).

- A variety of light, easily manageable and safe objects to carry.

- Laundry baskets and large cardboard boxes for pushing, pulling, and climbing in.

- Tunnels.

- Balls of all sizes.

- Small climbers and furniture that is safe to climb on.

- Ramps or inclines.

- Obstacle course created from objects in the setting.

Outdoor areas can provide hours of freedom and enjoyment, even if they are not full of equipment.

The description of Chelsea at the beginning of the chapter makes it obvious that the outdoors is the perfect place to enjoy gross motor movement. Even through the printed page we could feel her involvement, satisfaction, and joy. In our attempts to provide excellent care inside the center, we sometimes forget that there is a world outside — a world where children feel the wind on their faces, feel the leaves or the snow under their feet, see and feel flowers and rocks.

Weather permitting, outdoor time should be maximized. Outdoor areas for infants and toddlers need not be full of equipment. A grassy area for infants and toddlers (with provision for shade) and a hard surface for toddlers can provide hours of freedom and enjoyment. Fenced-off areas, high enough to prevent babies from being run over by older children, and low enough for toddlers to peep over, are advised.

Most toys and equipment that are suggested throughout this book can be easily moved outside. In addition, other equipment that stays outdoors should be available. Examples include large boxes to crawl in, play houses, tires, and low climbing frames. Greenman (1988) provides many more suggestions for outdoor space.

✔ *Caregiver Checklist*

DOES THE CAREGIVER:

1. Use own body to encourage babies' gross motor activity?

2. Demonstrate an understanding of the toddler's need for constant movement by avoiding activities that restrict or inhibit movement?

3. Recognize little achievements and encourage children by verbalizing their actions rather than offering constant praise? (e.g., "Oh! you crawled to the ball" rather than, "Good boy.")

4. Constantly remain aware of basic safety?

5. Vary toys and equipment according to baby's interest and capabilities?

6. Demonstrate enjoyment of the child's gross motor activities?

7. Observe closely, and occasionally demonstrate the fun use of equipment without intruding on the child's play?

8. Minimize conflict by making sure there are enough materials and equipment?

9. Plan and provide a variety of outdoor experiences?

10. Refrain from putting babies in restrictive devices (walkers, jolly jumpers)?

11. Encourage children to participate in movement but avoid "pushing" babies or toddlers into something they are not ready for?

12. Know the milestones of gross motor development and the variation or range of ages when skills might emerge?

13. Provide infants with frequent changes in position or location?

PRACTICAL APPLICATION

1. At a quiet moment, when the children are not in the center, list all of the toys and equipment available for gross motor activities.

2. Observe an infant, and then a toddler, for a twenty-minute period at some point during the day. List all of the movement activities that they engaged in during that period of time. How did the caregiver promote gross motor development?

3. What changes would you recommend to enhance gross motor development? What toys or equipment would help? What could the caregiver do?

4. If the director of the center said that a small amount of funding was available for outdoor equipment for babies and toddlers, what would you recommend and why?

12

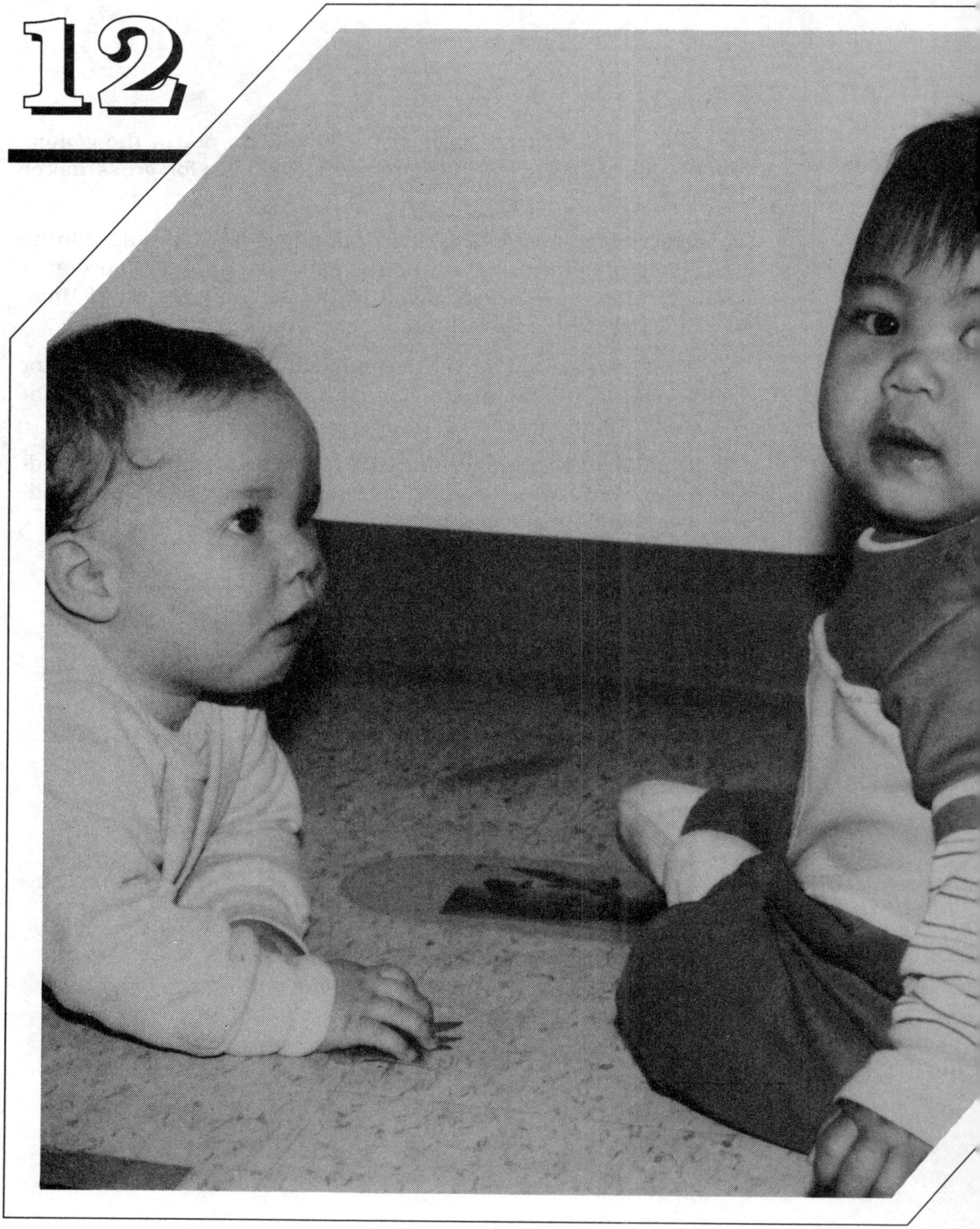

Cognitive Development

Objectives

❖ To review the sequence of cognitive development.

❖ To discuss the role of the caregiver in fostering cognitive development.

❖ To emphasize the importance of providing an environment rich in cognitive experiences for all children.

Opening Thoughts

Imagine that you suddenly found yourself in an airport in a strange city and you couldn't remember the address of where you needed to go. What would you do?

Comments on Opening Thoughts

❖ We use complicated problem solving skills daily, even if the situations are not as dramatic as the one above.

❖ We gain knowledge from daily interactions with people and things, and use that knowledge to solve problems. (We know that public phones work when we put coins in them, that the road map helps us find our destination, etc.)

❖ Experience is an important teacher. The development of thinking skills starts in infancy and infants and toddlers need lots of experiences and opportunities for practice, trial, and error. They also need guidance from the adult to learn how their world works. ❐

T wenty-month-old Melissa arrives at the day-care center bright and early. After coming through the door, without removing her jacket or saying good-bye to her dad, she says, "Baby?" with a puzzled look on her face. She walks over to the empty doll stroller, looks inside, and again says, "Baby?" Next, she tries the crib where the doll usually sleeps, but again no luck. In a final attempt, she moves a small stool over to the storage cupboard, opens the latch and locates the doll. "Baby!" she says, walks over to dad to show him and offers her lips for a good-bye kiss.

Consider all of the thinking that went on during this brief episode. Melissa remembers that she has a favorite doll here and she associates the doll with certain places in the setting. When the doll cannot be found, Melissa actively searches it out. The memory, the mental images of the doll and setting, the attention to the task of opening the latch are all quite remarkable for a toddler of this age. Already she has learned, through repeated experiences and manipulations, how her world operates. She has put together many pieces of information to solve this problem so early in the morning.

Cognitive development involves thinking, problem solving, intelligence, and language. It is a complex process of coordinating external and internal sensations. That means that we receive information via our senses, we process it, and we act upon it. Fogel (1991) suggests that infants are active in processing information by six months of age. This leads to understanding, to knowing, and to developing cognitive or thinking skills.

Cognitive development is likely one of the most fascinating areas to observe as caregivers watch the very dependent infant evolve into a thinking, problem-solving little person. Understanding the cognitive abilities of infants and toddlers requires that adults observe children closely, because many cognitive skills develop before language does.

The most widely known and read source on cognitive development information is the work of Jean Piaget. Piaget (1972) has outlined four major stages of cognitive development. The stage most relevant to infants and toddlers is the sensorimotor stage, from birth to twenty-four months. This stage is aptly named, since infants and toddlers actively experience the world through their senses and movements (Bee, 1989). This is a time when children actively explore and manipulate objects to get all the information possible so that they can then act on the world. The skills and abilities of the sensorimotor period of development will be the focus of discussion here.

Newborn babies enter the world with a number of reflexes that serve to protect them. For example, the rooting and sucking reflex ensure that babies can locate and get nutrition. Beginning at about one month, these reflexes fade and are gradually replaced with learned behaviors. The rooting reflex fades as babies learn that milk will come from mom. They learn to locate mom by smell and touch. They learn that she will be there to provide for their needs. When this occurs, the reflex is no longer needed; babies now know how to make sure they get fed. They know that if they cry, mom will appear. Through smell and touch, they will locate food with help from an adult.

During the first to fourth month, babies develop a number of skills related to thinking. They can watch an object and follow it as it moves. They begin to mouth objects. They will watch their own hands, grasp objects and reach out to objects that they see. An interesting development at this time occurs when the child accidentally causes something to happen, and then repeats the action on purpose. For example, the baby is lying in her bassinet and kicks up her leg. This unplanned movement causes the blanket to move, providing baby with a new sight and a slight breeze. The baby will then repeat this movement on purpose to cause the same result.

The next stage, which spans about four to eight months, sees continued development in a number of areas. The infant now explores objects in new ways by shaking, banging, pushing, and squeezing. A child who is holding two objects will drop one to get a third that is offered. If a wanted toy is just out of reach on a blanket, the baby will pull the blanket to get it. If the toy is partially covered, the baby will look and reach for it. This is the beginning of object permanence and is a major step for the baby who, up until now, had no idea that things will still exist even if they cannot be seen. Out of sight has been out of mind. This development has implications for the kinds of activities we engage in with babies. In a game of peekaboo, up until now, the baby would not realize that the adult was still there even though her face was hidden. The reappearing face was a surprise to the baby, sometimes even causing tears. Now, the infant realizes that the adult is still there and eagerly anticipates the reappearance of the player's face.

If an object falls to the floor, the baby will look for it too. The baby is gathering information about how the world works. If an object is dropped from the highchair, it will always go down. It will take many repetitions of this action to consolidate the information. Imitation of familiar movements such as clapping and waving are just beginning at this time and the baby is developing more interest in the sounds that he is able to make.

The next stage, from around eight to twelve months, takes on a new dimension since the baby is beginning to move. As infants move, their world gets larger and larger, with more to explore and discover (Bee, 1989). Young children will now move to obtain an object out of their reach or can pull a string to get the toy they see. In exploring objects, the child will drop objects on purpose or throw them. These actions are intended to increase understanding of the world, not to perturb caregivers! Baby will start to use familiar objects in a functional way; for example, they will feed their dolls with a spoon, or brush a doll's hair with a hair brush. This means that they are starting to associate objects with what they do, to learn how objects work. Putting objects in and out of containers is now an interesting activity. Not only are babies at this stage learning how things relate to one another (e.g., in and out) but they are also finding that they have control in manipulating objects. Babies can now put information together to get things to happen. They are beginning to realize that they can cause certain effects and can achieve simple goals such as getting a toy or making something interesting happen all by themselves.

From about the first-year mark to eighteen months, young children become more and more capable, able to do more things for themselves. They have largely conquered object permanence, so that they realize that objects exist even when they cannot be seen. They realize that mom is gone but will be back and that, when you play peekaboo, you are still there. Being able to anticipate that you will reappear makes the game fun. In order to get a toy that might be hidden under the sofa, children at this age will

Toddlers are able to make mental images of what they have experienced, and will replay daily events.

use a tool, such as a stick, to get it out. When toddlers want something to happen, they will guide an adult's hand or give the adult a toy, thus affecting the world in yet another way. Again, toddlers are learning about how the world operates and how much control they have.

The last stage of sensorimotor development, from eighteen to twenty-four months, really provides time for children to consolidate cognitive, sensory, and motor skills. Children, by now, have learned that objects exist even when out of sight (object permanence), that they can cause things to happen, either by acting upon them or by using language (cause and effect), and that they can achieve simple goals (means end). They are fine imitators of movements that they see and language that they hear (Fogel, 1991). Toddlers are now able to make mental images of what they've seen, heard, or experienced. They will represent mom or dad putting baby to bed, or will replay what happened at the doctor's office. They can solve problems by figuring them out in their heads rather than having to act directly on the world or problem solve with their hands. For example, they can figure out that they have to get a chair to climb on the counter to get a cookie. The child, through practice and many opportunities to explore, has learned to act upon the world and make things happen. For all intents and purposes, we can say that the child can think.

Role of the Caregiver

To Protect

Since much of the exploration required for healthy cognitive development involves the mouthing, touching, and feeling of new things, children will need to be protected in the following ways:

❑ Ensure that all toys are safe, non-toxic, and washable.
❑ Minimize interruptions when a child is concentrating.
❑ Protect the child from too much information or stimulation.
❑ Let the child explore at his own pace.
❑ Ensure that tasks are neither too difficult nor too easy.

To Support

Cognitive development is an interesting process that is not limited to certain activities or times of the day. As caregivers are changing diapers or taking the children for a walk, they are providing information about the world and how it works. These opportunities should be used as much as possible to promote cognitive development. In addition, the caregiver can:

❑ Provide lots of opportunities for the child to cause something to happen (e.g., ringing the doorbell, working pop-up toys).
❑ Provide toys where an object is hidden and reappears, usually after the child does something (e.g., a jack-in-the-box).

❏ Provide lots of time and space for exploration and play.

❏ Provide quiet times when children can practice what they've learned on their own.

❏ Be available during the child's play to imitate, explain, and offer new ideas (without taking over).

❏ Be aware of the child's successes.

To Enrich

Caregivers can enrich development by applying some of the following suggestions:

❏ Provide simple explanations of events, objects, and people to infants and toddlers to make the world more understandable.

❏ Play simple games where objects are hidden (partially at first, then totally) to aid the understanding of object permanence. Peekaboo and hiding familiar objects under a blanket or in a bag can be fun.

❏ Encourage imitation with simple action songs and finger plays.

❏ Provide words and labels for experiences.

❏ Set up simple problem-solving situations (e.g., how to get to a coat when the hall is blocked with boxes) and give children opportunities to solve their own problems (e.g., let the child figure out how to get the ball from under the chair).

❏ Model different movements, sounds, and words for the child.

❏ Demonstrate different ways to act on objects and show how things work (e.g., the light switch, the buttons on your calculator).

To Observe

Some questions to guide observations of thinking abilities include:

1. Is the infant using new and varied ways to explore objects?
   – Mouthing?
   – Examining?
   – Feeling?
   – Dropping?
   – Throwing?

2. Is the infant developing an understanding of object permanence?
   - Can he follow an object as it moves?
   - Will he stop and keep looking where he last saw it?
   - Can he find partially hidden objects?
   - Can he find totally hidden objects?
   - As you hide objects, will he follow along and search for them?

3. How does the baby or toddler attempt to get something she wants?
   - Does she always use the same method or try new ways?
   - Does she reach? Point? Move? Cry for it? Ask for it?

4. Does the child realize that she can cause things to happen?
   - Is this accidental or purposeful?
   - By communicating? By doing (using the light switch, turning a knob)?

5. Is the child imitating?
   - Familiar motor movements (waving, clapping)?
   - New motor movements?
   - Sounds, babbles, words that you make?
   - After you stop making the movement (e.g., you stop clapping, shaking)?

6. Can the child solve simple problems?
   - Where to find the toy that he wants?
   - How to get somewhere when the route is blocked?

7. Is the toddler beginning to pretend?
   - With a doll?
   - With a car?

Children with Special Needs

The most common difficulty related to cognitive development encountered by special-needs children has been termed the "Good Fairy Syndrome" (Raver, 1991: 314). Although it concerns primarily visually impaired children, it can be applied to most children with special needs. Many developmentally delayed, hearing impaired, visually impaired, and physically impaired children are passive and experience difficulties in exploring and understanding the environment. As a result, adults tend to do everything for them and they learn to rely on adults. An adult brings lunch, provides toys, takes them to the toilet, gets their jacket, and somehow gets mommy to reappear. This dependency interferes with developing cause-and-effect and problem-solving skills since the child never causes anything to happen and never solves a problem. All of the child's demands and wants are met. As time goes by, the child becomes less motivated to try or act the next time. Caregivers need actively to ensure that this does not occur by explaining the setting and objects within it, by setting up the environment so the child can explore, and by developing routines so that the child can anticipate what to expect. Caregivers should ensure that children can communicate their needs and that opportunities exist for the children to explore and figure things out on their own, even if they make mistakes.

Because children with special needs tend to be passive, caregivers often become more directive with them and forget about working from the babies' cues. This leads to another common concern. Caregivers are often so enthused about providing stimulation that they are always doing "to" the children rather than involving them. As a result, the children may be less willing to learn actively in their world. Encourage them by offering an interesting consequence when they are active or interested in something. For example, imitate their sounds or hand movements. When an activity is initiated by the child, it is more likely to maintain prolonged interest. Be careful not to tell the child always what to do, as the child will become dependent on your cues. For example, the child will respond to your instruction to go to the bathroom rather than to an internal cue or feeling. Be extra mindful to build in and practice cognitive skills in all daily routines during the day (e.g., "We're using blue cups today," "You can reach for your blanket; it's right over here").

Children with visual impairments may have other difficulties that cause problems in the development of cognitive skills. Visually impaired children often hesitate to explore their environment and things within it because they do not realize that things are even there. If the child is not yet moving around, provide foot and wrist rattles or mobiles so that he or she does not have to be too active to realize that something is there. A playpen can be useful for ensuring that toys stay close by and that a very young child will not push them out of reach. Be careful not to over-use the playpen though. Children with visual impairments need to learn to move around to explore. Once the child is mobile, caregivers should try to ensure that the environment is as consistent as possible. Toys and materials will always be moved around but larger pieces of equipment and furniture should remain relatively stationary. The setting will then be more predictable. If children know that the toys will be in the same spot from day to day, it is more likely that they will attempt to locate them on their own.

Children with visual impairments will experience difficulties in imitation, especially of movements. Describe and physically assist children to imitate different movements and encourage verbal imitation wherever possible. To help develop object permanence, use toys and objects that have either a sound or tactile quality to them so that the child can differentiate when they are there and when they are gone. This type of toy will also be easier for the child to find.

Children with hearing impairments usually do not experience difficulties with cognitive development (Raver, 1991). However, it is important to remember that such children will still need assistance in developing an understanding of the world, especially if sound is a factor. Caregivers will need to provide children with the visual cues and explanations of such things as doorbells, telephones, fire trucks, train whistles, etc.

Children with physical disabilities will experience few difficulties with cognitive development if caregivers are attentive to their special needs. Children with physical impairments may not move to explore their world. Make discovery possible by having toys close by and easily accessible. Alternatively, make the child mobile, on a scooter board or in a wheelchair that is easy to operate. Some children may experience difficulties manipulating objects. Have toys available that are easy to manipulate, or adapt some (e.g., make a switch larger so that it can be easily activated).

Caregivers need to be aware of the environment for all children. Providing toys and equipment and supporting children in their quest to develop thinking skills will be necessary at all stages of development.

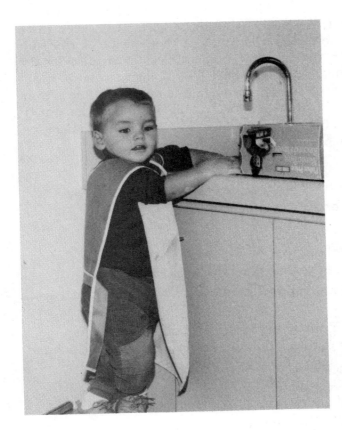

Toddlers can figure out that they have to get a chair to reach a high counter or sink.

TIPS FOR TOYS AND EQUIPMENT

Cognitive development occurs most often with things in the child's world. Adults often think that cognitive development or learning can occur only with educational toys. Yet every parent and caregiver knows how much infants and toddlers love to play with measuring cups, bowls, empty containers, shoes, and boxes. The kitchen cupboard and mom's purse provide hours of enjoyment. Furthermore, such objects are often easier to adapt to suit an individual child's level of development. For example, as the child begins to sort shapes, a shape sorter with even three holes may prove to be too frustrating. A "homemade" sorter with just one shape may be as enjoyable and less frustrating for the child. Another shape can be added later. Look at what is available and how it fits with what the child is doing. Get ideas from the child's cues — if the child loves using small cups for dumping and pouring, find (recycle and reuse) small cups. Here are some more specific tips:

- Mobiles.
- Busy boards or busy boxes.
- Feely blankets or activity quilts.
- Musical toys (e.g., toy radios, music boxes).
- Rattles that produce a variety of effects.
- Pots, pans, lids, spoons to play with together.
- Objects that fit into other objects (e.g., bowls, measuring cups, stacking blocks).
- Objects that can dump and be dumped out (e.g, carrying objects such as purses, dump trucks, or pails and safe, manageable objects such as blocks to fill them with).
- Set aside cupboards at the baby's level that can be emptied.
- Mirrors.
- Sorting games or objects to be used for sorting.
- Blocks of all shapes and sizes.
- Water play table.
- Sand table for toddlers.
- Puppets.

- Songs, finger plays, and action rhymes.
- Puzzles with large pieces after eighteen months.
- Dolls, baby bottles, furniture, and simple dress-up clothes.

Cognitive development occurs during play with many everyday items and materials such as spoons, bowls, water, and sand.

✔ *Caregiver Checklist*

DOES THE CAREGIVER:

1. Spend time observing children's actions and interactions with objects?

2. Offer simple explanations to the child without disturbing or disrupting?

3. Provide a safe, healthy environment where the child is free to explore (e.g., supply objects can safely be put in mouths or dropped)?

4. Encourage independence and freedom to explore?

5. Ensure that the environment promotes problem solving (e.g., provide objects that fit into one another)?

6. Interact with the child during play?

7. Remain available through child's play to model different actions?

8. Provide simple songs and games?

9. Provide opportunities and activities for problem solving?

10. Do things the child will want to imitate?

11. Imitate the child, with both movements and language?

12. Realize the value of real-life objects in addition to educational toys?

PRACTICAL APPLICATION

1. Several parents have asked you "Why are the children just playing all day long? Shouldn't you be teaching them?" Write a newsletter to parents in reply to this question.

2. Observe an infant and then a toddler as they play with a toy or piece of equipment. Describe the understanding they showed in their play. What was the role of the caregiver as protector, supporter, or enricher in promoting cognitive development?

3. Observe five toddlers for a twenty-minute period during the day. List all of the things they did that showed they understood that they could make things happen. What did the caregiver do to promote this understanding?

4. What changes could be made in this setting in terms of toys, materials, and the caregivers' actions to promote cognitive abilities?

13

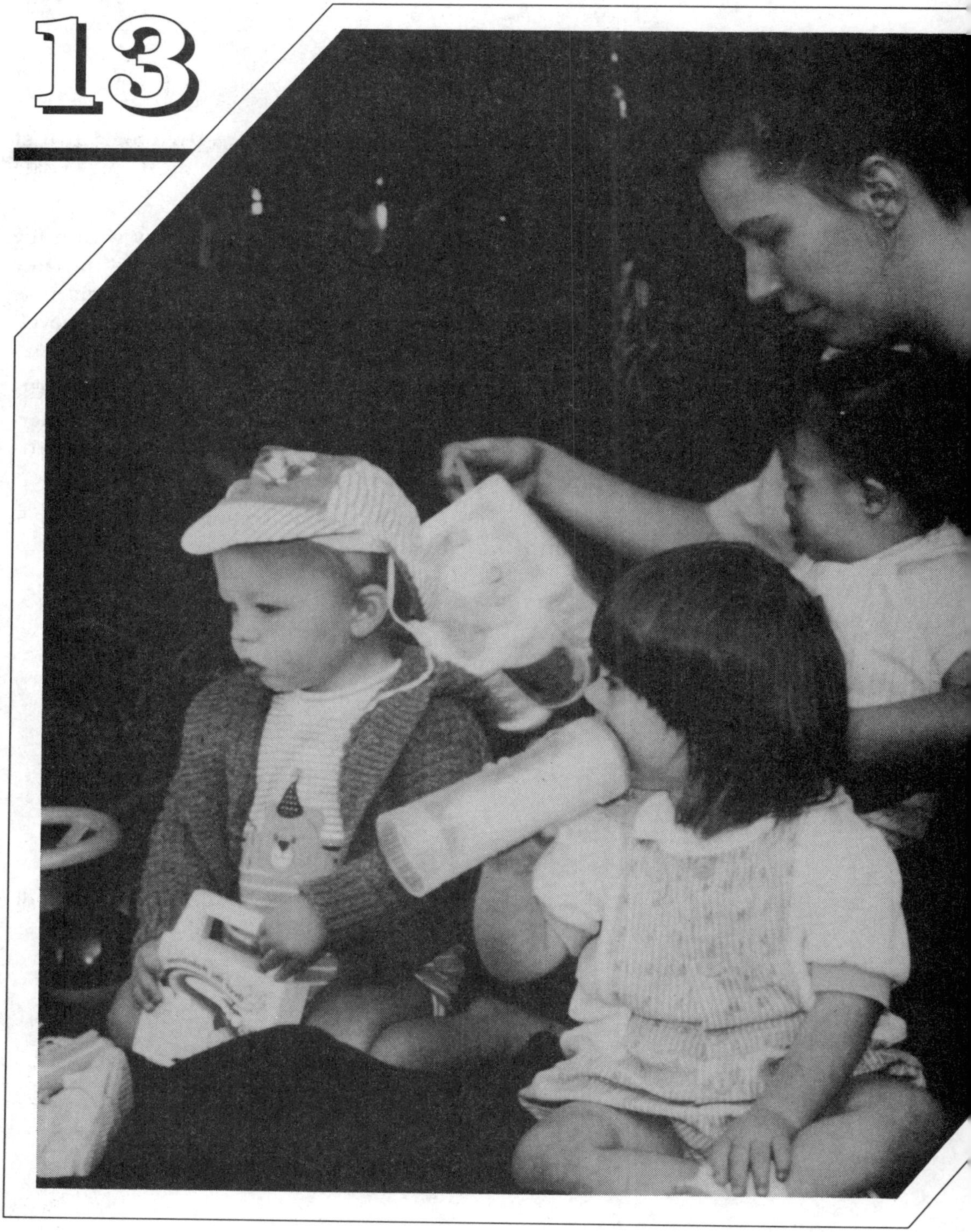

Language Development

Objectives

- ❖ To review the development of communication and language skills.
- ❖ To discuss the role of the caregiver in fostering language development.
- ❖ To outline the importance of providing equal language experiences to all children and to determine when a child may have special needs in this area.

Opening Thoughts

Think of a time when you were in a group of people who spoke a different language or used sign language. How did it feel to not understand? How did you communicate with these people?

Comments on Opening Thoughts

- ❖ Language is a powerful tool.
- ❖ We feel limited and frustrated when we are not understood, and competent and happy when we are understood.
- ❖ Non-verbal communication — pointing, shaking your head, looking perplexed — can be just as important as speaking.
- ❖ The development of language and communication skills is one of the most exciting achievements of infancy and toddlerhood. ❑

Six-week-old Nicky is lying, wide awake, in his mother's arms. Mom looks down at her baby and their eyes meet. "Well, you're awake, sweetie. Did you have a nice nap?" The baby continues to look intently at his mother and snuggles in a little closer. "Oh, you're such a good little baby. Would you like to rock a little bit?" Nicky looks up, makes a sound, and then looks back to his mother as if he is asking for a response. "You like to rock. Well, let's rock some more. Is that what you like? Is that what baby Nicky likes?" The baby makes eye contact again, makes a long cooing noise in response. "Is that what you like? Nicky likes to rock. Rock, rock."

This exchange between Nicky and his mother provides us with a glimpse of how amazingly communicative a baby can be. Long before the words are there, it appears that the baby is carrying on a conversation with his mother. The body movements, the facial expressions, and eye contact that initiates interactions are all present. All the necessities for communicating are there. Now all the baby has to do is learn the language that goes along with these non-verbal messages.

No area of development is as totally dependent on the adult who cares for the child as the learning of language (Fogel, 1991). Babies who are left alone with a few toys will explore and, on their own, discover and learn many important things. However, without hearing speech, they cannot learn to understand the language of their culture. It is crucial that we understand that language is not learned by a simple process of absorption. The key to language acquisition is *direct, responsive, one-to-one, face-to-face interchange between infants or toddlers and their "important" adults.*

Long before babies use language, they are powerful communicators. The communications that occur in the first stages of life set the stage for emerging language abilities. Newborn babies arrive with a reflexive cry that helps to ensure their needs are met. Eventually, the cries will be differentiated (e.g., "I am hungry," "I am in pain"), the baby will coo and begin to try making different sounds, and will laugh (Allen & Marotz, 1989). Very early on, around the sixth week, babies will appear to be engaged in a conversation where, like Nicky above, all the pieces are there but the words. Watch a mother talking to her young baby. Even without the words, their facial expressions, body movements, and eye movements look like a real conversation. The adult and baby are taking turns in communicating. As mother responds, baby becomes more and more motivated to continue and learn language.

The baby also must also learn to listen, to understand what others are saying. Newborns seem tuned into human voices: they will pay attention to a human voice from birth, and soon after can tell their parents' voices from others. Babies will move their bodies in rhythm to the language they hear (Bee, 1989).

At approximately six months, infants will begin to babble, usually when they are alone. They actively experiment with making a range of sounds. At approximately eight months, infants understand gestures such as pointing and waving bye-bye, and

Babies are powerful communicators, even without language.

will begin to use these shortly after. Socialized babbling begins around the same time — the babbling sounds as if the baby is talking, only the real words are missing. The child begins to realize that talking is something that people do and value, so babbling occurs more often when other people are present. This is when we often hear delightful sermons of meaningless sounds.

Somewhere around the first year the first word emerges. Although this word is not completely formed (e.g., "ba" means bottle, bath, blanket, ball), it is consistently used to refer to one object or person (Fogel, 1991). "Dada" is always used to refer to daddy and "wa" may refer to the dog (bow-wow). Early words that the child says and understands most often refer to objects in the child's immediate environment. In the beginning, as the child is developing thinking skills, the object that you are talking about must be within sight of the baby. The baby will understand if you are talking about the crib only when you are both in the bedroom and can see the crib. Later, the object will need to be in a predictable location for the child to think about it. The child does not have to see the crib but, because it always stays in the same place, he or she can think about it when others are talking. Eventually the child will understand and talk about objects not seen and in an unpredictable location — when looking for a blanket or jacket, for example.

For the next year, young children will build on their vocabulary and continue to use one word in a variety of meaningful ways. One word, "baba," can be a description (e.g., "that baby has a bottle"), a demand ("I want my bottle"), or a question ("Where is my bottle?"). Children select new words based on things they directly experience or manipulate and on objects that move and so attract attention.

At approximately the two-year mark, children begin to use two words together. At first this occurs when the child just happens to use two words close together, without relating the two (e.g., names "Mommy" then labels "car"). Later the two words become related in one thought (e.g., "Mommy car" now may mean "Look. Here comes mommy in the car").

Language development continues as the child begins to build vocabulary and develop more complex language, including questions, negatives and three- or four-word sentences. The child

puts more and more information together in meaningful, understandable ways. At two, a child may be using two words together,
or even talking in complex sentences. Paying close attention to
skills and providing a setting conducive to learning language will
be the most helpful approach for this age group.

In summary, babies are powerful communicators from birth.
As they hear more and more language, they develop incredible
skills in a very short span. As adults, it is important to observe
and listen to more than just the words. Facial expressions, tone
of voice, and gestures that accompany the sounds or words can
actually provide meaning. A child who feels that he or she is lis-
tened to and understood will feel important and will want to communicate.

Storytime, like action songs, offers an opportunity to enrich language development.

Role of the Caregiver

Regardless of the toys and equipment that are available, language development requires that the child hear language, and that the child's communications (verbal and non-verbal) be noticed and responded to.

To Protect

Since the first two years of life encompass so much growth in language skills, the caregiver must actively protect the child. Below are some ideas for protecting infants and toddlers as they develop language skills:

❏ Avoid bombarding the child with language all the time. Watch for children's responses. If they are tuning out, stop.

❏ Ensure appropriate noise levels. Infants and toddlers should not be bombarded with too many sounds.

❏ Provide some quiet times during the day so that infants and toddlers can play with sounds.

❏ Respond promptly to verbal and non-verbal communication.

❏ Listen and observe at the same time. A toddler whose message is not understood can become quite frustrated. Look for facial expressions, body language (e.g., pointing, the look in the eyes) to help determine what the child is referring to.

❏ Never make fun of a child's mispronunciations.

❏ Avoid correcting children's use of words (if you use the words correctly, the children will eventually learn).

To Support

Caregivers will want to be present and ready to interact with infants and toddlers to ensure that language development is stimulated. The caregiver can support the child in the following ways:

❏ Respond to the baby's non-verbal cues whenever possible.

❏ Listen very carefully to what babies and toddlers are trying to communicate.

- ❏ Show interest and delight in infant and toddler communications
- ❏ Talk to the baby or toddler. Hearing language lays the foundation for learning it.
- ❏ Vary your tone of voice (to show surprise, delight, firmness if necessary).
- ❏ Provide a variety of experiences. This will, in turn, provide a variety of things to talk about.
- ❏ Use short sentences that are more easily understood.
- ❏ Talk about objects in the child's immediate, here-and-now world. (Talking about something at grandma's house last Sunday will have little meaning to infants and toddlers.)
- ❏ Provide toddlers with opportunities to talk to each other (snack times, walks outside with two children).
- ❏ Don't just tell or command all the time; vary your language (e.g., ask questions, describe).
- ❏ Ask parents for babies' favorite words.

To Enrich

In the eyes of the child, the world is filled with things to explore, to talk about, and to tell people about. Share in these experiences with children. Dandelions may be weeds to you but they are beautiful, fragrant yellow flowers to the young child. Caregivers can enrich language development with the following activities:

- ❏ Use self talk. Talk about what you are doing as you are doing it (e.g., "I am picking up the diaper. See how big it is, see how white it is. It's soft; do you want to feel it?")
- ❏ Use parallel talk. Describe in words what the child is doing (e.g., as the toddler unpacks the diaper bag, you might say, "Ooh, you found your diaper bag. Yes, that's yours. Pick it up").
- ❏ Use expansions. When the child uses one word, expand upon it (e.g., "Baba?" — "Where is your blanket?" or "Bye-bye" — "Mommy is gone; bye-bye").
- ❏ Imitate the sounds that the child makes.

❑ Describe things, events, and activities over and over again. Don't overlook things because you have seen them before (e.g., Don't neglect to say, "Look how the water comes out of the tap").

❑ Sing to babies and toddlers.

❑ Do action songs and finger plays.

❑ Look at picture books with babies, point and label familiar objects.

❑ Look at picture books with toddlers, talk simply about what is happening on each page.

To Observe

Language development is often used as a measure of normal development because it is orderly and predictable. However, it is important to remember that all children will vary. One infant may utter a first word at nine months, and another not until sixteen months. One child will learn words on an ongoing basis, another will begin talking in two-word phrases. Although it is important to keep this variability in mind, caregivers also need to observe children to ensure that language is developing. Some of the following questions may help your observations:

1. Does the infant appear to be listening?

   – To sounds from toys?

   – To sounds from people?

2. How does she show she is listening?

   – Looks you in the eye, smiles, kicks and thrashes, body becomes slightly tense?

3. How does the infant communicate?

   – Cries? Reaches? Squeals? Points? Looks at the object?

4. Does the baby play with sounds and babble?

   – When alone?

   – When with others?

   – In response to sounds?

5. How does the toddler communicate?
   – Cries, points, looks at the object, uses words, pulls you over?

6. Can the older baby or toddler act when you ask him to do something?
   – In response to a simple request such as, "Pick up your bottle" or "Sit down"?
   – When the object is in view? When it is out of sight?

7. Does the toddler use specific sounds to refer to objects consistently?

8. Is the toddler adding more words and sounds? Using words together? Are the ideas related?

9. Does the toddler revel in words and sounds? Use language as needed? Seem to prefer other ways of communicating?

Children with Special Needs

Language is a complex set of rules for putting sounds, words, and meanings together. Caregivers may need to make language simple and understandable for children with special needs. Similarly, they may need to make special efforts to understand the child's attempts to communicate. All special-needs children need to learn that they can communicate and that their communications are meaningful in that their needs will be met. This will be the foundation for continuing to learn language.

Children who have difficulties in speaking may need to rely on non-verbal communication for a longer period of time. Caregivers are sometimes so anxious for the child to talk that they forget about letting the child communicate in other ways (e.g., pointing, using gestures). If talking is too difficult, the child may just give up, and a child whose attempts are not understood may become frustrated. Always be aware of what the child is saying, how he or she is saying it, and encourage communication. A child who is secure in knowing that he or she can communicate needs and wants will be more willing to try to talk.

Children with visual impairments develop language in much the same fashion as all children do. Caregivers may want to explain and describe objects to help the child develop a clear concept — by distinguishing between a baby's bottle and a bottle of milk in the fridge, for example. The word "bottle" is the same but the object is different, and the child needs help in understanding the difference.

Children with developmental delays will also develop language in the same order but at a slower rate. This is helpful to realize, because the caregiver can then know what to expect and can promote the next level of language development. For example, a child who is babbling will likely be ready to use one word soon. Use short sentences and check the child's understanding by letting him or her act directly upon objects often. Use techniques to promote speech development frequently, so that the child's world is filled with meaningful and understandable language.

Children with physical impairments may experience difficulties in making understandable sounds and words. A child who has difficulty eating will likely have difficulty talking, since the same body parts are used. If the child is trying to talk but is not easily understood, be extra attentive to non-verbal communication so that the child does get his needs met. If learning to speak is too difficult, an alternative communication system may be used. Interestingly, using an alternative system often lessens the pressure to speak in an understandable way, and the child's speech improves. Consultation with a speech therapist may be required.

Children with hearing impairments will usually cry, make sounds, and babble but language development will slow at this point because they simply do not hear any feedback they might get. Hearing difficulties are hard to detect because the child's behavior may be inconsistent (e.g., sometimes the child responds, at other times not). Therefore, delayed language development is often the first sign that there may be a problem. Don't stop talking to the hearing impaired child. At this young age, it is almost impossible to determine the extent to which the child can hear. Use short sentences and emphasize the key words. Use gestures, facial expressions, and body movements and encourage the child to do so too. It is critical that children with hearing impairments realize that they can communicate and be successful. Alternative communication systems and the assistance of a speech therapist will likely be required. The most commonly used approach is total communication (Raver, 1991), where all forms of communication are used together to maximize the use of hearing and speaking for all children.

TIPS FOR TOYS AND EQUIPMENT

Drawing up a list of toys conducive to developing language skills is a difficult thing to do. Caregivers need to ensure that the setting is filled with interesting toys and objects. If they are interesting, and if the caregiver is supportive, children will want to talk about them, will want to tell you what the objects do or how they sound. When children do something to a toy, they are proud of their actions and want to tell someone about it (e.g., "Look — clown!"). Children who are responded to, regardless of the toy in hand, will be motivated to talk. Toys used for sensory, fine motor, gross motor, social and cognitive development will all provide something to talk about.

Pictures and books are considered an excellent source for language learning and enrichment. Babies love to look at a picture and hear us talk about it ("That's a cow. Moo"). Books (washable ones) with simple stories, bright, clear, uncluttered pictures, and easy-to-turn pages are most suited to babies. At this age, the story may not be relevant, the interaction and sounds you make together will be. For young toddlers, each page may have a simple story and they will want to point and use words.

Songs and action songs will promote using language and imitation. Young children will enjoy short tapes and records of familiar songs. They may even carry a tune! However, tapes and records should be used mostly as a basis for interaction between the caregiver and children. Tapes left on while caregivers are busy elsewhere usually become extra noise and prevent young children from concentrating on language.

Essentially, for language learning, the best setting is the caregiver's warm lap, and the best equipment is the caregiver's skill in communicating with the baby.

✔ Caregiver Checklist

DOES THE CAREGIVER:

1. Engage in many face-to-face, one-to-one interactions?

2. Attend to all babies' efforts to communicate and respond to their needs?

3. Observe non-verbal gestures of infants, and give meaning to them?

4. Recognize the importance of non-verbal communication in language development and use it with infants and toddlers?

5. Present many opportunities for language to occur by providing interesting toys or activities?

6. Label everyday objects, events, and occurrences for infants and toddlers?

7. Talk to infants and toddlers about what is being done?

8. Talk to infants and toddlers about activities that they are involved in?

9. Check the infant's and toddler's understanding (e.g., "Where is your bottle?" "Can you bring me the train?").

10. Expand on a toddler's utterances by adding one or two words or completing a sentence?

11. Vary tone of voice?

12. Prevent "tuning out" by limiting noise?

13. Use picture books with children?

PRACTICAL APPLICATION

1. Visit a bookstore and select two books for an infant, and two for a toddler. Explain why you chose the books you did.

2. Spend an hour in an infant/toddler room. Record all the language used by the caregiver. What kinds of verbal messages is the caregiver giving (telling, labeling, scolding, etc.)? What recommendations would you make?

3. Observe an infant and caregiver when they are playing together with a toy. Describe what they did. How did the caregiver interact with the infant to promote language?

4. Observe an infant and toddler room for a morning, paying special attention to the noise level. Do you think it was appropriate? If it was too noisy at times, what steps do you think could be taken to minimize noise without disrupting play?

▼▼▼▼▼▼▼▼▼▼▼▼▼▼

PART III ROUTINE CAREGIVING

A large proportion of the child's day in group care involves the interactions with caregivers and other children that occur during the daily routines of arrival and departure, meal and snack time, diapering, dressing, and naptime. It is during these times that very basic needs for food, rest, and security must be met if infants and toddlers are to benefit from other aspects of the program. The familiarity of the routines and the responsiveness of the caregiver can go a long way in helping the child feel secure and happy in the group-care setting. In addition, the one-to-one interaction that occurs during routine care times provides an excellent opportunity for learning. Babies and toddlers learn self-help skills, language, problem solving, and social interaction through routine care.

Routine caregiving times should be pleasant and enriching experiences. The key to providing routines that are meaningful and enjoyable is to view them as excellent opportunities for quality interactions with the children, rather than as tasks to be completed. Rather than rushing through the routine to get on with the program, view the routine as an essential part of the program.

Routine caregiving practices must take into account the developmental capabilities of the children, health and safety considerations, and the feelings and requests of the parents of the children. These practices are affected by traditions, customs, and often deeply ingrained attitudes. It is important that caregivers examine their own practices and the values behind them, and make every attempt to respect and consider those of the parents.

In the beginning of this book we mentioned that being fair to infants and toddlers requires meeting their individual needs, rather than providing "equal" attention to each. This is true in routine caregiving practices as well. Some children can comfortably wait to receive their meals, others find waiting intolerable. Some children need a lot of comfort before going to sleep, others glide into naptime with ease. Prioritizing the routine caregiving activities according to these individual differences is important.

Finally, routine caregiving must be carried out in a manner that is respectful to children. Infants and toddlers must be treated not as objects to be fed, changed, or put to bed, but as active partners in these interactions, at whatever developmental level they may be.

Sometimes, in spite of all good efforts and planning, routine care activities do not go as smoothly as we would wish. We often feel too rushed and pressured to engage in pleasant conversation while diapering or providing meals. But many of the things that can make a qualitative difference in routine care practices take no more time and effort than lower quality practice. Telling a baby that you are going to take off a wet diaper while doing it does not make the task more time consuming, but it does make the interaction more meaningful. The "good" days can be maximized, and the "not so good" ones minimized, if time is taken to plan the routine care practices in the center.

The chapters in this part of the book provide guidelines for respectful routine caregiving practices. In the previous section we "divided up" the child according to areas of development to help understand how to provide supportive and enriching care. In this section we put the child "back together" and provide brief developmental reminders that are relevant to routine care activities. After each discussion, we provide questions to guide observations of the children and tips for ensuring that caregiving practices are healthy and safe.

14

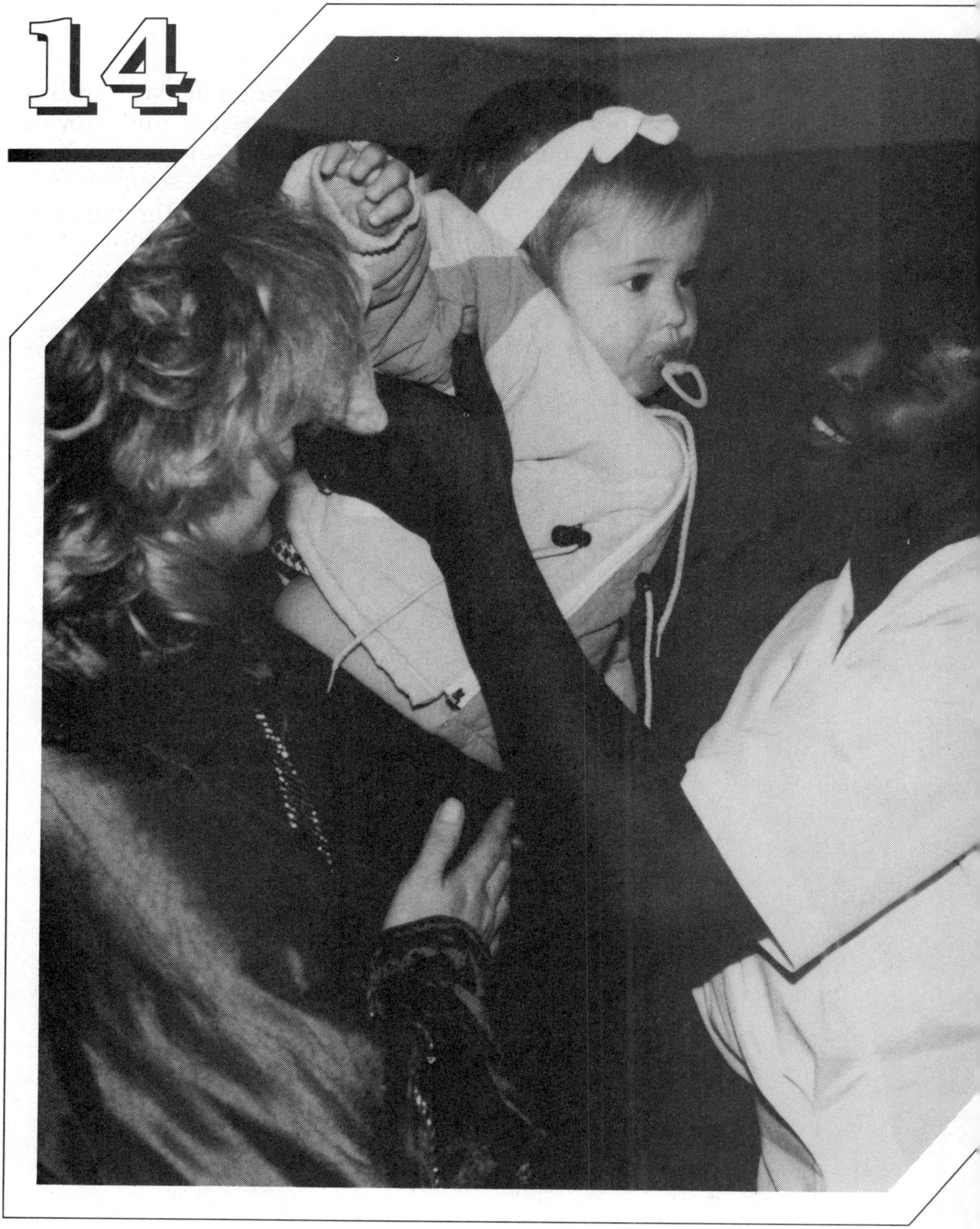

Easing Separation in Group Care

Objectives

❖ To examine the impact of separation on infants and toddlers.

❖ To provide guidelines for caregivers during arrival and departure.

❖ To discuss the caregiver's role in assisting young children to cope with separation throughout the day.

Opening Thoughts

Recall a time when you were left for a while by a loved one and expected him or her back by a certain time. Now, imagine that this person did not return when expected. What are some of the feelings you might experience? What skills and abilities do you possess that would help you understand and cope with the separation?

Comments on Opening Thoughts

❖ Separation evokes a number of emotions in adults: anger, fear, sadness, confusion, and guilt.

❖ Some of the skills or abilities that help adults to cope are understanding of concepts of time; memory; understanding the reason for separation; ability to distract themselves; communication (e.g., by telephone or letter writing).

❖ Adults are able to regulate their own emotional states. Infants and toddlers do not, on the whole, possess these skills and abilities, and are therefore much more dependent on adults to minimize the stress of separation. ❐

183

Developmental Reminders

— Attachment to parents is primary.

— Babies are developing trust in people so they need to attach to a significant other person.

— Stranger anxiety appears at around six months.

— Separation anxiety appears at around nine months.

— Babies are developing object permanence. Up until around the first birthday, out of sight is out of mind. Separation will likely be more difficult when children have acquired object permanence. They know that mommy and daddy exist somewhere, but where?

— After twelve to sixteen months toddlers can recognize and understand pictures.

— Separation anxiety is a normal occurrence throughout the years of childhood.

Separation, in the group-care context, refers to many things. The general problem of children being away from their homes and families for so many hours a day is a prime concern of the early childhood profession. New attachments are formed in group settings, and these attachments are disrupted when staff leave or change position. The child experiences separation regularly. A child leaves home in the morning and arrives at the day-care setting. In the afternoon, the parent arrives, the child leaves the caregiver, the other children, and the setting and returns home. It is customary to think of the morning time as coming and the afternoon as leaving. But each reception involves a separation, and each separation a reception. Therefore, the daily occurrences of coming to day care and returning home are closely related. At both arrival and departure the child undergoes a separation and is required to make an adjustment.

Some children with special needs use special transportation arrangements to arrive and depart, especially if they are involved in more than one program during the day. The number of arrivals and departures is increased and, because the child may not have a trusted caregiver present to help make the transition (e.g., it may be a taxicab driver who brings the child), the adjustments are more complex.

For infants and toddlers with limited understanding these daily transitions can be confusing and sometimes very problematic. One of the major responsibilities of day-care staff is to understand this psychological stress and adapt their own behavior in an attempt to help children and parents cope with separation.

One way of attempting to understand the impact of separation on children is to examine our own responses and coping strategies. Many of the emotions described in the opening thoughts are evoked from even minor separations: losing a wallet, car keys, or a favorite possession. Yet our sadness, confusion, or anger is filtered in many ways. We have some control over our lives, we can telephone or write letters to a friend whom we miss, we keep photographs of loved ones to bring them closer. We can mark passing days on the calendar or we can rationalize, understanding the reason for the separation. As infants and toddlers are not able to comfort themselves in these ways, the caregiver's role is crucial in helping the child cope with separation. Infants, toddlers, and special-needs children at an older age may not be able to express their emotions verbally, so act out in some way to indicate that they are feeling distressed. Caregivers must interpret these cues and give meaning to them.

The focus on separation at the beginning of the year sometimes creates the illusion for caregivers that the problem is dealt with at that time, and that indications of separation difficulty during the year are less significant. In many programs we see an awareness among caregivers of the initial difficulties that children and parents have when the child first comes to the center, but we need to ensure that children are provided with assistance and support for their separation difficulties throughout the year.

In order to assist infants and toddlers to cope with separation, we must understand the developmental competencies and abilities that affect reactions to separation. We must also consider the temperament of the child and family circumstances that might be related to separation difficulties. Finally, we must consider the ways in which staff and parents can ease the stress of separation.

What Factors Affect a Child's Reaction to Separation?

Although very young infants often do not seem to respond notice-ably to different faces and people, they may well be influenced by the differences in the way their behavior is interpreted by others around them and by the different sensations that different care-giving environments evoke. Consider, for example, the differences in sounds, smells, and tactile sensations between a home and the center.

Infants between the ages of six and twelve months may protest strongly when separated from parents, and react fearfully when exposed to strangers. As babies enter their second year of life, too, separation from parents can be very distressing. As they become more mobile and seek out their independence they seem to need the security of parents to help master the fear that their new-found world sometimes evokes. Fear of new people and new situations is still very common in this period of life. During this stage it is common to see toddlers refusing to go home at the end of the day, or suddenly expressing anger upon the arrival of their parents. They may be comfortable and involved in their activities and may not want to be uprooted once again.

At about the age of two many children simply prefer their parents to anyone else. They are struggling with issues of control over their environment and needs; they need, at the very least, to have a clear idea of what is going to happen to them. Often dur-ing this period there are significant changes in their lives (e.g., the birth of a sibling, a change in caregiver) during which times the toddler may, understandably, want to be at home.

While reactions to separation are influenced by developmen-tal milestones, there is tremendous variability in the responses and adaptability of children. Some are easy going, some find changes difficult. For some, all the changes in people, sights, sounds, smells, and textures arouse their curiosity. For others, new situations can result in intolerable levels of stress. It is very important to understand that the baby or toddler who finds sepa-ration difficult is not "spoiled" or "trying to get attention." The child's personality and temperament are such that separation is simply much more difficult.

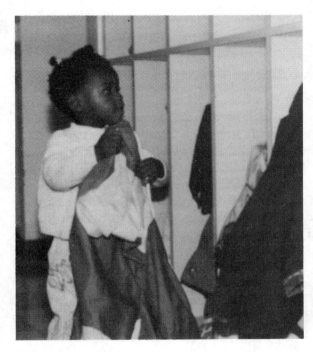

Developmental competencies and abilities affect a child's reactions to separation.

Previous Separations

The number of separations that young children have experienced, and the way in which these separations were handled, may well affect their coping skills. Caregivers should find out how many previous caregivers a child has had and how earlier transitions were made. In addition, knowing about separations the child has undergone as a result of moving, divorce, illness, or death can help the caregiver assess the child's vulnerability.

Special Family Circumstances

Babies and toddlers with a very unsettling or unstable home life are more likely to suffer from separation stress. A high level of family stress due to economic pressure, personal difficulties, or traumas such as a divorce or death in the family increase the baby's vulnerability. Babies of very young single mothers seem to have a higher risk of suffering from separation (Vaughn et al., 1980).

Feelings and Attitudes of Parents and Caregivers

The attitudes and feelings of the adults who care for the child affect the child's reaction to separation. A parent who is comfortable being a working parent, and feels confident that the day-care center is providing the child with quality care, will more likely transmit this positive attitude to the child. In many families, returning to work and having to leave a child in day care arouses feelings of guilt, loss and/or anxiety in the parents. A parent who feels guilty and lacks confidence in the center staff may negatively influence the child's responses.

Caregivers' feelings influence the children as well. It is understandable that a caregiver may feel angry at the child who cries incessantly when the parents leave. Often, a caregiver experiences a mild sense of victory when the child clings to her at the end of the day, refusing the open arms of his mother. Those feelings are natural. Caregivers invest a great deal of energy and emotion in caring for the children. However, feelings of jealousy and competition between parents and caregivers will be damaging to the child if they are not dealt with appropriately.

What Can Adults Do to Help Infants and Toddlers Cope with Separation?

Recognize Signs

In order to help babies and toddlers cope with separation, staff must be able to recognize signs of separation stress. Children do not always express this stress by crying, although this frequently does happen. Toddlers may behave aggressively — by kicking, hitting, or biting. Some children simply lose some of their liveliness, and seem to take little interest in toys or other people. Others may cling to the caregiver, and constantly seek her presence. Changes in eating habits sometimes occur. Some toddlers seem to have a tremendous increase in appetite, as if they are constantly trying to fill an empty spot. Others may lose their appetite. Similarly, sleeping patterns may change. Some children may be very wary of naptime, as closing one's eyes and falling asleep is another kind of separation. Other young children may feel quite exhausted from anxiety and will want to sleep for major portions of the day. Staff at centers often attribute these kinds of behaviors to problems at home. It is important to consider that these symptoms may be the result of being away from home.

Build Bridges

It seems that the more bridges there are between home and center, the more assistance the child is given in coping with separation stress. Frequent visits before enrollment help both children and parents feel comfortable at the center. Toys and other meaningful objects from home offer psychological comfort to the child. Pictures of families are a concrete reminder of home, and lots of conversation about mommy, daddy, siblings and even pets reassures the child that the separation is temporary. Caregivers often avoid these topics of conversation, thinking that they will just remind the child of home and upset him even more. This is usually not the case.

Make Gradual Transitions with the Parents Present

It is generally agreed that parents or parent substitutes who are very close to the child should stay a while when he or she first joins the center. It is difficult to say how long this should go on. Some children require a much longer transition period than others. However, it should be made clear to parents before enrollment that they may need to make special arrangements to help children make the adjustment.

It is not sufficient merely to suggest and encourage parents to stay with the children. Parents need to feel that they are welcome and needed. Many parents will be helped if the caregiver provides guidelines as to how they can help the child adapt. It is best for parents to assume a passive role — that is, to be there for security but to let the child become involved in the activities or with the caregiver. How active the parent should be will depend on the child, but some parents feel awkward just being at the center and should be assured by the staff that they are important and welcome. This provides an excellent opportunity for the caregiver to learn about how the infant or toddler responds to the parent and how the parent cares for the child.

Encourage Parents' Visits throughout the Year

While the importance of parents and babies making a gradual transition together is clear, children benefit from having parents visit throughout the year. Many staff feel that if parents drop in for visits and then leave, the babies become upset, and indeed, this can happen sometimes. However, more often when parents visit frequently the babies adapt and benefit from their presence.

Personalize Reception

Every effort should be made for the same person, preferably the primary caregiver, to receive the child each morning with warmth and friendliness. Greetings should be personalized. Some children are helped by a welcoming ritual. For example, going to the mirror with a caregiver to see their reflection or having the child help the caregiver to turn on some music can become morning rituals which the child looks forward to. Often the young child is still very tired and would prefer to be cuddled and/or rocked for a while, until ready to explore and play, or gently guided to any activity. Some babies and toddlers wander off to play without much fuss.

Respect and Reassure

Respectful caregiving requires that children are not tricked or their feelings denied. Parents should say goodbye when they leave. Parting need not be emotional or lengthy but the parents must not sneak away. It may seem easier for both child and parent, but at a time of life when learning to trust is so important, the easiest way is definitely not the best. Caregivers need to respect a child's feelings. Helping them to understand their feelings ("You are sad because daddy left") and reassuring them that their parents will come back ("After our snack mommy will come") are the kinds of constant reassurances that children require.

Make the Center an Interesting Place to Be

Certainly an interesting program that is geared to the child's developmental capabilities helps alleviate some of the stresses of separation. Bored or frustrated children are likely to miss home and family more than children who have interesting things to do.

Work with the Parents

If parents know that their child is well taken care of, their own feelings of separation anxiety will be lessened. Though communication with parents should occur throughout the year, it is natural that at the beginning many will want as many details as possible about their child's day. Details such as the exact amount of formula the baby had, how long the baby slept, and what the baby played with may be very reassuring to the parents. Asking parents for information about how the baby likes to be held, the baby's favorite toys, and so forth helps the caregiver and helps the parents feel that they are working together with the caregiver to help the baby make the transition into the center.

Prepare for Departure

Attention should be paid to the transition when it is time to go home. Seeing the parent appear suddenly at the end of the day often evokes emotions that the child may have been "saving up" for when the parents arrive. Before parents arrive it is advisable that children be involved in activities that can be terminated easily so that they can prepare to leave. Parents understandably want to get home quickly at the end of the day, but sometimes an extra three minutes of patience goes a long way towards a smoother transition. Involving parents in the activity by having them come to look may be helpful.

Children with Special Needs

Children with special needs who arrive by special transportation may need extra attention when they get to the center because of the time between the separation from family and their arrival to their caregiver. Though some may not show signs of distress by the time they arrive, they may well need an extra warm reception. If we approach the problem of separation for children with special needs with understanding and empathy, as we do for all children, there are few special considerations. The child who is developmentally delayed may need to have more of the assurances and reminders that his parents love him and will return. For children with visual impairments more voice, talking, or singing may be required at separation and departure time. For hearing impaired children, make sure that the words of reassurance and rituals around arrival and departure are accompanied by non-verbal cues (a big hug, a wave) and pictures.

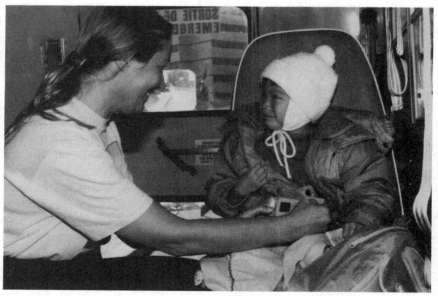

Children with special needs who use special transportation may require extra attention at arrival and departure.

OBSERVATION QUESTIONS

1. How does the infant or toddler appear when she arrives?
   – Sleepy? Alert? Crying? Happy?

2. How does the infant or toddler respond to your greeting?
   – Smiles? Reaches out? Remains passive? Withdraws?

3. How does the toddler behave when her parent says goodbye?
   – Clings? Runs off to play? Seeks the caregiver? Stares quietly?

4. How does the infant or toddler react when his parents arrive to pick him up?
   – Gets excited? Stays calm? Is happy? Is upset?

5. How does the infant or toddler respond when her caregiver goes on coffee break?
   – Watches the caregiver go? Cries? Becomes involved in play and doesn't react?

TIPS FOR HEALTHY AND SAFE ARRIVAL AND DEPARTURE

- Provide information to parents regarding car seats.
- Check and record any daily medications. Store medications safely.
- Report any accidents or unusual behavior (e.g., lack of appetite) to the parents, and ask parents to do the same.
- Report contagious diseases in the center to the parents.
- Provide information regarding symptoms and managing them to the parents.
- Have clear policies concerning who may pick the child up from the center.

✔ Caregiver Checklist

DOES THE CAREGIVER:

1. Receive each child by name and relate to the child personally upon arrival, verbally and/or through warm body contact?

2. Show initiative and readiness to talk with each parent upon arrival and/or departure?

3. Show understanding and acknowledge children's feelings when they display unhappiness at separation?

4. Accompany each child from reception to activity?

5. Talk with the children about their parents during the day, show them pictures or books that relate to the family?

6. Understand the importance of and encourage bringing objects from home and, when possible, from the center to home?

7. Understand the importance of and carry out small rituals, both at reception and departure (going to the window or mirror, a special song)? Are the rituals adapted to the needs and likes of the particular child, rather than stereotyped?

8. Provide a wind-down time when parents come to pick up their children?

9. Show understanding of parents' difficulties at separation?

10. Show awareness that separation symptoms arise through the day, not just in the morning, and respond to them appropriately?

11. Show flexibility when siblings accompany the child to the center?

12. Attempt to obtain information from home to help the child throughout the day (e.g., about schedules)?

13. Provide parents with schedules and written comments about the child's experiences throughout the day?

PRACTICAL APPLICATION

1. Observe the interactions that take place among parents, caregivers, and children at arrival and departure. Record as much information as possible about what was said to each child (include tone of voice and body language) by both parents and caregivers, and what the parents and caregivers said to each other.

   a) Reflect on the observation. Was the separation handled sensitively? Respectfully?

   b) Based on the observation and the information in the chapter, make a list of recommendations that would help minimize the stress of separation.

2. Make a list of the information you would like to obtain from parents to help ease the baby or toddler's transition from home to day care. What information at the end of the day would help the parents?

3. Write a newsletter to prospective parents explaining why your center requests that parents plan to be available for the child's gradual transition into the center.

15

Mealtime and Snack Time

Objectives

❖ To emphasize the connection between caregivers' backgrounds and values and the way in which mealtime is planned in a group setting.

❖ To review the potential learning opportunities that mealtime provides.

❖ To provide guidelines for planning quality mealtimes.

Opening Thoughts

Recollect a mealtime situation from your own life, and describe it in as much detail as possible (e.g., the food, the manner in which it was served, the conversation, general atmosphere, and so forth). Analyze what you enjoyed, or what you did not enjoy about the experience. Think about meals in different settings (e.g., a fancy restaurant, a noisy cafeteria, at home). What were some of the mealtime rules and traditions you had in your family when you were a child? Did these vary from daily meals to special occasions?

Comments on Opening Thoughts

❖ The physical setting of the mealtime significantly influences the nature of the experience.

❖ A wide variety of personal tastes and preferences determines the way different people enjoy different mealtime situations.

❖ There is a tremendous variety of expectations and rules concerning mealtime behavior, from extremely informal "eat what you want and when you want" to very formalized settings.

❖ There are no right and wrong ways to organize meals, just differences in family traditions and patterns. Experiences from your own childhood will likely serve to determine how you deal with these situations in your own family life and in your caregiving role. ❏

Developmental Reminders

Newborn to Four Months

— Sucking and swallowing are reflexive actions, but become voluntary.
— Will push food out of mouth with tongue.
— Exclusively nurses or sucks a bottle.
— Develops eating schedules.
— Will need six to eight feedings the first month and will reduce to three to five by the end of the first month, and three to four after the fourth month. At around six months the baby will eat three meals plus two snacks per day.

Four to Six Months

— Opens mouth when a spoon is brought to it.
— Pushes out food less often.
— Grasps objects.
— Can bring hands to mouth.

Six to Eight Months

— Chewing begins.
— Holds spoon, cup, or bottle.
— Puts objects into mouth.

Eight to Ten Months

— Sits unsupported.
— Uses a pincer grasp so begins self feeding.

Ten to Twelve Months

— Chews better so textures of food can vary more.
— Can manage table food.
— Bites off the right amount.
— Begins to drink from a cup.

Twelve to Eighteen Months

— Drinks independently.
— Uses a spoon independently.
— Increases in independence; mostly self feeds, can be a picky eater.
— Some use a bottle less, drink from a cup more.

Food is necessary for existence but much of society's concern with food goes far beyond the need for survival or even the nutritional value. Food becomes an expression of individual and cultural differences. It becomes a way of marking special events or a way of expressing concern and care. From the time children are born, issues around what they eat, when they eat, and how they are fed become a prime focus of discussion for all those involved in their care. When an infant appears to have eating problems, caregivers can become overly concerned and inadvertently increase stress during mealtimes.

For very young babies, the feeding experience is perhaps the most important single situation for close contact and interaction with an adult. Through this experience they learn basic trust. Security revolves around food. As babies grow, mealtime can become a medium through which they learn much about themselves, those caring for them, and the world around.

For young babies, feeding should be associated with close contact and interaction.

The responsibility in any child-care setting is, therefore, to provide good food with nutritional value, and also to ensure that the children are not deprived of all the other, equally important aspects of mealtime. Often children who present feeding problems *are* deprived, as mealtime focuses on the mechanics of eating only. The stress caregivers feel, along with the stress of the child, can be alleviated somewhat by emphasizing other aspects of the mealtime experience such as talking or socializing.

Though discussions of food and feeding are popular among caregivers, coming to agreement about policies and procedures and establishing changes in caregiving practices is far from an easy task. Eating brings forth a variety of emotions in most people. Adults bring to a feeding situation feelings, ideas, and traditions that are often deeply ingrained. They have strong feelings about what should or should not go on, and this affects the way in which we handle mealtime situations (Gonzalez-Mena & Eyer, 1989). For example, one young caregiver working with toddlers had the expectation that children should eat, and then talk or play afterwards away from the table. In discussing her own childhood experiences, she stated that this is what had happened at her house all the time. It was then that she realized that she brought this expectation to the children she worked with. Nevertheless, consistency in practice and agreement among staff members regarding feeding procedures is very important if we are to ensure that mealtime is emotionally and educationally satisfying.

While provincial regulations and guidelines determine feeding practices to some extent, where possible, parents' requests and practices should be considered. Religious dietary laws must be respected (for example, many people of Jewish or Muslim faith are forbidden to eat pork) and alternatives provided. An attempt should be made to offer variety in food preparation, reflecting the cultures of the children present.

Planning Mealtime

Three main points should be considered in the planning of mealtime. First, what are the goals of mealtime for the child? Second, what are the individual differences in the needs and personalities of the children? Third, what are the attitudes of parents and caregivers towards food, feeding, and expectations of behavior during mealtime?

Developmental Goals of Mealtime

Perhaps the primary developmental goal of mealtime for infants is the learning of trust. By providing nourishment to relieve the discomfort of hunger, the adult reinforces the child's sense that the world is a good, secure place to be. Mealtime provides the earliest socialization experience for the child. The baby who is cuddled, talked to, and responded to while being fed is part of this social experience. Mealtime provides an important opportunity for socializing among the older babies, provided that the group is small (two to three babies) and the atmosphere relaxed.

At mealtime, toddlers can begin to learn the cultural values of appropriate behavior (e.g., manners). However, great care needs to be taken not to expect too much from them. Waiting quietly at the table — either to receive food or to sit until others have finished — is an impossible task for a toddler. The best way to begin socialization is for the caregiver to sit at the table with the toddlers and model the eating behaviors and the social behaviors that they should learn.

Much language learning can occur at mealtime. This begins in infancy, as the baby learns that the caregiver responds to smiles, vocalizations, and body movements. At feeding time the baby initiates and responds to both direct, verbal interactions and non-verbal communication. Mealtime continues to be an excellent opportunity for language learning as the baby develops. Caregivers can describe their actions, the children's actions, the food, and so forth. Since vocabulary is based on concrete, immediate experiences, mealtime provides a prime opportunity to develop language for all children. It can also be an excellent vehicle for encouraging basic vocabulary and decision-making skills (e.g., choosing between two foods or drinks, where the result of the choice is immediately reinforced). Caregivers can encourage conversation at the table as the toddlers acquire language skills.

The variety of colors, smells, tastes, and textures at mealtime provides rich sensory experiences for infants and toddlers. In addition, children can learn about properties of foods (e.g.,

Much learning can occur at mealtime, especially if the caregiver sits at the table with the children and models desired behaviors.

mashed potatoes stick to the spoon; peas roll off) and utensils. While many adults oppose playing with food, a certain degree of experimentation can be incorporated into the mealtime (mixing the milk into the cereal, for example).

Mealtimes provide a forum for teaching and practicing fine motor skills. Babies can improve their pincer grasp if they are offered small foods such as dry cereal, and can practice a variety of grasps with utensils. Mealtimes also call for eye-hand coordination and hand-mouth coordination.

Finally, mealtime can provide an excellent opportunity for all infants and toddlers to practice self-help skills, from holding the bottle or cup to managing finger foods, managing utensils, and eventually serving themselves. Mealtime is an excellent situation in which to begin teaching self-help abilities, along with fine motor skills, because foods and drinks are usually enjoyable and immediately reinforce a child's success.

Individual Differences in Personality and Needs

Small babies often require individualized feeding schedules. Each baby has a unique rhythm and comes from a home with its own rhythms. Babies and toddlers who are hungry should not have to wait for their food. While some babies adapt fairly rapidly to a fixed schedule, others cannot cope with the interference with their basic body rhythms. A child-care setting must make provisions for these irregular schedules. Staff who can adapt to a flexible schedule often find that it is easier to make mealtime a quality time when the babies are not all eating together. However, when special-needs children require one-to-one attention and feeding becomes a long process, it is important to plan a workable schedule. The caregiver should ensure, for example, that mealtime and snack time do not consume the entire day.

As children get older, mealtimes become more regular. However, many factors affect appetite (teeth, sickness, fatigue) and schedule adjustments for individual children are necessary. Ongoing communication with parents regarding changes in eating patterns will help to understand the babies' and toddlers' cues. Certainly communication is crucial in determining babies' and toddlers' likes and dislikes, although some children seem to enjoy certain foods at the center that they are unwilling to eat at home.

Mealtime can mean different things to different infants. Some infants enjoy and need close body contact while feeding, others need to be unrestricted, with more eye contact and less body contact. For one toddler, mealtime may be a good time for a stimulating conversation, for another it might be important that mealtime be quiet enough to allow the child to concentrate on food and eating. Meeting all those varying needs in a group situation is not always easy, but if caregivers are aware of them, meals can be planned accordingly. Difficulties are more likely to arise when mealtime is planned without taking into consideration the different needs of children. Sometimes the fine details of planning (for example, changing where the caregiver sits or making lunch-time fifteen minutes earlier) can make a big difference in terms of meeting the individual needs of the children.

Parents' and Caregivers' Attitudes toward Mealtime

Some adults feel that a child who does not finish a meal should not have dessert. Others feel that dessert should be as nutritious as the meal and not seen as a reward for finishing. Some adults feel that children should not be allowed to smear their food, others feel that this is a valuable experience and should be tolerated. Some worry that babies who are allowed to play with food will acquire messy eating habits. Different cultures have different food favorites and different ways of eating that food. In some cultures it is considered polite to eat chicken, but not steak, with your fingers; in others all foods are eaten using fingers. In some cultures burping is considered rude; in others it is a way of complimenting the host or hostess for a fine meal. Such differences in what is considered tasty or polite need to be discussed in an atmosphere of acceptance.

Parents often focus much of their anxiety about group care on feeding issues. It is the parents' right to know what and how much their child eats. Much of their anxiety will be alleviated by frequent communication with caregivers, not only when a feeding problem arises, but also when the child eats well. If a parent is concerned that the child is not eating enough, a record of food intake over a period of time can be a helpful basis for discussion.

Maximizing the Quality of the Mealtime Experience

Mealtime should be quality time for children and the caregiver. Whether a baby is bottle fed on the caregiver's lap, eats finger food in a highchair, or sits at a table with other toddlers, he or she needs the caregiver's full attention. The role of the adult here needs to be seen as much more than the provider of food or manager of messes. The adult has to be part of the child's mealtime experience. Babies and toddlers should have the company of their primary caregiver at mealtime, because she will best know their habits, likes, and dislikes. While it is common practice to see groups of children seated and the caregivers standing, serving, and fetching, every effort should be made to sit with the children for most of the meal.

Giving a choice is important in feeding situations, from a very early age. Choosing between eating and not eating and how much to eat and even what to eat (from a limited number of choices!) should be up to the child. Mealtime is one of the best environments for teaching choice and decision making to children, especially those with special needs, because the items are observable, concrete and provide immediate reinforcement. Finger foods are important for helping the baby make the transition to self feeding. It is important to provide an assortment of colors, tastes, and textures in foods that are safe and convenient for the babies to handle. Eating with their fingers is important for their "I can do it" feeling and good practice for fine motor skills.

While a certain amount of messiness must be tolerated, it can be controlled by providing suitable utensils and foods. Thick mixtures stick better to spoons. Bowls with suction cups under them, or plates placed on damp cloths, will not slide. If caregivers agree on reasonable limits of experimentation, mealtimes will be more relaxed.

With all the best intentions, planning, and efforts, sometimes feeding situations go wrong, and this can arouse feelings of frustration, anger and guilt among caregivers. It is important to recognize this difficulty as a fact of life in day care. However, if feeding problems persist, it will be necessary to analyze the mealtime procedures in terms of their suitability for an individual child, or in terms of general organization. Sometimes minor changes, such as having the food available before the children sit at the table or having small groups of two to three, can make a tremendous difference in the atmosphere.

Children with Special Needs

Children with special needs, like all children, may find mealtime either a frustrating or rewarding and interesting social experience. Understanding how and what to feed the baby or how to assist the toddler is a starting point for ensuring that mealtime is a positive experience. Parent involvement is of paramount importance, and parents and caregivers alike can benefit from sharing experiences and information about feeding. For example, certain foods or eating in certain positions might be helpful.

The caregiver needs to have a clear idea of what the child is capable of. Can he or she swallow? Chew? Hold food alone? As for all children, the food provided must be suited to developmental and physical abilities. For example, if the child is beginning to finger feed, provide foods that are easily picked up and not easily choked on.

Adaptive equipment is often used to aid children with physical disabilities to eat independently. Built-up handles on utensils that are easier to grasp, velcro straps to hold utensils in place, rubber mats, or secured plates that cannot move are several examples. All adaptations can be quite useful. However, it is

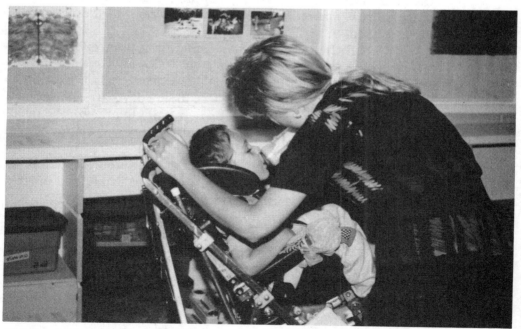

Children with physical disabilities may need to be placed in positions that allow maximum comfort for eating or drinking.

important to stop using them when and if the child is ready. A child who can use only one hand, for example, may always require the use of a placement that sticks to the table because it is impossible to hold a bowl and eat with just one hand. When possible, gradually discontinue using adapted tools (e.g., built-up handles should get smaller) or keep trying to reintroduce regular items.

It is important to place children with physical difficulties in positions that allow maximum comfort and assistance in eating. Points to consider in positioning are:

❑ Feed directly facing the child (not from one side).

❑ The child should be in an upright position with the head tilted forward slightly to reduce the risk of choking.

❑ Support the child's feet (e.g., on the foot rests of the highchair.)

❑ Place the child's hands directly in front of his or her body in preparation for self feeding.

Correct positioning will facilitate muscle tone and eating. A physiotherapist or occupational therapist can provide extra help if needed.

A child with a visual disability will develop eating skills more easily if the setting is predictable. For example, put the drink in the same spot each time so it doesn't get knocked over, and put the spoon and plate in the same place so the child knows where to find them.

Children with developmental delays or hearing difficulties should present no other concerns and would benefit from the same considerations that are provided to all the children. Ensure that mealtimes are social times, a time for choices to be made and words to be learned, and a time for enjoyment.

OBSERVATION QUESTIONS

1. How does the infant or toddler usually react to mealtime?
    - Very hungry, anxious to eat and impatient?
    - Interested in eating but not anxious?
    - Rather disinterested in food; not wanting to come to eat?

2. How does the infant or toddler react to food?
    - Likes most foods?
    - Has some preferences?
    - Is very particular?

3. Does the infant or toddler
    - Want large quantities?
    - Eat moderate amounts of food?
    - Eat small amounts of food?

4. At mealtime does the infant or toddler
    - Enjoy socializing with the caregiver? With other children?
    - Scan the environment?
    - Focus on food and not want to be distracted?

5. Does the older infant or toddler
    - Want to self feed with fingers or spoon?
    - Like to be helped?
    - Get annoyed when the caregiver tries to help?

6. Does the older baby who has just learned to stand up
    - Like sitting in the highchair at mealtime?
    - Want to stand up all the time?

7. Does the toddler
    - Remain seated happily throughout the meal?
    - Want to eat more but can't sit still?

TIPS FOR HEALTHY AND SAFE MEALTIMES

- Check local regulations regarding health and nutrition.
- Food preparation area must be clean and sanitary. There should be adequate spaces for food preparation, serving, and storage to minimize accidents.
- Prepare food away from diaper changing area.
- Remove garbage regularly.
- The garbage storage area should be clean and sanitized often.
- Wash hands — your own and those of the children.
- If a baby is breastfeeding try to arrange the feeding schedule so that baby is ready to nurse when mom arrives. Baby should eat about two and a half hours before she comes.
- Safely store milk or formula.
- When babies begin eating solids at four to six months, introduce new foods one at a time. Allow the child time to adjust (three to five days) and note difficulties (e.g., allergies, dislikes).
- Provide food at the consistency children are ready for (e.g., thick soups when first using a spoon; food that melts, such as cereal, when learning to chew).
- Help to establish good eating habits and a nutritious diet.
- Use the Canada Food Guide as a guide to food choices.
- Avoid peanuts, popcorn, hotdogs, grapes, hard candies, and gum, as these items are easily choked on.
- Try to offer less food, rather than too much, so the toddler can ask for more.
- Try new foods. It may be best to serve new foods with familiar foods, or to serve new food only when the child is hungry.
- Encourage tasting; don't force.
- Serve preferred with non-preferred foods.

✔ Caregiver Checklist

DOES THE CAREGIVER:

1. Relate to babies while bottle feeding — maintain eye contact and talk softly to the baby, rather than to other caregivers?

2. Show patience with the slow eater?

3. Use food to satisfy hunger, not as a pacifier?

4. Encourage self feeding, use finger food, and tolerate a reasonable amount of messiness?

5. Show willingness to change schedules when a child is too sleepy to eat or hungry earlier than planned mealtime?

6. Sit with toddlers in a relaxed manner while they eat, and talk and respond to them?

7. Allow toddlers to choose foods and amounts of food?

8. Encourage babies and toddlers to try new foods, without forcing or tricking them?

9. Not expect toddlers to sit for long periods waiting for meals or after meals?

10. Point out names of food, colors, and textures and encourage children to notice smells of foods?

11. Allow toddlers to participate in preparation — bringing bread to the table, helping themselves from serving bowls, wiping up, etc., when possible?

12. Make provision for smooth transition for each individual child from eating to next activity?

13. Ensure that health and safety issues concerning food preparation and eating are dealt with?

14. Relate to parents' concerns over feeding with patience and understanding?

PRACTICAL APPLICATION

1. Observe a mealtime in a group setting and record:

   a) the general atmosphere;

   b) the conversations that occurred between the caregiver and a child;

   c) the behavior of the child;

   d) the opportunity provided to make choices and practice skills.

   Based on the discussion in this chapter, make a list of recommendations that would improve the quality of mealtime at the center observed.

2. Observe and compare the way two different caregivers interact with children during mealtime (consider verbal and social interactions, body language, etc.). What recommendations would you make?

3. What are some of the difficulties that infants and toddlers may encounter during the transition to and from mealtime? How can staff help minimize these difficulties?

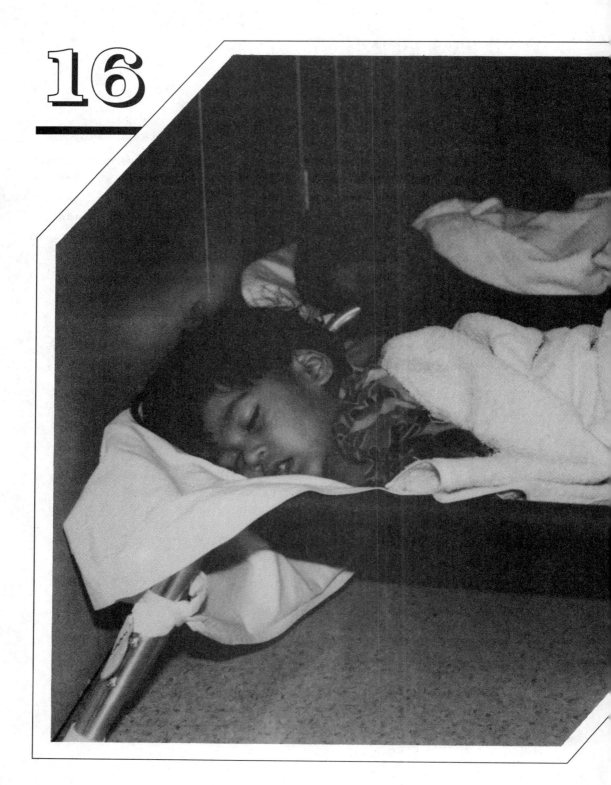

Rest and Naptime

Objectives
❖ To emphasize the individual needs of children for resting and napping.
❖ To highlight the role of the caregiver in responding to an infant's need for rest in an individualized, respectful manner.
❖ To emphasize the importance of communicating with parents about naptime.

Opening Thoughts
Imagine that you are away at a conference and are given a two-hour break to rest. Write down briefly how you would use this time.

Comments on Opening Thoughts
❖ There are vast differences in what people consider rest to be. Some people will engage in passive activities such as watching TV or sleeping. Others will be active; they may jog or shop.
❖ There are differences in how people make the transition from activity to rest.
❖ There is a wide variation among infants and toddlers in sleep patterns, and their differences need to be taken into account when planning for rest and naptimes. ❏

Developmental Reminders

—Newborns sleep approximately eighteen to twenty hours per day.

—Babies will sleep about four to six times per day starting at four weeks.

—Most infants sleep fourteen to seventeen hours per day between one and four months.

—Most infants require two to three naps per day starting at four months.

—One afternoon nap is often enough starting at about ten to twelve months. Babies will entertain themselves briefly when awake.

—Toddlers may display difficulties going to sleep (they have too much to do).

—There is great variability in the sleeping habits of infants and toddlers.

All infants and toddlers in group care will require a rest or nap during the day. Physically and emotionally, children require periods of quiet and rest away from the activity of the group. The amount of sleep needed, the ease with which very young children settle into naptime, and their needs upon awakening vary from child to child. However, the needs of the adults and the needs of the group as a whole sometimes make it very difficult to ensure that each child's individual needs are met. Every program must ensure that children who require rest may do so but, at the same time, children who are not tired should not be forced into a state of inactivity. Meeting the individual needs of babies and toddlers for rest and sleep requires a planned, flexible daily schedule in a calm and reassuring environment.

Young infants come to group care with very different sleep patterns. As they get older, the rhythms of the center can influence their sleep patterns, but the need for flexibility always exists. Even if patterns do emerge, they will vary according to age, changing patterns at home, teething, illness, and changes in the group environment.

It is the adult who often has to determine when a child needs a nap, based on careful observation of his or her behavior. Children indicate they are tired in different ways: rubbing eyes, crying, clinging, losing interest in play, becoming frustrated easily, or sometimes by becoming increasingly active or aggressive. As infants and toddlers seldom ask for a nap, it is important that the caregiver who knows each child well makes the decision for the child, or as the child grows older, with him or her (e.g., "It looks like you are getting sleepy; you have your blanket, are you ready for a nap?").

Children should not be put to bed when distressed and the caregiver should always attempt to calm a child before naptime. It is likely that many children associate going to bed with their home and their family, so naptime can evoke strong feelings of separation anxiety that require comfort and attention (Provence et al., 1977). Some babies cry themselves to sleep, but prolonged distressed cries should never be left unattended. It is often easy to tell the difference between a distressed baby and one who cries himself

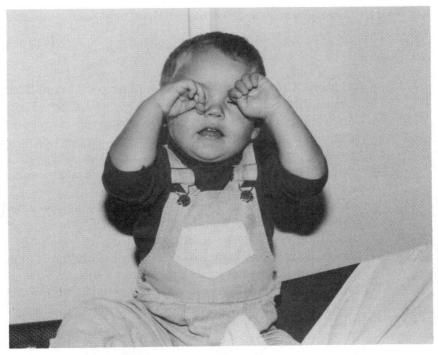

Children indicate they are tired in different ways.

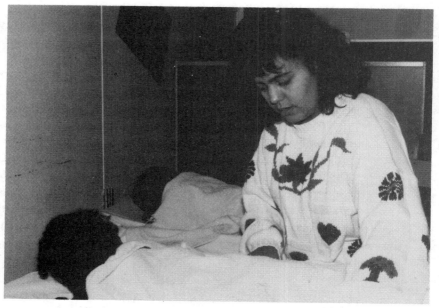

Caregivers should put each child to bed in a warm, individualized manner.

to sleep. Cribs or cots should be in as permanent a place as possible so that children have the security of a familiar and predictable environment. Toddlers should be allowed to have special objects in their beds since, for some, naptime evokes feelings of sadness and longing for their parents. In addition, caregivers should always be available during naptime in case a child awakens early or has difficulties (e.g., is coughing, needs a diaper change).

A smooth transition to naptime is usually aided by a quiet preceding activity, such as a song, story, or cuddle. Some infants and toddlers require rocking, patting, or stroking to help them sleep. Caregivers sometimes feel that if one child receives special attention in this manner, the other children will demand it as well. Experience has shown that this is not usually the case since this kind of comparison requires a level of cognitive sophistication that toddlers do not yet have.

Infants generally fall asleep easily and remain sleeping regardless of the environment, but it is preferable to dim the lights and arrange for a quiet time. Toddlers will be much more affected by noise and lights than infants will, so naptime routines (i.e., setting the atmosphere) will become more important during this stage.

Infants and toddlers have very different waking behaviors. Some will want to play in their beds, some are quite cranky and need some individual attention, and others may be ready for action immediately upon waking. Caregivers should be aware of these differences and be available as needed.

Sleep time, like other areas of routine care, is often a source of concern for parents. Some parents want their children to have a lengthy nap at the center so that they will be able to spend time with them after work. Other parents want their children to have shorter naps (or no naps at all) so that they will go to bed early. As with all other areas of routine care, the needs of the infants and toddlers must come first. However, there should be a willingness to cooperate with parents when possible. For example, if a parent wishes to take the child home earlier to nap at home, it may be possible to engage the child in a quiet activity rather than putting him or her to bed. In all cases, how much children sleep, when they sleep, and other relevant information needs to be communicated regularly to the parents.

Children with Special Needs

If caregivers are intent on meeting the individual needs of all children in their care, they will adequately meet the needs of children with special needs as well. Several points may assist special-needs children at naptime. Children with special needs may not always provide consistent cues about being tired. Observing the child and getting information about sleep times from parents may be helpful. Developing a routine will help the child prepare and be ready for naptime.

Children with physical disabilities might need to be positioned correctly so that they are able to rest. For example, a child with cerebral palsy may relax lying on one side. A floppy baby with Down's syndrome may need to be supported with rolled up blankets or not laid tummy-down. The child may need to be repositioned at some point during the rest. The child's parents are the best source of information regarding rest.

Children with visual impairments may need extra considerations in transition to and from naptime. Developing a routine for naptime that includes auditory cues such as playing soft music or singing may help the child prepare. When approaching the baby after a nap, the caregiver should call the child's name to announce gently that someone is approaching.

Children with hearing impairments may require similar considerations with visual cues. Smooth transition to naptime may be achieved with pictures or objects such as a blanket or teddy that is set out just before rest so the child can prepare. When the rest is over, let the child make visual contact with you before you pick the child up. If possible in the setting, turning the lights on will give the child a bit of notice that you are coming.

Children with developmental delays should pose no special difficulties at naptime. Giving extra attention to transition times and building routines into the day will best benefit these children.

A fussy baby should be calmed down before being put to bed.

OBSERVATION QUESTIONS

1. What signs indicate that the infant or toddler is tired?
2. Does the child settle to sleep easily?
3. Does the child need a longer transition to naptime?
4. Is the child active immediately following sleep?
5. Does the child require attention or comfort upon waking?
6. What toys or objects does each child prefer to have in bed at naptime?

TIPS FOR HEALTHY AND SAFE REST AND NAPTIMES

- Bedding and blankets must be laundered regularly.
- The setting will need to be organized for individual, flexible sleeping schedules. Infants will be different from toddlers, and other factors may interfere (e.g., what time the child arrives, teething, illness).
- Cribs or cots should be spaced far enough apart to allow privacy but close enough for children to feel secure (i.e., they should know others are close by).

✔ Caregiver Checklist

DOES THE CAREGIVER:

1. Provide each child with a consistent sleeping place?

2. Notice and respond to infants' and toddlers' signs of tiredness?

3. Provide quiet calm transitions to naptime?

4. Assist the child who has difficulty in falling asleep?

5. Show flexibility in the timing of naptime according to the needs of the child?

6. Allow the child to have a favorite toy or object in bed?

7. Put each child to bed in a warm, individualized manner?

8. Ensure that the setting is suitable for sleeping (dimmed lights, quiet, etc.)?

9. Individualize the transition from naptime according to the child's behavior and temperament (allow the slow waker time; calm the fussy baby)?

10. Communicate with parents regularly about children's rest and sleep behaviors?

PRACTICAL APPLICATION

1. Observe a caregiver's interactions with three different children at naptime. Based on the discussion in this chapter make a list of five recommendations that will ensure that each child's needs for rest are met in an individualized, respectful manner.

2. What are a number of activities that you would recommend prior to naptime? Why did you choose these activities?

3. In many toddler centers, mealtime occurs at a set time and is followed by naptime. Observe the toddlers eating and their transition to naptime. Does this schedule work for them? What made you think so? If you think you observed a child for whom this schedule did not work, what made you reach this conclusion, and what recommendations would you make?

17

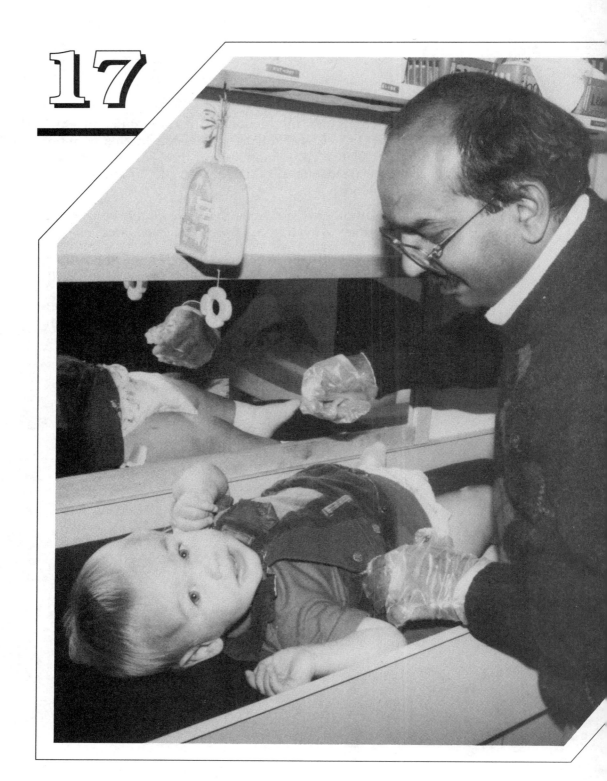

Diapering and Dressing

Objectives

- ❖ To emphasize the importance of diapering and dressing as quality interactions between caregivers and children.
- ❖ To discuss the learning potential of diapering and dressing interactions.
- ❖ To emphasize the importance of respectful caregiving in diapering and dressing routines.

Opening Thoughts

Think of a situation where someone took control over your body — for example, when you were hospitalized or in a dentist's chair. What kinds of behavior on the part of the person in control added to or hindered your feelings of being respected or in control?

Comments on Opening Thoughts

- ❖ We often find ourselves in situations where someone temporarily takes control over us. The stress is reduced when we are informed what is happening.
- ❖ The stress is reduced when we have some input into the decisions that are being made or if we have some choices.
- ❖ Infants and toddlers can have input and choices when we involve them in diapering and dressing. ❐

Developmental Reminders

Up to Six Months
— Some infants do not like clothing pulled over head.
— May enjoy wearing no clothes.
— Many enjoy changing time.

Six Months to a Year (Approximately)
— May fuss at diaper change time.
— Likes to roll, twist, and turn.
— May like to pull off hats, socks, etc.

Twelve to Eighteen Months
— May want to stand when being diapered.
— Shows natural interest in genitals.
— Begins to cooperate more actively in dressing.
— Learns to unzip zippers.

Eighteen Months On
— Can pull off loose shirt.
— Pulls down pants.
— Washes and dries hands "alone with help."
— Wants to do things himself or herself.
— May like to brush teeth.

Each infant is diapered thousands of times in the first few years of life. Diapering and dressing infants and toddlers is one of the most time-consuming elements of their care. Yet it is an element that infants do not normally feel a strong need for, and older infants and young toddlers may often resist, preferring to move about and play. Dressing and undressing are repeated routinely throughout the day: taking off coats when children arrive; changing a shirt that got soiled at feeding; dressing to go outdoors; undressing when back indoors; and again dressing the children in preparation to go home. In addition, often a sudden need arises for a diaper change or change of clothing when the caregiver is busily involved in another activity.

Diapering and dressing are sometimes difficult tasks for which there is little immediate gratification for either the child or caregiver (compared, for example, with feeding, where caregivers usually can notice the child's gratification). On the other hand, diapering and dressing are times when infants, toddlers, and their caregivers can interact on a one-to-one basis. They offer an excellent opportunity for quality time, if carried out properly. They present an opportunity for babies and toddlers to learn about themselves, to practice self-help skills, and to feel pleased about the way they look.

Making Diapering and Dressing Quality Interactions

In order to maximize the potential of these one-to-one activities, caregivers must understand the learning potential of these routines, the individual needs of the children, and the attitudes and needs of the adults who care for the children. Only then will they be able to plan the experiences in a manner that is appropriate, respectful, and suited to the individual personality of each child. In addition, attention must be paid to the health and sanitation aspects of diapering.

Learning Potential of Dressing and Diapering Routines

Diapering and dressing routines can encompass all the developmental goals commonly established for infants and toddlers in group care. When the discomfort of a soiled or wet diaper is relieved by a caregiver who responds to the child's cry, the trusting relationship is reinforced. Children's developing images of themselves are going to be influenced by the manner in which the adult relates to and handles their bodies during dressing and diapering routines.

Certainly these routines provide for a rich variety of sensory experiences —the warm wash cloth; the different textures of clothing; the feeling of being bundled up, or the freedom of having no clothes on. The dressing and diapering routines provide an opportunity for young children to practice skills (infants can pull off their socks, toddlers can practice with zippers), to engage in conversations that stimulate language development, and to master problem-solving challenges. Diapering and dressing provide an excellent opportunity for physically disabled children to become aware of and recognize body parts and perhaps to attempt to exert some control over their bodies (e.g., in moving their arms or lifting their heads). In addition, the repetitive routines of dressing provide the children with concrete clues as to how the day will evolve. As infants mature they may come to associate a change of clothing with an event — a meal or an outdoor time. This building of routines is particularly helpful for children with special needs, but can help foster a sense of security for all children. The manner in which the caregiver relates to the infant or toddler during diapering and dressing will have an impact on the child's self image. If babies are treated with respect, and have the opportunity to participate in the activity, they will feel good about themselves. If caregivers relate to dressing and undressing as opportunities for learning and practicing skills, these exchanges become more enjoyable for children and caregivers alike, and can promote all areas of the child's development.

Diapering and Dressing in a Manner that Respects Children and their Individual Differences

Changing an infant requires respectful body contact. Children must never be insulted, even in fun. Calling babies "stinky" or "poopy pants" is simply unacceptable, even if there is no mean intention. Respectful caregiving is reflected in the caregiver relating to the child as a person, not an object. A child should not be picked up without warning or explanation of what the caregiver is doing or why. Babies and toddlers can be involved in caregiving tasks from a very early age, according to their ability. A small baby can be told what the caregiver is doing, can be shown the diaper, and allowed to feel it. An older baby can "help" by lifting a leg, or pulling off a sock. A toddler can bring the bag and find the diaper inside, or go to the cupboard to fetch the diaper. The toddler can partially undress and dress alone. Caregivers must read the children's cues to gauge how much they want to participate.

Older infants and toddlers often resist being dressed, preferring to move around and play.

Most diaper changing times are not urgent enough to justify disturbing a child who is very involved in an activity. It is best to try to time the change for when the child is not involved in activity or when the child is in transition from one activity to another. When a child must be disturbed in order to be changed, caregivers can empathize with any unwillingness to cooperate! While repetitiveness in routines is a good thing, routines need not become monotonous. Varying the procedure sometimes, by introducing a new activity while changing (clapping hands, playing peekaboo, or gently massaging), can turn changing time into a fun time for babies and caregivers. Changing practices must be adapted to individual differences in the personality and mood of the child. Some babies will love to play or be tickled gently while being changed. Others want a more gentle experience. Some toddlers find it easier to be dressed standing up, others may prefer to lie down and hold a toy.

A decision as to how much the child should wear is not always based on the temperature of the room. Emotional factors, such as separation problems, come into play. Not wanting to part with a sweater or coat is a common reaction to stress in young children. In addition, babies differ in the way they respond to tactile stimulation. Some children find the restriction of tightly buttoned clothing intolerable, others find comfort in being bundled up. Some children are very sensitive to heat, and suffer discomfort while waiting to have their coats removed. Caregivers must be aware of these temperamental differences and take them into account.

Resistance to being changed or dressed is developmentally appropriate as babies get older. Caregivers can help themselves with two different approaches. One is to use as many distraction techniques as possible, such as giving the child a favorite toy while he or she is being changed. The other approach, which is considered preferable by some experts, is to make great efforts to involve the child in the task. This second approach helps to provide the child with additional information about the experience.

Needs and Attitudes of Parents and Staff

Sometimes diapering and dressing issues can become a source of tension between parents and caregivers. Parents sometimes send clothing that staff feel is inappropriate. Parents sometimes feel that staff are not prompt enough in changing their children. There are no easy solutions to these issues, but if centers have clear policies regarding the kind of clothing that is appropriate, communicate regularly with parents, and are willing to listen to parents' concerns, these problems can be somewhat alleviated. It is important to respect parent's wishes whenever possible.

The needs of the caregiver must also be considered when planning diapering and dressing. Caring for infants involves lifting, carrying, and bending. A caregiver who is suffering back discomfort will have difficulty engaging in pleasant interactions. The height of the changing table and the location of the sink and supplies should be planned to maximize comfort and convenience.

Some centers have provided in-service training programs for staff to teach them exercises and body positions that prevent back problems.

Children with Special Needs

Children who have special needs deserve the same respectful diapering and dressing practices as all children. Because it may be harder for some of these children to participate actively, we must be very conscientious about ensuring that they are involved as much as possible. If, for example, a physically disabled toddler is unable to fetch her coat like the other toddlers do, she can be given other ways to participate, or be given choices as to how the coat will be put on ("Shall we put this arm in first, or your other arm?").

Some children who have been subjected to painful medical treatment may be hesitant about being touched. This needs to be understood and respected. Caregivers should approach gradually and gently, and offer assurances that they won't hurt. Even if the child doesn't understand the words, the voice can be very reassuring.

Children with visual impairments will require descriptions or explanations of dressing and undressing to supplement the tactile feelings they are getting while being changed (e.g., "That's powder; doesn't it feel soft and smell nice?").

Children with physical impairments such as cerebral palsy may be difficult to diaper and dress. Knowing how to position and handle the child will be necessary. See Finnie (1981) for a detailed overview of this topic.

Developmentally delayed children and children with hearing disabilities should pose no extra difficulties in diapering and dressing.

Diapering and dressing provide a perfect one-to-one time to develop cognitive (e.g., "Where's your foot?"), sensory ("Let's rub powder on your tummy"), and motor skills in undressing and dressing for all children. These interactions should be capitalized on for the young child with special needs to promote development in all areas.

Dressing helps to promote development in all areas.

OBSERVATION QUESTIONS

1. How does the infant or toddler respond to the feel of clothing?
   - Likes shirts buttoned to the top?
   - Finds close-fitting clothes uncomfortable?

2. How does the baby participate in the dressing activity?
   - Reaches for the caregiver?
   - Pulls at his sock?

3. How does the infant or toddler react to having diapers changed?
   - Squirms and fusses?
   - Enjoys the attention?
   - Doesn't seem to mind?

4. How does the toddler respond to hand washing?
   – Enjoys the experience?
   – Resists?

TIPS FOR HEALTHY AND SAFE DIAPERING AND DRESSING

- Change diapers only in the area set up for that purpose. Use the area only for diapering.
- Diaper area should be far removed from food preparation.
- A sink should be nearby to wash hands before and after.
- Provide a diapering surface that is easy to clean.
- Have disposable gloves available (to use if a child has diarrhea, for example).
- Avoid contact with blood. Use disposable rubber gloves.
- Clean and disinfect areas contaminated with blood, vomit, or feces immediately.
- The child should be restrained with a guard rail and belt when on the change table.

   RULE: One hand must be on the child at all times.

- Keep creams, diapers, etc. within easy reach so your attention need not be diverted from the child.
- Lotions, creams, etc. should be out of the child's reach.
- Cleaning supplies for the area must be stored out of the child's reach.
- The change area should be close to the play area so caregivers are in hearing range and won't need to feel that they have to rush back.
- The change area should be at an adequate height so caregivers are not uncomfortable, and need not strain their backs.
- Caregivers need to be cautious in lifting babies and toddlers. Repeated lifting of heavy toddlers may cause back problems.

✔ *Caregiver Checklist*

DOES THE CAREGIVER:

1. Inform the baby or toddler of the intention to pick her up to dress or change her?

2. Focus attention on the baby or toddler while changing and dressing?

3. Describe the process and label body parts or items of clothing, but refrain from irrelevant and constant chatter?

4. Encourage babies to participate in the task (e.g., to lift a leg, find the hole in the shoe)?

5. Utilize changing and dressing for enriching sensory experiences (e.g., feeling the diaper, touching the wet cloth, smelling the soap)?

6. Enjoy the interactions of diapering and dressing?

7. Refrain from insulting (e.g., "How does such a small boy make such a big smell"), even in a joking manner?

8. Understand that toddlers will often resist being attended to, understand that this is natural, and acknowledge their feelings?

9. Occasionally introduce humor to the dressing situation for the toddler (e.g., try to put a sweater on upside down or the toddler's clothes on herself)?

10. Show the child how pretty, handsome, special he or she is after changing or dressing?

11. Pick up the baby's verbal and non-verbal communications while changing or dressing, and respond to them?

12. Allow toddlers to help in dressing and changing (e.g., bringing the diaper, holding the rubber pants)?

13. Manage to create quality dressing time for each child, yet remain aware of the other children?

PRACTICAL APPLICATION

1. After observing the diapering and dressing routines in an infant/toddler setting, explain the different ways in which the staff:

   a) communicated with the children; and

   b) involved the children in the activities.

   Based on your observation and the discussion in this chapter, would you have any recommendations for the staff?

2. Describe some of the interactive activities that could be incorporated into diapering and dressing routines.

3. Write a newsletter to parents explaining how caregivers consider diapering and dressing as learning time. What suggestions could you make to parents regarding the kind of clothing that helps children become more independent?

18

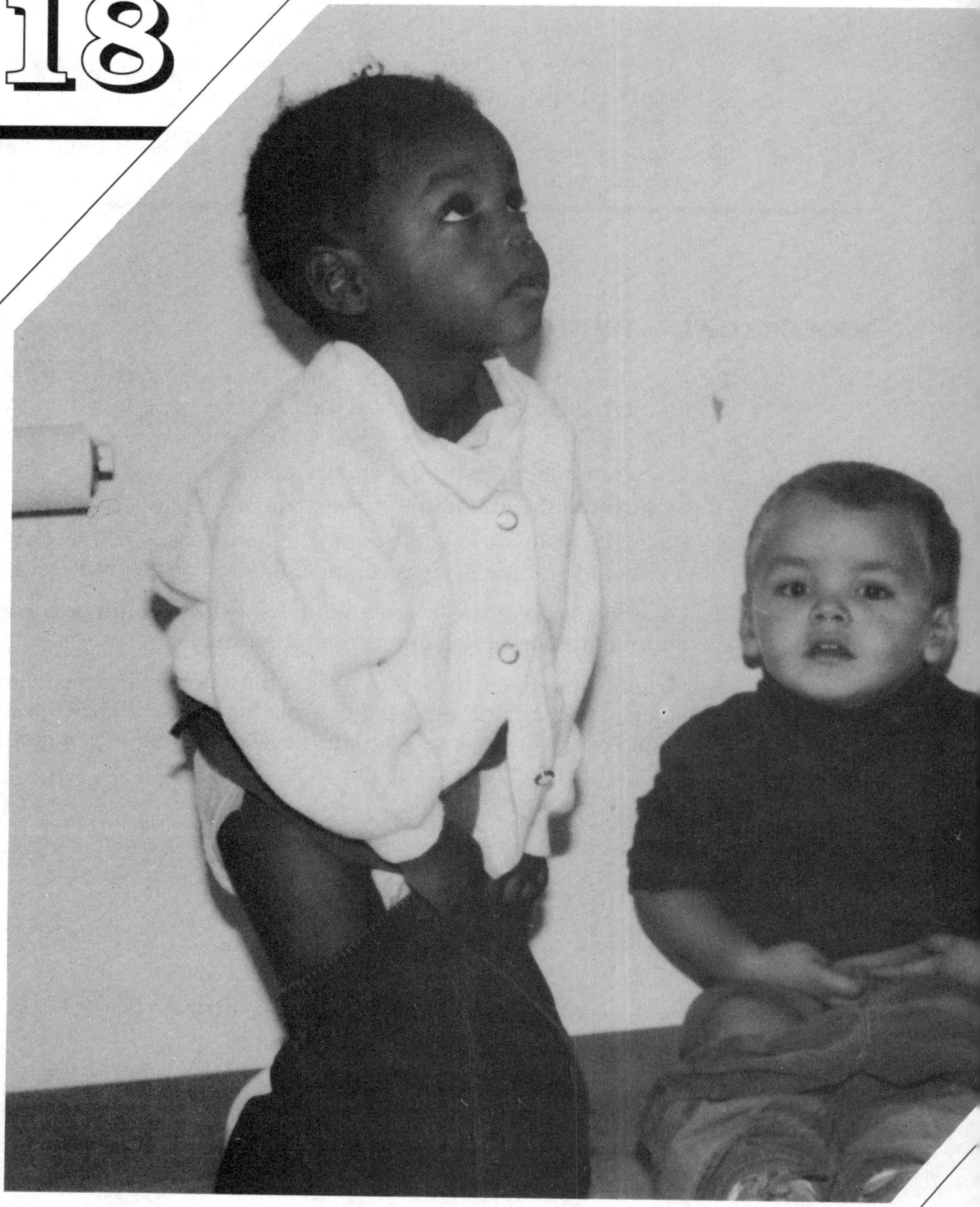

Preparing for Toilet Training

Objectives

- ❖ To review the developmental needs and capabilities of toddlers related to toileting.
- ❖ To discuss attitudes related to toilet training.
- ❖ To review the recommended practices for supporting toilet training.

Opening Thoughts

Think about different methods of toilet training that you have heard or read about. Which of these are in accordance with the child's developmental abilities and which are respectful of the child?

Comments on Opening Thoughts

- ❖ There are many different ways of toilet training and it is difficult to know which is best for which child.
- ❖ Successful toilet training requires that toddlers are mature enough to be successful.
- ❖ Pressuring children to toilet train prematurely usually benefits no one. ❑

Developmental Reminders

Most of the following developmental capabilities should be evident before attempting toilet training:

— The toddler is dry for about two hours at a time.

— The toddler has regular bowel movements.

— The toddler shows some signs of knowing when diapers are wet or soiled, or is bothered by it.

— The toddler imitates behavior.

— The toddler shows interest in the toilet and others using it.

— The toddler can hold and wait after indicating the need to go to the potty.

— The toddler likes to put things where they belong.

— The toddler is not in a highly resistive "no-no" period.

— The toddler can assist in undressing and dressing.

There are very few children who reach school age and still use diapers. Among the very few children who have difficulty with bowel and bladder control, many of the difficulties can be traced to too much pressure to become trained too soon. Why then does toilet training seem such an important issue, for parents and staff alike? Toilet training is often an emotionally charged experience for both the child and the parent, and also for the center staff who are not always in agreement on how to proceed (Weinstein & Flynn, 1982). Expert advice on issues of toilet training sometimes confuses more than assists, largely due to the fact that much of the advice is conflicting.

It is interesting to note that, even though infants and toddlers need the guidance and assistance of an adult in learning to eat or to master the stairs, we never hear the term "eating training" or "stair-climbing training." Yet helping a child master the skills involved in toileting is referred to as "toilet training." The use of the term "training" implies that the focus is on what the adult (the trainer) does, rather than what the child does. Indeed, many of the methods used for toilet training have little to do with what the child is doing, thinking, or feeling. The child is placed on the toilet when the adult thinks it the right time, and encouraged to stay there (often being entertained by the adult to be kept sitting longer) until he or she has produced something. We prefer, however, to think of toileting as a combination of skills that the child will acquire with guidance and assistance from parents and caregivers. We use the term "training" only because that is the common way to refer to the process. Really, we don't want to train children — we want to help them learn.

Toilet Training in Group Care

How then should the issue of toilet training be handled in group care? First, as with all issues of routine care, needs and abilities of infants and toddlers need to be considered. Second, differences in the attitudes of the adults caring for the children need to be examined and clarified. Finally, the way in which this aspect of the child's growth and development will be supported in a respectful, individualized manner needs to be determined.

Developmental Needs and Abilities

The ability to control bowel movements and urination is not an isolated achievement. As with many emerging skills, successful toilet training depends on a number of other developmental milestones. First of all, the ability to hold urine for a reasonable time depends partly on the size of the bladder. When a toddler urinates frequently, the chances are that his or her bladder is not large enough to make toileting reasonable. The control of bowel movements also requires a physiological readiness that training cannot rush. Therefore, toilet training should be delayed until bowel movements are fairly regular and the child remains dry for a reasonable length of time (e.g., about two hours).

In addition to physiological readiness, toddlers usually display a number of associated abilities before they learn to use the toilet successfully. Motor skills that are usually prerequisites for toileting are the ability to stand, sit, walk, and have good balance. Toddlers are usually able to undress themselves partially before they can successfully use the toilet. Many children do not feel discomfort in a wet or soiled diaper, so their motivation to use the toilet has to come from other sources. Therefore, the desire to imitate and the desire to please others are important for successful training. If a toddler is in a phase of oppositional behavior (the "no-no" stage), toilet training is difficult.

A toddler should have the verbal and conceptual skills to be able to understand what is expected during toilet training. Having words for urine and bowel movements and understanding that certain things belong in certain places (and liking to put things where they belong) are characteristics that are associated with successful toilet training.

A toddler who likes to put things where they belong may be ready for toilet training.

All these are simply developmental signs. They are not absolute requirements, and not all children will display all these signs before they begin to use the toilet. However, they can be used as useful guidelines in the consideration of when to start toilet training.

Clarifying Attitudes and Feelings about Toilet Training

Why is toilet training such an emotionally charged issue in many families and toddler centers? Sometimes it relates to the general pressure that is prevalent in our society for children to grow up. Sometimes parents or caregivers see early toilet training as their own accomplishment. The desire to save money on diapers or energy on changing diapers is a prime factor. Certainly staff in centers often feel judged by parents according to their success or lack of success in toilet training. The entrance criteria for certain programs, especially for special-needs children, often include being toilet trained, which places extra pressure on parents and caregivers. Whatever the reasons are, attitudes need to be discussed openly and weighed very carefully. In all quality infant and toddler centers the emotional well-being of the children must be given first consideration, and caregivers need to ensure that pressure for early training does take precedence over the needs of the children to develop and master skills at their own pace.

Supporting Toilet Training in a Respectful, Individualized Manner

Children have their own feelings about toilet training. They are being asked to do something that they often cannot see any reason for. Their compliance will depend on their readiness. If a child is not ready, toilet training can become a battle of wills! The way toddlers feel about their caregiver may well be a factor in successful toilet training. A primary caregiver who knows the child well, and with whom the child has a loving, secure relationship, is the appropriate adult to guide the child in learning to use the toilet.

It is recommended that, well before children are to be toilet trained, they have exposure to the potty or toilet, including flushing. Also, children should have the opportunity to practice related skills, such as pulling up pants or sitting on the toilet.

Potties should be placed in a consistent, pleasant location. For sanitary reasons it is recommended that this area be separate from other activity areas. Toilets and sinks must be kept sanitary, and caregivers must rigidly adhere to handwashing practices after each contact with the toilet.

In the early stages of toilet training toddlers may not want to sit on the toilet for more than a few seconds. It is not recommended to try to encourage them to remain seated by providing toys, books, or other entertainment. Early successes should be recognized and certainly toddlers often are proud of what they have produced in the toilet! Yet somehow it seems artificial to praise elaborately a very natural occurrence. A matter-of-fact recognition (e.g., "There, you have a bowel movement in the potty") may be more appropriate than over-praise. Children should never be insulted or otherwise punished for being unsuccessful when accidents occur. Sometimes toddlers between eighteen and twenty-four months show an initial interest in toilet training and will, for example, want to sit on the toilet without removing their clothes. Often, however, the interest subsides as soon as someone interprets it as a cue to begin toilet training. This is an indication that the efforts to begin toilet training should be set aside for a while.

For many of the issues surrounding toilet training there are no clear cut or right or wrong answers. Questions include, What amount of privacy do children require? Should going to the potty be suggested, or left up to the child? What vocabulary is used for urinating and defecating in the child's family? Questions such as these need to be discussed and clarified according to the wishes of staff and parents. However, coordinating the efforts at home and the center is often not easy. If parents feel that their toddler is not ready to begin, this should be considered carefully by staff. If parents want toilet training to begin at the center before the child is ready, it will be important to explain the center's policy to the parents. Parents may want to know how frequently a child urinates or has bowel movements to assist in making decisions about toilet training. Having written records available is important. Clear policies on toilet training will reduce the potential for conflict.

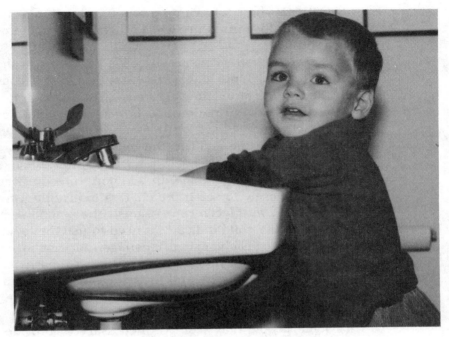

Washing hands should become part of the toilet routine.

It must be remembered that toilet training is a highly individualized process. Some children simply graduate smoothly from diapers to toileting, and that usually happens when children are not pressured. The process is often easier with young children in group care because other children are using the toilet, but many ups and downs occur. If toddlers are given the time to develop toilet skills gradually, at their own pace, they will learn to use the toilet regularly.

Children with Special Needs

Some children have more difficulty than others in learning to use the toilet. The training process may need to be more intensive to ensure success. Caregivers are cautioned to be careful and critical when referring to toilet training manuals, since some are punitive in nature while others may be impractical in a group setting.

Some children with special needs learn to use the toilet by dividing the tasks into stages. The first task is to become familiar with the routine of toileting. The caregiver would first record the time of the child's urination and bowel movements, to learn the child's "schedule." Based on this schedule, the caregiver would then try to take the child to the toilet at set times, often upon arrival, prior to or after snack, prior to or after lunch, after nap-time, and before going home. In addition, the caregiver needs to watch very closely to see if the child is indicating a need to use the toilet (e.g., with facial expressions). The second step might be to wait until the child indicates a need to use the toilet. Again, it is important to teach related language, but not to make it the main focus. Special-needs children have to learn to go to the bathroom independently, and in this case, the related language skills may be of secondary importance. Keeping these two goals distinct is important.

Some people may feel it is necessary to provide the child with a treat after successful use of the toilet, to reinforce the learning that has occurred. If additional reinforcements are necessary, it is crucial that they be removed when no longer needed. The special-needs child may require more practice over a longer time period to ensure mastery of skills. In this case, consistency, breaking down of skills, and reinforcements may be required. Although extra procedures may need to be added (e.g., more time, more practice), toilet training — generally speaking — should be the same as it is for other children.

OBSERVATION QUESTIONS

1. What words does the toddler use to indicate that her diaper is soiled?

2. How does the toddler indicate a need to use the toilet?

3. When the toddler is on the toilet does he want to:
   – Be alone?
   – Have the caregiver nearby?

4. When going to the toilet, does the toddler:
   – Try to undress herself?
   – Wait for the caregiver to help her?

5. How long does the toddler sit on the potty?

TIPS FOR HEALTHY AND SAFE TOILETING

- Caregivers must wash hands thoroughly with soap after assisting each child.
- Toilet area should be cleaned and sanitized regularly.
- Keep cleaning supplies stored safely, out of children's reach.
- Centers that are not equipped with child-size toilets will need a toilet seat adapter that fits over the regular seat and a stool (caution will be required as toddlers climb on and off).
- Soiled clothing and diapers should be put into plastic bags immediately.
- Clothing should be easy to remove since toddlers often give little advance warning.
- Ensure that children always wash their hands so it becomes part of their routine.

✔ *Caregiver Checklist*

DOES THE CAREGIVER:

1. Consult with parents about their expectations and methods for toilet training?

2. Know the developmental abilities of infants and toddlers to ensure that the child is ready?

3. Ensure that the child has had exposure to the toilet beforehand to encourage its use?

4. Provide opportunities to model others using the toilet?

5. Have potties or toilets in a consistent location?

6. Maintain cleanliness of potties and toilets?

7. Encourage children to wash their hands after toileting.

8. Wash his or her hands?

9. Recognize successful attempts and praise appropriately?

10. Decide on vocabulary to use in conjunction with parents?

PRACTICAL APPLICATION

1. Prepare a short brochure for parents explaining the procedures you use for toilet training at the center. Be sure to include an explanation of why you prefer the process you describe.

2. Observe toilet training procedures in two infant centers. Give examples of respectful practices. What recommendations would you make based on the discussion in this chapter?

▼▼▼▼▼▼▼▼▼▼▼▼▼▼▼

PART IV MAKING SURE IT'S HAPPENING

In this final section of the book we look at two important issues. Chapter 19 discusses working with parents. Although the importance of good communication and respectful relations between caregivers and parents is addressed throughout the book, we devote a chapter to a more in-depth discussion of the topic.

All quality programs benefit from a systematic objective look at themselves. Thus, Chapter 20 discusses the evaluation of infant and toddler programs with the object of scrutinizing and improving the services that centers offer.

19

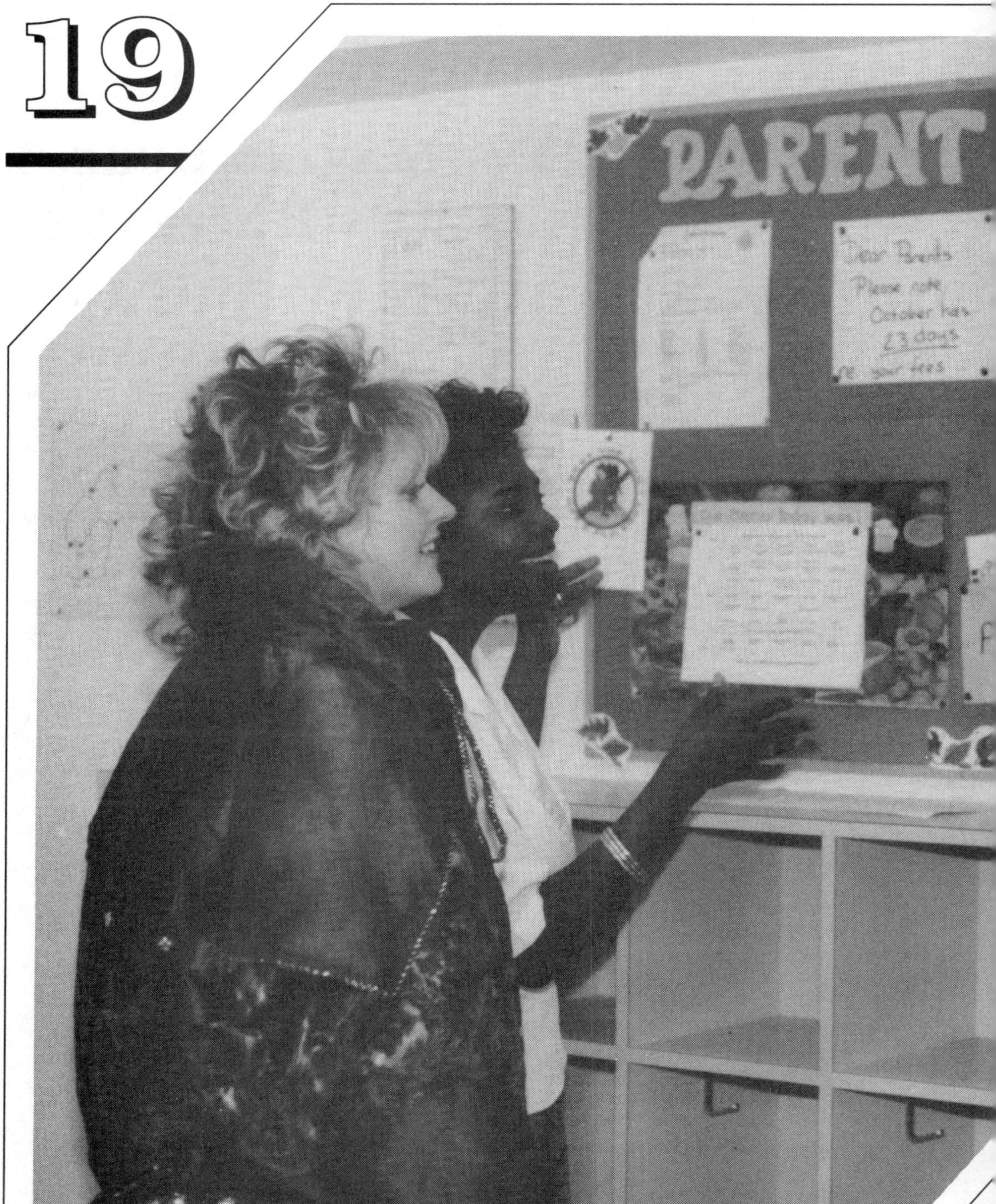

Working with Parents

Objectives

❖ To review the need for parent involvement in programs for infants and toddlers.

❖ To discuss the different types of involvement possible.

❖ To elaborate upon tensions and conflicts that may exist between parents and caregivers.

❖ To discuss strategies for working effectively with parents.

Opening Thoughts

If you were a parent of a baby or toddler, how would you complete the following sentence: I wish my child's caregiver would _____.

If you were a caregiver in an infant and toddler room, how would you complete the following sentence: I wish all parents would _____.

Comments on Opening Thoughts

❖ Parents and caregivers often have different perspectives. There are few right or wrong ways of childrearing.

❖ Understanding the sources of conflict between caregivers and parents can help overcome some problems.

❖ As professionals we recognize the importance of communication and cooperation with parents and involving them in the life of the center. We must also be respectful of the practical realities or constraints from the parents' point of view. ❐

Joey is an energetic little boy with a mild temperament. He speaks in two-word sentences. Joey arrived in the morning and was greeted by the caregiver. In a hopeful voice he said, "Boat — see boat." The caregiver took Joey to the book corner to see if there was a picture book on boats. No boat! They tried the water table, and several other areas that they thought had the boat that Joey wanted to see. None of these ideas seemed to lead to what Joey intended, and his frustration was visibly mounting, as was the caregiver's. His mother also reported that he had repeated those words at home and became quite upset when she had tried to guess his intention. During the last shift of the day the caregiver who was with Joey from four o'clock to departure time related how excited Joey had become when they went to the college swimming pool and watched the kayak team practice.

By virtue of his being at the center, Joey has several adults involved in his care. While all of them may provide good care, if they do not communicate regularly, his experiences will be disjointed. It is difficult for him to communicate what is important and meaningful to him, and his developing language skills depend on his being understood by those providing care. The younger the children are, the more important it is that adults who share their care communicate and attempt to provide links between experiences. This is done by developing positive relationships between parents and caregivers and ensuring a constant flow of two-way information.

At the beginning of this book, positive relations with parents was identified as one of the crucial components of quality day care. In almost every subsequent chapter the importance of sharing information with parents has been stressed. The involvement of parents in the care and education of their children who are in day-care centers is such an important matter, and often so problematic an issue, that it warrants a separate chapter.

While it would be difficult to find an early childhood program that did not believe in the importance of good relations and communication between parents and staff, this is an area of caregiving that often is associated with tension, frustration, and anger. Part of the difficulty may stem from unclear expectations concerning the nature of the relationship between parents and staff and the extent of parent involvement in day care.

Traditionally in early childhood programs, the parent involvement component has often meant parent education. The assumption on the part of caregivers has been that parents may be lacking in childrearing skills and knowledge of child development. Staff members, through formal structured sessions with parents and through continuous informal contact, have been supposed to help parents gain a better understanding of their children's needs and the ways in which to meet those needs.

The appropriateness of parent education in the day-care context has been questioned recently (Shimoni, 1991). First of all, although many parents (especially first-time parents) have benefited from the knowledge gained through parent education programs, many parents do a fine job of raising their children and do not need our assistance in that area. Second, many people feel that day-care staff need to focus their concerns on the children and have little time to devote to extra activities with parents. Child-care staff may feel that they have not had the training or experience to enable them to be parent educators. Third, many working parents have little free time to devote to parent education activities and adding one more demand on their time might be more detrimental than beneficial. It may be more appropriate, then, to consider caregivers as a resource for the parents. That is, caregivers have knowledge that they can share with parents, if and when parents are interested. The caregiver will most likely be used as a resource for parents if pleasant, comfortable relations exist between them. And we must also remember that parents can be an excellent resource for the caregiver. It is not just a cliché that most parents know their young children better than anyone else does.

Parent involvement is often sought to ensure the maximum degree of continuity for the child. The assumption is that if parents and staff communicate with each other, children will experience less discontinuity in the two environments in which they spend most of their time — home and center. Certainly the story about Joey in the opening of this chapter highlights how communication could have provided parents and staff with the information required to understand what Joey was trying to convey when

It is helpful to provide new parents with an opportunity to meet staff, review policies, and see the center.

his language skills were inadequate to convey his experience. Communication, however, does not ensure continuity. There are vast differences in the way in which mealtime, toilet training, or discipline occur at home and at the center. The fact that staff communicate to parents will not result in continuity of experience unless either staff or parents change their practices. And childrearing practices are often deeply ingrained, influenced by culture and life histories as well as knowledge. It is quite presumptuous to assume that caregivers' communication can or should alter parents' practices. Moreover, we don't really know how children are affected by discontinuities in their experiences. Children do make adjustments to changes in environments, and these adjustments can be thought of as positive signs of growth. Different experiences needn't always cause stress — they can also enrich the life of a child. Perhaps we need to think of communication not in terms of increasing continuity between home and center, but rather in terms of enabling some bridging between the experiences, or ways of linking the experiences. Communication between staff and parents would have helped Joey's mother understand that he wanted to talk about the boat.

It is safe to say that all parents are delighted to receive information about their child's day. Many mothers have stated that the guilt feelings they endure when they leave their babies in day care are alleviated considerably by a sensitive caregiver who clearly enjoys sharing information. For infants, especially first babies, a detail that may seem unimportant to staff can be crucially significant to parents, even if it is that there was only one ounce of milk left in the bottle.

Understanding parents' need for information and details of both the delightful and the not-so-delightful behavior of the child will motivate staff to work out flexible ways of ensuring two-way communication. More intense communication, such as discussions of family problems or childrearing practices, must be done with sensitivity and thought. A good guideline to follow is to ask yourself what the goal of the communication is. If the goal remains the well-being of the child, it is likely that communication will be appropriate. For example, at one day-care center, staff members were concerned that one toddler seemed to be receiving a series of snacks "on the run" through the day, rather than regular meals. If the child, however, showed no signs of distress, and seemed healthy and well-nourished, it would probably not be appropriate to discuss this practice with the parents unless they, themselves, brought up the subject. The need for parent contact and communication cannot be overstated.

Prior to discussing practical strategies that can be employed, it is helpful to understand the sources of tension and conflict that may exist. These conflicts may originate from either parents or staff.

Sources of Tension and Conflict

Preconceived Ideas

A study by Shimoni, Creighton and Carnat (1990) demonstrated that staff often have preconceived and incorrect ideas about parents. More specifically, they think that most parents do not have time or do not want to be involved, and generally that they just want a place to dump their children. Parents interviewed in the study presented a very different perspective. That is, they indicated that, even though they are very busy, if they were given advance notice and if the timing was flexible, they would be very willing to be involved. As professionals, it is important not to make assumptions or be judgmental.

Misconceptions may occur in the opposite direction — that is, parents may have preconceived and incorrect ideas about staff. For example, there is a story regarding a caregiver who had a particularly long and exhausting day because the center was understaffed and several children were ill. The caregiver had neither breaks nor lunch and was desperately attempting to hold everything together until the center closed. Just before closing, the last parent called to say that she would be delayed. Exhausted, the caregiver cuddled up with the child on a rocking chair with a picture book. Shortly after, the parent arrived and greeted the caregiver with, "Gee, I wish I had nothing to do all day but sit around in a rocking chair!" Clearly, respect is an issue in caregiver-parent relationships.

Prejudging Parents

Innes and Innes (1984) found that staff tended to feel that parents who leave their children in day care are neglectful. One expert on parent-staff relations (Galinsky, 1988) tells of parents judged to be neglectful because their child came in rather shabby clothing with mismatched socks, even though the family was quite wealthy. The parents believed, on the other hand, that it was important to let their daughter choose her own clothing. They believed in promoting independence.

Prejudging may be a result of cultural differences or differences in values. Some people adamantly believe that mothers must stay home with children, especially babies. These sorts of ideas or values will clearly affect the caregiver's attitude and approach toward working mothers. It is essential that caregivers examine their own values and then their approach toward parents.

Status Differences

Day-care workers are often underpaid and undervalued as professionals (Whitebook et al., 1990). Parents often treat caregivers as "just the babysitter" (Daniel, 1990), or so caregivers feel. Parents in executive clothing, planning exotic holidays, may not support pay increases but expect staff to provide excellent care for their children and to be understanding when they arrive late. These differences, perceived or real, may be a source of conflict.

The Group vs. the Individual

Parents' primary focus of concern will be their individual child. The caregivers' focus of attention will be on all the individuals in the group. Parents can and should insist that their child's needs be considered on an individual basis. Further, it is difficult to expect parents to consider the needs of the group as a whole. Caregivers must, on the other hand, consider the group and each individual in it. Both parties need to realize this difference to ensure that conflict does not arise (e.g., caregivers being angry at parents for being parents, for caring about their individual child).

This difference is likely more pronounced for parents of children with special needs. Some parents become focused on the needs or deficits of their child and want desperately to see progress, so that it becomes difficult to maintain a balance between the needs of that child and those of the group.

Unclear Policies or Lack of Communication

Arguments often arise over late pick-ups, insufficient changes of clothing, forgetting to provide outdoor clothing, or late payment of fees. Similarly, parents may be concerned that their children are going outside in cold weather, or that caregivers are not careful enough about keeping the clothing clean.

Strategies for Working with Parents

Set Clear Policies, Goals, and Principles

When programs have outlined philosophies, goals, and principles, parents will know what to expect. It is good practice to determine which policies are flexible and which are not, and then to communicate that information. For example, are you willing to allow parents to send alternatives for lunch if the child does not like the food served? Are parents welcome to drop in whenever they wish without prior notice? (This would be a most desirable practice.) Once the policies have been established, attempt to adhere to them, but review periodically to ensure that these policies are as realistic as possible. Changes or updating may be required from time to time.

It may also be helpful to explain the rationale behind the policies (for example, as related to toilet training) and to explain which policies are derived from provincial regulations.

Provide Orientation

Providing new parents with a good orientation where they have the opportunity to meet staff, review policies, and see the center will be beneficial. A short period of time taken with the director and appropriate staff initially will serve to make parents feel welcome, comfortable, and informed. Informing parents about helpful resources in the community should be part of the orientation to the center.

Inform and Involve Parents

Wherever and whenever possible involve parents in changes. This may include introducing parents to practicum students or new staff members. Or it may involve keeping parents updated by use of a newsletter that informs them about staffing changes, asks for their input regarding purchases of new toys or equipment, or provides articles of interest.

Communicate

Communication is the key to strong relations with parents. Several factors must be considered in order for communication to be successful. First of all, communication must be flexible and fit into the plans of working parents. A parent meeting announced only two days in advance is destined for failure, especially when parents have to struggle with child-care arrangements. When parents do not show up, staff generally assume that they are not interested. Mutually agreed-upon times to meet and talk in person or by telephone will enhance communication.

Second, communication must be two-way so that parents feel that their voices are heard and that they can be involved if they so choose. Newsletters and information boards are good but may not provide parents with the opportunity to have input. Talking to parents daily or providing an open forum for questions at parent meetings might be useful.

Third, personal contact where caregivers and parents share information on a daily basis may be difficult to achieve. Some staff share that information on a daily basis by doing it in written form. This may consist of a communication book or a sheet for each child detailing "My day." The essentials on this sheet would include what the child ate, how long or the times the child slept, diaper change information, and highlights of the day. Caregivers will assume this duty for young children but may involve older children by, perhaps, having them color the sheet. This practical strategy ensures that the essential information is readily available to parents. It also makes departure time less hectic as the caregiver does not have to scramble to remember all the details of the day. It is important to bear in mind, however, that written communication is not a substitute for personal contact. In addition, care and sensitivity need to be taken when requesting that parents participate in written communication. Not all parents are able to write and read English well.

Parents of children with special needs may have less direct contact with staff if the children are transported by bus or taxi. A communication book provides a vital link where both parent and caregiver can exchange basic information (e.g., regarding eating, sleeping, illness) and anecdotes regarding progress or change and

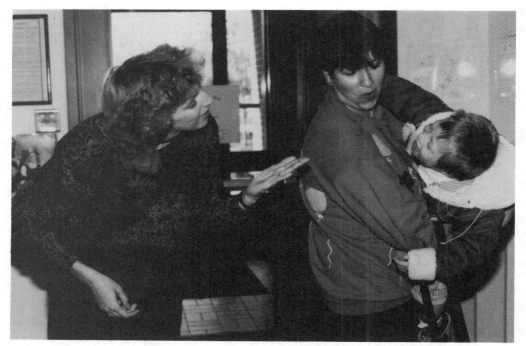

Frequent communication with parents of special-needs children can be especially helpful.

helpful approaches. Since children with special needs often have communication difficulties, this exchange of information will be more critical, especially in the absence of face-to-face contact.

Show Respect

A sound relationship between parents and professional care-givers is based on mutual respect. Parents, with their individual styles and approaches, must be respected even though caregivers may not necessarily agree with their practices. For example, dis-cipline styles may vary. Staff should be aware of different styles and approaches, ask for information where appropriate, and be willing to respect the differences.

In addition, caregivers need to think of themselves as professionals and treat themselves with respect. This entails setting limits and boundaries and not allowing oneself to be overextended or exploited. Respecting oneself means sometimes politely declining and considering one's own needs first. This attitude of self-respect, which should not be confused with smugness or superiority, will be evident to parents who will then treat caregivers with respect in turn.

Seek Support

Caregivers require support from supervisors or administration. This may involve having the opportunity to take professional development courses to build skills in working with parents or simply having supervisors available to help when difficulties arise. Support begins with the recognition that working with parents can be a difficult process, as is working with other adults generally. If this awareness exists, then staff should feel comfortable in seeking support.

To conclude, working with parents is integral to working with infants and toddlers. As professionals, caregivers must build the skills necessary to form and maintain healthy relationships. This process, however, may not be as simple as it appears. Relationships with parents can be marred by conflicts, lack of communication, and different perspectives. Caregivers must always bear in mind that they and the parent are committed to the best interests of the child both professionally and personally. In that sense, the relationship is a cooperative one with a strong common bond or focal point — the child.

✔ *Caregiver Checklist*

DOES THE CAREGIVER:

1. Greet all parents in a friendly manner?

2. Regularly inform parents of their child's activities and interests?

3. Ask parents for information that is relevant to caregiving practice, without intruding on their privacy?

4. Always demonstrate respect for parents?

5. Encourage parents to visit the center, and welcome them when they do?

6. Arrange the environment so that it is welcoming and comfortable for parents?

7. Provide written policy information to parents?

8. Provide an orientation for all parents?

9. Provide information about community resources to parents?

10. Show empathy with parents?

PRACTICAL APPLICATION

1. List the different opportunities for staff and parent communication at your center. How could you expand these opportunities?

2. Ask parents what kind of information they would like to receive from you and in what form (written notes, phone calls, meetings). What changes would you recommend, based on this information?

3. Think about the kind of information you would want from parents. Write down what you would want to know and how you would use that information. How would you assure parents that any private information would remain confidential?

Evaluating Infant and Toddler Settings

Objectives

❖ To emphasize the importance of ongoing and systematic evaluation in quality infant and toddler programs.

❖ To provide guidelines for choosing evaluation tools.

❖ To discuss the ethical issues involved in evaluation.

❖ To provide helpful resources specifically relating to infant and toddler program evaluation.

Opening Thoughts

Recall some evaluation you have been through, for example, a driving test, a final exam, or a job interview. Identify some of the feelings associated with that process.

Comments on Opening Thoughts

❖ Evaluation often provokes fear and anxiety.

❖ Evaluation can mean pass or fail, hired or fired — so often the stakes are high.

❖ When done properly, evaluation offers an excellent learning opportunity. ❐

Many people feel uneasy at the thought of evaluation. This is not surprising when we think of how evaluations are normally used. The most common form of evaluation undergone by most people is the examination. Examinations pass or fail students, or label them as poor, fair, or excellent. We seldom have the opportunity to learn from the evaluation process and try to improve. It is, therefore, not surprising that the very word "evaluation" makes many people nervous. One's self-esteem, job, or entrance to a college or a profession might depend on the outcome of an evaluation. Yet evaluation is an essential component of quality programs (Bredekamp, 1987). Professionals running infant and toddler programs have an obligation to evaluate regularly the care that is provided. This obligation is not only to the children, but also to the parents, who often do not have the time and knowledge required to evaluate the care their children receive.

Perhaps the most important reason for regularly evaluating programs is that, if done properly, evaluation can be an invaluable tool for improving the quality of care in the center. It can be used for staff training and can provide the necessary information for wise decision making. Evaluation can be an invitation to grow, can increase our potential as adults working together with young children, and can enable the creation of better program environments (Catron & Kendal, 1984).

In order to design, implement, and grow from program evaluation it is necessary to understand the process, to choose a method of evaluation that best meets the program needs, and to resolve the ethical dilemmas involved in program evaluation.

What Is Evaluation?

Evaluation is defined as a systematic, objective way of acquiring information. "Systematic" refers to the fact that evaluation needs to be done according to a formulated method or plan. "Objective" refers to the fact that evaluation should be, as far as possible, not influenced by personal feelings, judgments, or prejudice. Program evaluation should be an ongoing process. We evaluate an aspect of our program, use the evaluation to make improvements, and re-evaluate to see what progress has been made.

Deciding What to Evaluate

The first step in developing an evaluation is deciding what it is we want to know about the program. Realistically, most centers do not have the time or resources to do a major comprehensive review of the entire program on a regular basis. Therefore, clear priorities need to be made in the formulation of evaluation questions. The best way to formulate questions is to focus on the program's philosophy, goals, and objectives. Are your criteria for quality care being met? How much individual attention does each child receive? What kind of communication occurs with parents and how often does it occur? What kinds of verbal interaction occur between children and caregivers? Are there enough toys and equipment and are they arranged to maximize free play and exploration? These are but a few of the questions that might be the focus of a program evaluation to assess the degree to which certain goals are met or principles of caregiving adhered to. The questions asked must be relevant to the specific program being evaluated.

Designing a Means for Gathering Information

Once the questions have been defined, a method of gathering that information must be decided upon. The method selected will depend on the skills and resources available as well as the kind of information sought. Usually information is gathered through observation, questionnaires, interviews, and focus groups. A combination of these methods is often useful.

Observation

The three most common observation methods used in program evaluation are event sampling, time sampling, and checklists.

Event Sampling   Event sampling consists of defining a certain behavior or occurrence and then recording specific kinds of information that are associated with the event or behavior. For example, staff members might notice an increase in aggressive behavior in the toddler room and might feel that perhaps some aspects of the program are too stressful. They then might do daily event sampling over a period of two weeks to see if any patterns emerge. They could first define the behaviors (hitting, biting, kicking) and then list the factors influencing the behavior (e.g., the time of day, location, activity, and number of children in the group).

Event sampling of this kind can lead to valuable insights. For example, staff in one program found that the most frequent occurrence of these behaviors took place just before lunch time, when many toddlers were hungry and tired. A slight change in the schedule and the transition process to lunch time yielded a significant improvement.

Time Sampling   Time sampling is a useful strategy for determining how often desirable or undesirable events occur in a program. The occurrences, events, or behaviors have to be clearly defined, and then regular intervals of observation decided upon. One example of a time sampling was devised by Jay Belsky and Ann Walker at Pennsylvania State University (Shimoni et al., 1990). They identified several desirable caregiver behaviors such as elaborating on a verbal response of the child, expressing empathy, using routines for learning, and so forth. Negative behaviors such as leaving babies unattended in restrictive devices and using prohibitions ("No — don't do that!", etc.) were defined. Observing a playroom at regular intervals (say two minutes every half hour over a period of a few days) and checking the number of times the behaviors occurred gives some indication of the balance between desirable and less desirable caregiver activities.

Checklist   A checklist is basically a list of items that one looks for while observing in a center. A number of checklists have been devised to assist in evaluating preschool programs and, more recently, checklists have been devised for infant and toddler programs. Checklists provide a clearly defined list of behaviors and/or toys, equipment, use of space, and policies that are used as a guide to evaluating aspects of programs or entire programs. An observer would spend as much time as necessary in a playroom to determine whether the items on the checklist were present or absent.

Examples of checklist items might be:

❑ Does each child have his own storage space?

❑ Are provisions made for irregular meal times?

❑ Are children allowed to bring "security" objects from home?

When using a checklist, it is important to check the appropriateness of each item for the particular program being evaluated. For example, infant and toddler programs should be evaluated against criteria for such programs, not preschool programs.

Questionnaires and Interviews

Questionnaires and interviews are common ways of obtaining information from adults. Questionnaires may be distributed to parents, for example, asking them to rate their satisfaction regarding a number of program issues. Similarly, staff members could be asked to complete a questionnaire rating various aspects of the professional development program, and so forth. Interviews can be carried out on a one-to-one basis with parents and staff, providing that the wording of the questions is consistent in each interview. Putting together a questionnaire may seem like a straightforward task but great care needs to be taken to ensure that the questions are not biased or leading. At a bilingual school that had a policy of hiring only French teachers who came from France, parents were given a questionnaire that asked if they would rather have a French teacher who was an excellent teacher but not a native French speaker, or a teacher whose mother tongue was French. The lack of a third option — an excellent teacher whose native tongue was French — made the questionnaire leading, biased, and invalid. Centers that do not have staff trained in evaluation methods should consult an expert in that field for advice on how to construct questionnaires.

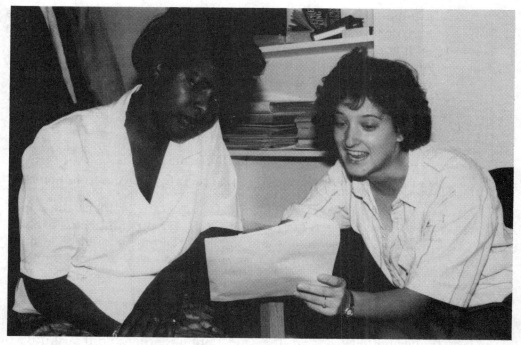

When done properly, evaluation offers a valuable learning opportunity.

Focus Groups or Discussion Groups

Recently attention has been given to the importance of gathering information from parents or staff by holding informal discussion meetings and recording the contents of the discussion. It is often difficult to arrive at clear-cut conclusions from discussion groups but they do often generate useful information.

Other Methods

Methods of obtaining valuable information need not always be complicated. At one center, staff members were concerned that, at the end of their busy days, they were not sure each child was getting a fair share of special attention. Their imaginative director helped the caregivers devise the following plan to evaluate the situation. A glass jar for each child was placed on a high shelf in the infant room and a box of large beads (big enough to be safe) was purchased. The director and staff defined what they meant by quality interaction. After each quality interaction, the caregiver placed a bead in the jar labelled with the child's name. At the end of the day the beads were counted and the number of quality interactions with each child was recorded. This method of gaining information took very little time on the part of the staff, and provided a colorful reminder of the importance of quality one-to-one time.

Another easy method is to monitor children and evaluate the way they respond to toys, equipment, and activities on a chart similar to the one shown below. The chart, if used regularly, can provide information about the room as a whole and can help to determine each child's interests. Caregivers might, for example, notice that a particular child repeats the same activity over and over and may need some encouragement to try new things. They might also be able to conclude that certain toys are very infrequently used or seem to cause frustration.

Response Chart

Date:

Name of child:

Age:

Name of primary caregiver:

Toys and equipment used the most:

Second favorite toys:

Toys that seemed to cause frustration:

Did the child play mostly alone?

Did the child play mostly with the caregiver?

Did the child initiate interactions with other children?

Did the child respond to other children's interactions?

What Does the Information Tell Us?

Unless the information from the evaluation is analyzed and summarized in a clear manner, it is difficult to draw conclusions and use effectively what we have learned. Here, too, there are definite advantages in consulting with experts to learn effective ways of computing and analyzing data. If done inappropriately, the results can be misleading. For example, in several centers caregivers were asked to give recommendations on how to improve the scheduling of staff shifts. The information was not sorted properly or analyzed according to the centers. The general recommendations that came out of this evaluation were not very useful to specific centers.

Who Gets the Information?

Once the information has been summarized, it needs to be reported. It is important to decide who gets what information at the beginning of the evaluation procedure. The ethical issues concerned in reporting the evaluation will be discussed in further detail below.

Deciding How the Information Will be Used

The main purpose of an evaluation is to decide on program improvements. Therefore, a course of action based on the evaluation should be included as part of the evaluation process. This may involve rearranging the playroom, providing staff with more training in dealing with behavior problems, devising systems for improving communication with parents, or a vast number of other actions. Whatever the course of action may be, it is essential to determine who will take responsibility for implementing it, how it will proceed, and within what time line.

Who Should Implement the Evaluation Process?

A major question that arises concerning program evaluation is, Who should do it? Should centers hire an outside agency to evaluate their program or should they try to do it themselves? The two approaches are not mutually exclusive and, in an ideal world, centers could benefit from both. A professional external evaluator might be able to devise a more objective procedure. However, if an outsider does the evaluation, it is still essential that staff be involved in its formulation. Not only will staff know what goals or aspects of the program they feel are important, but also their input — based on their familiarity with the organizational aspects of the center and their familiarity with the children, parents, and programs — greatly assists the complete evaluative process. However, for most centers this question is hypothetical, as it is difficult to find suitably qualified evaluators and formal evaluations done by external professionals are often expensive.

Internal evaluation is often viewed as second best but actually has many benefits. Although it is time consuming, it can be an extremely valuable learning experience for staff. It can provide the occasion for staff to examine and analyze their center. Often the evaluation process opens communication channels among staff members. Moreover, staff members usually feel less threatened by internal evaluation and are more likely to contribute. If the internal evaluation is carried out appropriately and staff feel part of the process, the results can be most useful (Kontos & Stevens, 1985).

Ethical Issues in Program Evaluation

Resolving some ethical issues before embarking on an evaluative process can eliminate many of the anxieties associated with evaluation. Caregivers should be informed of the program evaluation process at the time they are hired. An evaluation of a staff member or a playroom must never take place without the knowledge of those being evaluated. Furthermore, the goals of the evaluation must be clarified with the caregivers. Is the evaluation taking place to assess certain aspects of the program for future planning? To isolate needs for training? To assess the need for special programming for individual children?

These and other, similar questions must be addressed honestly at the beginning of the process. Then the information used in the evaluation must be used for the declared purpose. It would be unethical to tell staff that the use of equipment is going to be monitored, and then to use the information gathered to evaluate staff-child interaction in a playroom. Caregivers should be familiar with the method of evaluation and, preferably, should have some input into that method. They should, for example, be able to say that the evaluation day is a very untypical day, or to request a change of time in the scheduled observation, or a repeat observation.

In addition, every staff member involved in the evaluation has a right to know the results although, at the same time, specific caregiver performances must be kept confidential. Careful means of relating information to staff must be developed. For example, information could be communicated as follows: "In all the playrooms observed, staff used the words 'No' or 'Don't do that' between four and twenty times a day. We recorded seven times in your classroom." This gives each caregiver an indication of how his or her program was rated in relation to the others without saying specifically what happened in any other room.

Finally, caregivers should be involved in deciding what to do with the information gathered from evaluation. If, for example, the evaluation revealed that there was very little social interaction during mealtime, caregivers may decide that a problem-solving approach should be used to develop strategies to improve mealtimes.

Evaluation Tools

Evaluation should be an ongoing component of infant and toddler programs. If caregivers are involved in the process from the beginning (e.g., in the formulation of the evaluation questions) to the final stage (using the information to develop strategies for improvements), they will likely see evaluation as a positive learning experience. Many excellent evaluation tools for infant and toddler programs are in existence.

There are four evaluation tools that may be particularly useful for infant and toddler programs:

1. Regular and consistent use of the caregiver checklists presented in each area of discussion in this book could easily be used as a basis for evaluation. The items contained within each checklist give information regarding the essentials of good, respectful, responsive caregiving that all infants and toddlers should receive.

2. The Infant and Toddler Spot Observation Scale formulated by Jay Belsky and Anne Walker (Shimoni et al., 1990) uses a fairly easy time-sampling method that focuses on interactions between caregivers and babies (see Appendix B).

3. Harms, Cryer, and Clifford (1990) have developed a comprehensive evaluation tool for infant and toddler programs (see Appendix C). Their detailed checklist covers all aspects of most day-care programs including the physical setting, toys and equipment, and interactions between caregivers and parents.

4. The National Association for the Education of Young Children has published guidelines for the care of infants and toddlers entitled *Developmentally Appropriate Practices in Early Childhood Programs Serving Children From Birth Through Age 8* (1987). This document provides an overview of all aspects of a quality program and is an invaluable source for thinking about and devising an evaluation.

PRACTICAL APPLICATION

Isolate a problem area in a day-care program for infants and toddlers. Then design an evaluative process that might help improve the situation. The steps referred to in this chapter should be included in the evaluation plan.

APPENDIX A

Guidelines for Recognizing Child Abuse and Neglect

These guidelines are adapted from *Protocols for Handling Child Abuse and Neglect in Day Care Services* by Alberta Family and Social Services (1990)

Responding to the Abused Child

❑ If a child discloses abuse, listen to the child. Take the child to a quiet place and allow the child to tell what happened in his or her own words.

❑ Reassure the child. Let the child know you believe what you have heard. Children rarely lie, particularly about sexual abuse. Comfort the child by saying that it was a good thing for the child to tell you.

❑ Remain calm. Do not over-react or show horror or anger or any other reaction that would lead the child to believe the abuse or neglect was his fault. Tell the child it is not his fault. Support and acknowledge the child's feelings — whether anger, fear, sadness or anxiety — and assure the child that you will do something to help.

❑ Call the child welfare services in your area for help as soon as possible. A worker will advise you what to do next.

What You Should Look For

Child abuse and neglect take many forms. "Abuse" can mean actively hurting a child or depriving the child of affection and acceptance. "Neglect" means failing to take proper care of a child. Abuse and neglect can range from constantly humiliating a child, to denying the nurturing he needs, from hard shaking or slapping, to the sexual abuse of a child. It also means doing nothing to stop abuse or neglect from happening — in other words, "permitting" abuse is against the law.

Your first indication that a child may be in need of protective service may be your observation of the relationship between the parent(s) and child. If you sense something is wrong, trust your instincts. Do not over-react, but do watch the situation closely. Look for indicators and if a child or parent provides information, contact your child welfare services.

Child abuse and neglect fall into four basic categories: physical, sexual, and emotional abuse, and neglect. The form of the maltreatment in a particular case may be a single form of abuse or a combination of abuse and neglect.

The child may:

❏ be anxious, depressed, unhappy

❏ have poor relationships with peers

❏ show extremes of behaviour — may be very passive or aggressive, outgoing or withdrawn or swing between two opposite extremes of behaviour

❏ be frequently absent

❏ be over-anxious to please

❏ show distrust of others

❏ have low self-esteem

❏ fear and avoid physical contact with adults

The adult may:

❏ suggest or indicate loneliness, isolation, carrying a heavy burden of responsibility for the child

❏ react with hostility/anger/indifference when you discuss concerns regarding the child

❑   have been abused as a child

❑   misuse drugs and/or alcohol

If any of these indicators is present, monitor the situation carefully. Look for the more specific indicators listed in the following section and decide whether a report should be made immediately.

If, under any circumstances, a child tells you that he or she is being abused or neglected, believe the child and take action!

Remember to write down any information you have related to the suspicions: physical signs, conversations you had with the parent or child, the date, time and any other details.

The following charts show the indicators of specific forms of abuse and neglect. In any given situation, the abuse and neglect may be of one specific type or may be a combination of several of the types described.

INDICATORS OF PHYSICAL ABUSE

The Child

Physical signs might include:
- bruises and welts
- bite marks
- burns
- lacerations and abrasions
- dislocation of shoulders, hips, etc.
- head injuries

The Child may:
- be wary of physical contact with adults
- seem afraid of parent or other person
- be frightened in the face of adult disapproval
- be apprehensive when others cry
- show extremes of behaviour — aggressive/withdrawn
- be over-anxious to please
- may approach any adult, including strangers

The Adult may:
- be angry, impatient; frequently lose or almost lose control
- appear unconcerned about child's condition
- view child as bad or as the cause of life's problems

- resist discussion of child's condition or family situation
- view questions with suspicion
- use discipline inappropriate to child's age, condition and situation
- offer illogical, contradictory, unconvincing or no explanation of injuries
- show poor understanding of normal child development (for example, may expect adult-like, mature behaviour from a young child)

INDICATORS OF EMOTIONAL ABUSE

The Child

- Child's appearance may not indicate or suggest the extent of the difficulty. Child may appear clean, well groomed and well nourished.
- Child's facial expression and body carriage may indicate sadness, depression, timidity or held-back anger.

The Child may:

- appear overly compliant, passive, shy
- show episodes of very aggressive, demanding and angry behaviour
- fear failure, have trouble concentrating or learning and give up easily
- be either boastful or negative about himself
- constantly apologize

The Adult may:

- blame or belittle child in public and at home
- withhold comfort when child is frightened or distressed
- treat other children in the family differently and better, showing more acceptance and loving, and less criticism
- tend to describe child in negative ways: "stupid," "bad," "trouble-maker"; and see failure or poor future for child
- hold child responsible for parent's difficulties and disappointments
- identify child with disliked relatives

INDICATORS OF SEXUAL ABUSE

The Child

Physical evidence of sexual abuse is rare. Often with young children, abuse is not intercourse but touching, which may leave no physical signs. Where physical evidence is present it may be:

- torn, stained or bloody clothing
- pain or itching in genital area or throat, difficulty going to bathroom or swallowing
- bruises, bleeding or swelling of genital, rectal or anal areas
- vaginal odour or discharge

The Child may:

- display unusual interest in sexual matters
- use language and make drawings that are sexually explicit
- fantasize excessively
- show fear of closed spaces
- resist undressing or diaper changes
- masturbate excessively
- exhibit seductive behaviour

The Adult may:

- often be domineering but emotionally weak
- suggest or indicate marital or relationship difficulties with adults
- indicate own social isolation, loneliness, especially as a single parent
- cling to child, both physically and emotionally; hold and touch the child in an inappropriate way
- tend to blame others for life's problems and child's sexual behaviour — may even accuse child of causing sexual abuse

INDICATORS OF NEGLECT

The Child may:

- be underweight by more than 30%, and gain weight when offered proper nutrition
- show improvement of developmental delays following proper stimulation and care

- demonstrate signs of deprivation: cradle cap, severe diaper rash, diarrhea, vomiting, anemia, recurring respiratory problems
- be consistently dirty or dressed inappropriately for weather, or wear torn clothing
- often be hungry or thirsty
- often be tired or listless
- demand much physical contact and attention
- assume role of parent or adult in the family
- lack proper medical and dental care

The Adult may:

- maintain a chaotic home life with little evidence of health routines
- not supervise child for long periods of time or when child is involved in potentially dangerous activity
- leave child in the care of inappropriate persons
- give child inappropriate food, drink, medicine
- consistently bring child early and pick up late
- be apathetic towards child's progress, hard to reach by phone and fail to keep appointments to discuss child and concerns
- overwork or exploit child
- show evidence of apathy, feelings of futility

APPENDIX B

Evaluating Programs:
A Time-Sampling Technique

The evaluation methods presented here and in Appendix C can be used by caregivers observing their co-workers, by center directors, or by outside evaluators.

This evaluation guide is taken from "Evaluating Programs," an article by Rena Shimoni, Denise Maclean, and Cathy MacWilliam (*Day Care and Early Educator*, Spring 1990). It is based on the Infant and Toddler Spot Observation Scale by J. Belsky and A. Walker.

The evaluation uses the time-sampling technique. The observer should enter the room at steady intervals (every hour, for example) and observe the room for two minutes. Immediately following the observation, the observer should record what he or she has seen on the score sheets shown.

Note that several examples of a center are required to obtain a reliable picture of the proportion of positive to negative events.

A description of both the positive and negative events the observer should note follows.

Score Sheet

Positive Items

Playroom _____
Date _____

Time of Observation

1. Caregiver expresses affection and/or positive regard.											
2. Caregiver responds to and expands on child's gestures, sounds, and words.											
3. Caregiver uses tone of voice, gestures in an expressive manner.											
4. Caregiver expresses empathy.											
5. Caregiver turns routines into learning opportunities.											
6. Caregiver involved with one child yet responsive to other children.											
7. Caregiver involved in non-child task yet remains responsive to children.											
8. Caregiver makes use of teachable moments.											
9. Caregiver assists children in getting along with others.											
10. Caregiver distant from child but still involved.											
11. Caregiver at eye-level with children while interacting.											
12. Child engaged in exploring a non-toy object.											
13. Most of the children look happy.											

1. **Caregiver expresses affection and/or positive regard for the child.**

   Positive regard is displayed by hugging, kissing, genuine praise, or indicating verbally or otherwise that the child is special. Children need to feel liked and to be nurtured for their own self-esteem, self-worth, and overall emotional well-being.

2. **Caregiver responds to and expands upon child's vocalizations or words, or body language.**

   When a prelinguistic infant babbles, coos, or makes a gesture, the caregiver should respond as if the child is speaking. With a linguistic child, the caregiver responds by repeating and expanding upon the utterance (e.g., Child: "Dog"; Caregiver: "Yes, a dog, a big, brown dog.") By being responsive to a child's vocalizations, the caregiver is indicating that the child is an important individual, which in turn encourages the development of language. Talking to or at a child (i.e., giving directions, commands, etc.) does not count for this item.

3. **Caregiver uses tone of voice, facial expression, and body language in a way that noticeably expresses her or his emotional state.**

   When the caregiver expresses happiness, laughter, sadness, or enthusiasm, she or he is facilitating communicative understanding in children and provides a more stimulating environment.

4. **Caregiver expresses empathy to child.**

   The caregiver in this way acknowledges how the child is feeling, that she or he understands the child, and that "it's okay" to express emotions. An empathic response to a child who has fallen and is crying could be "Ouch! I know that your knee must really hurt."

5. **Caregiver turns routine experience (an everyday occurrence) into a learning experience.**

   The caregiver is utilizing valuable interaction time to expand upon a child's knowledge of his or her surroundings. For example, while rinsing out a cloth, the caregiver might take the opportunity to teach how to turn a faucet on and off.

6. **Caregiver is involved with one child but remains responsive to other children.**

   In group care, it is important to ensure that all children are included and that all needs are met. Being involved with one child gives that child one-to-one time, and being responsive to the other children is letting the children know that they are still important and the caregiver is there for them.

7. While caregiver is busy with task not related to caregiving, he or she still remains responsive to children.

Examples of non-child tasks are cleaning, filing, and arranging the room, which are unrelated to the children's present activities. The caregiver should be aware of and able to interact with the children even while doing a non-child task, not merely keep an eye on them.

8. Caregiver makes use of teachable moments.

This means that a caregiver spontaneously focuses a child's attention on an object, event, or person and elaborates. It is not planned as part of a structured activity. The caregiver verbally labels, describes, or shows how something works to the child (e.g., "Look at the light. You can turn it on and off. Would you like to try?")

9. Caregiver assists children in getting along with each other.

Facilitating peer relations is essential for social skill development. This may be accomplished by the use of distraction to avoid conflict, providing enough toys to avoid conflict, establishing clear limits, etc. Arranging and planning the environment will minimize the need to intervene when children are at play.

10. Caregiver is at a distance from child but still involved.

When a caregiver is at a distance from a child but still involved — maybe verbally commenting, smiling at, or showing something to a child — she or he is displaying awareness of what the child is doing and readiness to assist the child if necessary.

11. Caregiver is at eye level with children while interacting.

The caregiver is able to establish eye contact with the children and is more easily heard and understood, and the children will not feel that they are being talked down to.

12. At least one child is engaged in exploring a non-toy object.

A non-toy object is any object which has not been manufactured for the sole purpose of being a child's toy (e.g., pots and pans, wooden spoons, bowls). This encourages the child to be more creative and constructive with objects available in the environment.

13. Most of the children (all but one or two) look happy and/or content.

This should speak for itself! Everyone would like to see children happy, and the best indication that a program is suiting the needs of the children is a room full of happy and/or contented children.

Score Sheet

Negative Items

Playroom _____

Date _____

Time of Observation

1. Child crying and fussing.										
2. Caregiver physically or verbally prohibits child from doing something.										
3. Child placed in restrictive device and left unattended and/or unobserved for 1 minute or longer.										
4. Children unoccupied and waiting for something to happen.										
5. Caregivers involved in conversation among themselves that is unrelated to immediate tasks.										
6. One or more children bored, uninvolved and/or aimless.										
7. Routine care task done with little or no interaction.										
8. Caregiver behaves negatively towards children.										

---

1. **Child is crying and fussing.**

   Although it is quite normal for children to cry or fuss sometimes, if this occurs in more than 15% of the observations, it may suggest a need for changes in the program or the responsiveness of the caregiver.

2. **Caregiver physically or verbally prohibits child from doing something.**

   The room arrangement and activities should be planned in such a way as to minimize prohibitions (e.g., "Don't run." "Don't touch.") Every child must have a safe environment to allow for freedom of choice and movement. As well, the social environment should not prohibit children from expressing emotions (i.e., "Don't cry").

3. **Child is placed in a physically restrictive device (e.g., walker, highchair, crib, Jolly Jumper) and is unattended and/or unobserved for one minute or longer.**

   When a non-ambulatory or an ambulatory child is placed in a restrictive device, she or he is solely at the mercy of the caregiver. The child is unable to remove herself or himself from the device at will; therefore, the child loses control and choice within her or his environment.

4. **Children are not occupied and are waiting for something to happen.**

   Transitional times (i.e., lunch, naptime, going outside) are when children most often have to do some waiting. To expect a child to be patient and wait without being occupied in some way causes children to become frustrated and irritable. Recognizing transitional times and planning accordingly (i.e., songs and stories) will minimize the waiting.

5. **Caregivers are involved in conversation among themselves that is unrelated to immediate tasks.**

   When caregivers are conversing with each other, they are in fact ignoring and unaware of the children if the topic of conversation is unrelated to the immediate tasks. Communication between caregivers is essential, but it does not need to be lengthy or completely exclude the children. In addition, if planning is done properly beforehand the necessity to ask each other questions will decrease (caregivers should not discuss children in front of children).

6. **One or more children seem bored, uninvolved, and/or aimless.**

   Although children need time to rest, integrate and absorb experiences, and day dream, too much time spent uninvolved could mean that the child is bored and may need some direction or a more stimulating, challenging, and interesting activity.

7. **Routine care task is done with little or no interaction.**

   When the caregiver treats the caregiving tasks (e.g., diapering, feeding, putting child to bed) as chores and the child is related to as an object rather than as a person, valuable one-to-one interaction time is lost and the caregiving is disrespectful.

8. Caregiver behaves negatively (sarcasm, teasing, belittling, threatening, yelling) toward the children.

Respecting children is the foundation of quality care. Sarcasm, teasing, belittling, threatening, and yelling at the children are disrespectful behaviours which are hurtful to the children. In addition, as children learn so much from the examples adults provide, these behaviours should not occur.

The adaptation of the Belsky and Walker scale is intended for program evaluations and training for practitioners rather than for strictly research purposes. However, measures should be taken to ensure systematic and objective use of this scale. The procedure recommended below may be varied to meet the time and staff limitations of the various centers employing this scale as long as whatever schedule of observation has been decided upon remains consistent. That is, if it is decided to do a time sampling of 2 minutes every 30 minutes, for the entirety of the evaluation the time intervals should remain at 30 minutes.

Before using any observation tool, it is important to be very familiar with it and to have memorized almost all the items. Read and reread the scale, and discuss with colleagues what kinds of observations would constitute positive and negative scores.

As a note of caution, when evaluating a room, the observer must rate only what is observed during the two-minute period, not what is believed to be the normal occurrence. For example, if the observer is observing in a room that is familiar, and knows that the caregiver frequently expresses empathy, the observer can only check this item positively if it is observed during the two-minute observation period.

If possible, it is advisable to complete the evaluations in pairs. In this way, if two evaluators' results differ significantly, then clearly the items on the checklist must be studied and clarified before the room is reevaluated. If it is not possible to work in pairs throughout the entire evaluation, it is strongly recommended that initially the evaluators pair up and the scale be used in a pretest situation until there is an agreement on how what is observed should be scored on the checklist.

For example, two observers may have observed a caregiver changing a diaper. The caregiver placed a rattle in the child's hand and said, "That will keep you busy while I am changing your diaper" and proceeded to change him with no further verbal interactions. One observer gives a negative score for #7: Routine task done with little or no interaction. The second observer does not. The observers must then compare and justify their own scores. In this way, they will eventually agree upon what kinds of behaviour constitute a positive or negative score. Aside from clarifying the points on the observation scale, this process of dialogue can be an extremely valuable learning tool for staff.

Procedure

1. Decide upon the time intervals between the 2-minute observations. (Recommended timing of observations is 2 minutes, at 20-minute intervals over a period of a day, to be repeated over at least 3 days.)
2. Select the room to observe.
3. Observe intently for 2 minutes.
4. Leave the room immediately and mark with a check mark all the items observed during the 2-minute observation.
5. Repeat the procedure every 20 minutes for a period of at least 3 hours according to the prearranged schedule.
6. Calculate the scores.

The manner in which the scores are calculated will depend upon how the information gleaned from the observations is to be used. If, for example, the primary goal of the evaluation was for staff training, it will be necessary to calculate the number of times each positive and negative item was displayed during the observation period. In this way, staff will be able to see what positive behaviours were not observed frequently, and what negative behaviours were observed too frequently. For example, one negative behaviour that staff tend to use frequently without being aware of is #2: Caregiver physically or verbally prohibits a child from doing something. Often, after seeing the results of the evaluation, caregivers will monitor their own behaviours and attempt to reduce them. Similarly, if over the entire period of observation some of the positive behaviours are infrequently seen (e.g., #11: Caregiver is at eye level with children while interacting), caregivers can make a conscious attempt to get down to eye level more and monitor the number of times this behaviour occurs.

Therefore, if you are trying to isolate the staff behaviours that need to be increased or decreased, an item-by-item score should be recorded.

In order to have some overall evaluation of the quality of interactions, scores may be calculated in percentages. That is, over the course of the evaluation process, there may be 60 time samplings. The frequency of positive and negative items may be calculated individually (e.g., #13: Most children happy) scored 30 check marks; therefore, 30-60 (time samplings) = 50% of the time).

The percentages of negative and positive items are totaled, and the respective totals are divided by the number of possible items to be seen (e.g., 13 positive, 8 negative). The end results are the percentages of time that positive and negative interactions occur over the course of a day.

If the negative interactions were observed 25% or more of the time, there is cause for concern. Likewise, the positive interactions should be observed 25% of the time. A lower score of positive items indicates the need for caregivers to make a conscious effort to increase positive interactions.

APPENDIX C

Evaluating Programs: The Checklist Method

The following sample is taken from the evaluation checklist designed by Harms, Cryer, and Clifford (1990).

	Inadequate 1	2	**Minimal** 3

PERSONAL CARE ROUTINES

6. Greeting/ departing
   – Greeting is often neglected; departure not prepared for.
   – Parents discouraged from entering area used for child's care
   – Parents do not have direct contact with caregiver.

   – Caregiver usually greets child and parent and acknowledges departure.
   – Parents allowed to enter area used for child's care.
   – Parents and staff[1] share information related to child's health and safety (Ex. special diets, accident reports).

7. Meals/ snacks
   – Meal/snack schedule does not meet individual needs.
   – Food service[2] not sanitary (Ex. caregiver does not wash own hands before preparing food or feeding; same sink used for meals/snacks and diapering).
   – Food served is of questionable nutritional value[3] or not age-appropriate.
   – Infants[4] not held for bottle feeding.
   – Infants/toddlers put to bed with bottles.

   – Meal/snack schedule meets children's needs (Ex. infants on individual schedules, toddlers fed lunch when hungry).
   –Sanitary food service.
   – Well-balanced, age-appropriate foods served for meals and snacks.
   – Infants held while bottle fed.
   – Infants/toddlers not put to bed with bottles.
   –Children who finger feed selves have hands washed.
   –Children encouraged but not forced to eat.

[1] The term staff means all the people working in the center including the caregivers, director, and all support personnel.

[2] In this case, food service means simple preparation completed in the room, such as opening baby food jars, mixing cereal or formula, and preparing simple snacks, but not more extensive preparation of food done outside of the room.

	Good		**Excellent**
4	**5**	**6**	**7**

– Caregiver greets each child and parent warmly and provides pleasant organized departure (Ex. conversation on arrival; clothes ready for departure).
– Parents bring child into care-giving area as part of daily routine.
– Separation problems handled sensitively.
– Written record of infant's daily feeding, diapering, and naps available for parents to see.

– Staff use greeting and departure as information-sharing time with parents.
– Staff give parents specific information about how the day went (Ex. play activities, mood, new skills).

– Children fed separately or in very small groups.
– Meals/snacks are relaxed (Ex. caregiver patient with messiness, slow eaters).
– Children encouraged to feed selves.
– Menus posted for parents.
– Caregiver talks with children and provides a pleasant social time.

– Caregiver sits with children and uses feeding time to help children learn (e.g., names foods, encourages toddlers to talk and develop self-help skills).
– Staff cooperate with parents to establish good food habits (Ex. plan together to help child give up bottle, coordinate introduction of new foods).

---

3 Nutritional value is rated only if the program provides the food. The United States Department of Agriculture Child Care Food Program standards may be used to judge nutritional adequacy when program provides the food.

4 Infants and young toddlers who can sit up independently and hold their bottles may be allowed to feed themselves.

	Inadequate **1**	**2**	**Minimal** **3**

LEARNING ACTIVITIES

17. Eye-hand coordination

– No age-appropriate eye-hand materials available for daily use.

–Some age-appropriate eye-hand materials available for daily use.
– Some materials accessible to children for independent use daily for much of the day.

18. Active physical play

– No outdoor or indoor space used regularly for active physical play.
– No age-appropriate equipment/materials.
– Equipment/materials generally in poor repair.

– Uncluttered space provided indoors for infants and toddlers to crawl and walk around much of the day.
– Outdoor physical play provided for infants/toddlers at least 3 times a week year-round except in very bad weather.
– Some age-appropriate toys and equipment used daily; all equipment in good repair.

Good
5

4   6

Excellent
7

– Variety of age-appropriate eye-hand materials of different type, color, size, shape, texture in good repair, accessible daily for independent use.
– Materials that cannot be left out for independent use are offered to toddlers daily for free choice with supervision (Ex. crayons, toys with many small pieces).

– Caregiver helps children develop skills (Ex. plays with infant using appropriate toys; helps toddlers with crayons, puzzles, peg-board).
– Eye-hand materials rotated to provide variety.

– Convenient outdoor area where infants/toddlers are separated from older children used for at least one hour daily year-round, except in very bad weather.
– All toys and equipment for physical activity used both indoors and outdoors are age-appropriate.
– Materials used daily stimulate variety of large muscle skills (Ex. crawling, walking, balancing, climbing, ball play).
– Active play areas are not crowded.

– Physical play equipment changed or rotated weekly to provide new challenges either indoors or outdoors (Ex. crawling tunnel, games with bean bags, tumbling on mat, ball games).
– Caregiver talks to children about their activities (Ex. explains safety rules, names up/down, in/out).

Recommended Readings

Allen, K. E. & Marotz, L. (1989). *Developmental profiles: Birth to six.* Albany, NY: Delmar.

Bailey, D.B. & Wolery, M. (1984). *Teaching infants and preschoolers with handicaps.* Columbus, OH: Merrill.

Bayless, K.M. & Ramsey, M.E. (1982). *Music: A way of life for the young child.* St. Louis, MO: (C.V. Mosby).

Bee, H. (1989). *The developing child* (5th Ed). New York: Harper & Row.

Canadian Child Day Care Federation (1990). *National statement on quality child care* (2nd Draft). Ottawa: CCDCF.

Cataldo, C. (1983). *Infant and toddler programs: A guide to very early childhood education.* Reading, MA: Addison-Wesley.

Chud, G. & Fahlman, R. (1985). *Early childhood education for a multicultural society.* University of British Columbia: Pacific Educational Press.

Finnie, N. (1981). *Helping the young cerebral palsied child at home* (2nd Ed). London: William Heinemann Medical Books.

Gonzalez-Mena, J. & Eyer, D.W. (1989). *Infants, toddlers, and caregivers.* Mountain View, CA: Mayfield.

Greenman, J. (1988). *Caring spaces, learning places: Children's environments that work.* Redmond, WA: Exchange Press.

Honig, A.S. & Lally, R.J. (1981). *Infant caregiving: A design for training.* Syracuse, NY: Syracuse University Press.

Karnes, M.B. (1982). *You and your small wonder: Activities for busy parents and babies. Book 1: Birth to 18 months.* Circle Pines, MN: American Guidance Service.

Lally, R.J. (Ed) (1990). *Infant/toddler caregiving: A guide to social-emotional growth and socialization.* Sacramento, CA: Center for Child and Family Studies, Far West Laboratory for Educational Research and Development, California State Department of Education.

Lally, R.J. & Stewart, J. (1990). *Infant/toddler caregiving: A guide to setting up environments.* Sacramento, CA: Center for Child and Family Studies, Far West Laboratory for Educational Research and Development, California State Department of Education.

Lane, Mary B. & Signer, S. (1990). *Infant/toddler caregiving: A guide to creating partnerships with parents.* Sacramento, CA: Center for Child and Family Studies, Far West Laboratory for Educational Research and Development, California State Department of Education.

Leavitt, R.L. & Eheart, B.K. (1985). *Toddler day care: A guide to responsive caregiving.* Toronto: D.C. Heath.

Miller, K. (1984). *Things to do with toddlers and twos.* Marshfield, MA: Teleshare Publishing.

National Association for the Education of Young Children (1987). *Developmentally appropriate practice in early childhood programs serving children from birth through age 8* (Expanded Ed). Washington, DC: NAEYC.

Network of the Federal/Provincial/Territorial Group on Nutrition & National Institute on Nutrition (1989). *Promoting nutritional health during the preschool years: Canadian guidelines.* Ottawa: Health and Welfare Canada.

Raver, S.A. (1991). *Strategies for teaching at risk and handicapped infants and toddlers: A transdisciplinary approach.* New York: Merrill.

Shapiro, K.A., Kaufmann, R., & Messenger, K.P. (Eds) (1988). *Healthy young children: A manual for programs.* Washington, DC: National Association for the Education of Young Children.

Surbeck, E. & Kelley, M.F. (Eds). (1990). *Personalizing care with infants, toddlers and families.* Wheaton, MD: Association for Childhood Education.

Thomas, A. & Chess, S. (1977). *Temperament and development.* NY: Bruner/Mazel.

Weiser, M.G. (1991). *Infant/Toddler care and education* (2nd Ed). Toronto: Merrill.

Willis, A. & Ricciuti, H. (1975). *A good beginning for babies: Guidelines for group care.* Washington, DC: National Association for the Education of Young Children.

References

Ainsworth, M.D.S., Blehar, M.C., Waters, E., & Wall, S. (1978). *Patterns of attachment: A psychological study of the strange situation*. Hillsdale, NJ: Erlbaum.

Allen, K. E. & Marotz, L. (1989). *Developmental profiles: Birth to six*. Albany, NY: Delmar.

Anslemo, S. (1987). *Early childhood development: Prenatal through age eight*. Columbus, OH: C.E. Merrill.

Appoloni, T. & Cooke, T.P. (1978). Integrated programming at the infant, toddler, and preschool levels. In M. Guralnick (Ed). *Early intervention and the integration of handicapped and non-handicapped children*. Baltimore: University Park Press.

Aronson, S. (1982). Health and safety in the child care program — an update. In R. Lurie & R. Neugebauer (Eds). *Caring for infants and toddlers: What works, what doesn't* (Vol. 2). Redmond, WA: Child Care Information Exchange.

Bailey, D.B. & Wolery, M. (1984). *Teaching infants and preschoolers with handicaps*. Columbus, OH: Merrill.

Bala, N., Hornick, J.P., & Vogl, R. (Eds). (1991). *Canadian child welfare law: Children, families and the state*. Toronto: Thompson Educational Publishing Ltd.

Bayless, K.M. & Ramsey, M.E. (1982). *Music: A way of life for the young child*. St. Louis, MO: (C.V. Mosby).

Bee, H. (1989). *The developing child* (5th Ed). New York: Harper & Row.

Belsky, J. (1986). Infant day care: A cause for concern. *Zero to Three, 7*, 1-7.

Bloom, B.S. (1964). *Stability and change in human characteristics*. New York: John Wiley & Sons.

Blum, M. (1983). *The day care dilemma*. Lexington, MA: Heath and Co.

Bowlby, J. (1951). Maternal care and mental health. *Bulletin of World Health Organization, 3,* 355-534.

Braun, S.J. & Edwards, E.P. (1972). *History and theory of early childhood education.* Belmont, CA: Wadsworth.

Brazelton, T.B. (1977). The infant's world: How babies learn about taste, touch and smell. *Redbook Magazine, 11,* 24-25.

Bredekamp, S. (Ed). (1987). *Developmentally appropriate practice in early childhood programs serving children from birth through age 8.* Washington, DC: National Association for the Education of Young Children.

Bricker, D.D. & Bricker, W.A. (1973). *Infant, toddler and preschool research and intervention project report:* Year III IMRID Behavioral Science Monograph No. 23. Nashville, TN: Institute on Mental Retardation and Intellectual Development.

Caldwell, B.M. & Rorex, J. (1977). A day at the Kramer Baby House. In M.D. Cohen (Ed). *Developing programs for infants and toddlers.* Washington DC: Association for Childhood Education International.

Canadian Child Day Care Federation (CCDF) (1990). *National statement on quality child care* (2nd Draft). Ottawa: CCDF.

Canning, P. & Lyon, M.E. (1990). Young children with special needs. In I.M. Doxey (Ed). *Child care and education: Canadian dimensions.* Scarborough: Nelson Canada.

Caruso, D.A. (1988). Play and learning in infancy: Research and implications. *Young Children,* September, 63-70.

Cataldo, C. (1983). *Infant and toddler programs: A guide to very early childhood education.* Reading, MA: Addison-Wesley.

Catron, C.E. & Kendall, E.P. (1984). Staff evaluation that promotes growth and problem solving. In J.E. Brown (Ed). *Administering programs for young children.* Washington: DC: National Association for the Education of Young Children.

Cayley, D. (1984). The world of the child. *Canadian Society for the Prevention of Cruelty to Children, 7* (1), 7-14.

Center for Child and Family Studies (1988). *Visions for infant/toddler care: Guidelines for professional caregiving.* Sacramento, CA: Far West Laboratory for Educational Research and Development, California State Department.

Chud, G. & Fahlman, R. (1985). *Early childhood education for a multicultural society.* Vancouver: University of British Columbia, Pacific Educational Press.

Clarke-Stewart, A. (1982). *Daycare.* Cambridge, MA: Harvard University Press.

Clarke-Stewart, K.A. (1988). The "effects" of infant day care reconsidered. *Early Childhood Research Quarterly, 3* (3), 293-319.

Cosby, S.R. & Sawyers, J.K. (1988). *Play in the lives of children.* Washington, DC: National Association for the Education of Young Children.

Craig, G.J. (1989). *Human development.* Englewood Cliffs, NJ: Prentice-Hall.

Croft, P.J. (1976). *Be honest with yourself.* A self evaluation handbook for early childhood teachers. Belmont, CA: Wadsworth Publishing.

Daniel, J. (1990). Child care: An endangered industry. *Young Children, 45* (4), 23-26.

Decker, C.A. & Decker, J.R. (1988). *Planning administrative early childhood programs* (4th Ed). Toronto: Merrill.

Dittmann, L.L. (Ed). (1973). *The infants we care for.* Washington, DC: National Association for the Education of Young Children.

Dittmann, L.L. (Ed) (1984). *The infants we care for* (Rev Ed). Washington, DC: National Association for the Education of Young Children.

Doxey, I.M. (Ed) (1990). *Child care and education: Canadian dimensions.* Scarborough: Nelson, Canada.

Erikson, E.H. (1963). *Childhood and society.* New York: Norton.

Evans, E.D. (1971). *Contemporary influences in early childhood education.* New York: Holt, Rinehart & Winston.

Feeney, S., Christensen, D., & Moravcik, E. (1991). *Who am I in the lives of children? An introduction to teaching young children.* New York: Merrill.

Fein, G. (1980). The informed parent. *Advances in Early Education and Day Care, 1,* 155-187.

Field, T., Masi, W., Goldstein, S., Perry, S. & Parl, S. (1988). Infant day care facilitates preschool social behaviour. *Early Childhood Research Quarterly 3* (3), 341-359.

Finnie, N. (1981). *Helping the young cerebral palsied child at home* (2nd Ed). London: William Heinemann Medical Books.

Fogel, A. (1991). *Infancy: Infant, family, and society* (2nd Ed). St. Paul, MN: West Publishing Company.

Fowler, W. (1980). *Infant and child care.* Boston: Allyn & Bacon.

Galinsky, E. (1988). Parents and teacher-caregivers: Sources of tension, sources of support. *Young Children, 43* (3), 4-11.

Garvey, C. (1990). *Play: The developing child.* Cambridge, MA: Harvard University Press.

Godwin, A. & Schrag, L. (1988). *Setting up for infant care: Guidelines for centers and family day care homes.* Washington, DC: National Association for the Education of Young Children.

Gonzalez-Mena, J. (1986). Toddlers: What to expect. *Young Children 42 (1),* 47-51.

Gonzalez-Mena, J. & Eyer, D.W. (1989). *Infants, toddlers, and caregivers.* Mountain View, CA: Mayfield.

Goosens, F.A. & van IJzendoorn, M.H. (1990). Quality of infants' attachments to professional caregivers: Relation to infant-parent attachment and day-care characteristics. *Child Development, 61* (3), 832-838.

Greenspan, S.I. (1990). Emotional development in infants and toddlers. In J.R. Lally (Ed). *Infant/toddler caregiving: A guide to social-emotional growth and socialization.* Sacramento, CA: California Department of Education.

Greenman, J. (1988). *Caring spaces, Learning places: Children's environments that work.* Redmond, WA.: Exchange Press Inc.

Grusec, J.E. & Lytton, H. (1988). *Social development: History, theory and research.* New York: Springer-Verlag.

Guralnick, M. (1976). *Early intervention and the integration of handicapped and nonhandicapped children.* Baltimore: University Park Press.

Guralnick, M. (1981). The efficacy of integrating handicapped children in early education settings: Research implications. *Topics in early childhood special education, 1* (10), 57-71.

Harms, T., Cryer, D., & Clifford, R.M. (1990). *Infant/toddler environment rating scale.* New York: Teachers College Press.

Honig, A.S. (1975). How good is your infant program? Use an observational method to find out. *Child Care Quarterly* (Fall).

Honig, A.S. (1985). High quality infant/toddler care: Issues and dilemmas. *Young Children, 41* (1), 40-46.

Honig, A.S. (1990). The baby: Birth to 12 months. In E. Surbeck and M.T. Kelly (Eds). *Personalizing Care with Infants, Toddlers and Families.* Wheaton, MD: Association for Childhood Education International.

Howes, C. (1989). Infant child care. *Young Children, 44* (6), 24-27.

Howes, C. (1987). Quality indicators in infant and toddler child care: The Los Angeles Study. In Deborah A. Phillips (Ed). *Quality in child care: What does research tell us?* Washington: National Association for the Education of Young Children.

Hughes, F.P., Noppe, L.D., & Noppe, I.C. (1988). *Child development.* St. Paul, MN: West.

Hunt, J. (1961). *Intelligence and experience.* New York: Ronald Press.

Huntington, D.S., Provence, S., & Parker, R.K. (1973). *Day care: Serving infants.* Washington, DC: US Department of Health, Education and Welfare.

Hutt, C. (1976). Exploration and play in children. In J.S. Bruner, A. Jolly, and K. Sylva (Eds). *Play — Its role in development and evolution.* New York: Basic.

Innes, R.B. & Innes, S.M. (1984). A qualitative study of caregivers' attitudes about childcare. *Early Childhood Development and Care, 15,* 133-148.

Jones, E. (Ed.) (1979). *Supporting the growth of infants, toddlers and parents.* Pasadena, CA: Pacific Oaks.

Kaplan, P.S. (1991). *A child's odyssey: Child and adolescent development.* St. Paul, MN: West.

Karnes, M.B. (1982). *You and your small wonder: Activities for busy parents and babies. Book 1: Birth to 18 months.* Circle Pines, MN: American Guidance Service.

Kontos, S. & Stevens, R. (1985). High quality child care: Does your center measure up? *Young Children, 40* (2), 5-9

Kostelik, M. (1975). Program evaluation: How to ask the right questions. *Child Care Information Exchange.* (Fall).

LaGrange, A. & Read, M. (1990). *Those who care: A report on child caregivers in Alberta day care centres.* Red Deer, Alta: Canada: Child Care Matters.

Lally, R.J. (Ed). (1990). *Infant/toddler caregiving: A guide to social emotional growth and socialization.* Sacramento, CA: Center for Child and Family Studies, Far West Laboratory for Educational Research and Development, California State Department of Education.

Lally, R.J. & Stewart, J. (1990). *Infant/toddler caregiving: A guide to setting up environments.* Sacramento, CA: Center for Child and Family Studies, Far West Laboratory for Educational Research and Development, California Department of Education.

Langenbach, M. & Neskora, T.W. (1977). *Day care curriculum considerations.* New York: Merrill.

Leach, P. (1984). The world of the child. *The Journal of the Canadian Society for the Prevention of Cruelty to Children, 7* (1), 7-14.

Lero, D. & Kyle, I. (1985). *Day care quality: Its definition and implementation.* Background papers for the report of the task force on child care: Standards and quality. Ottawa: National Action Committee on the Status of Women.

Lieberman, A.F. (1991). Attachment and exploration: The toddler's dilemma. *Zero to Three, 11* (3), 6-11.

McCartney, K., Scarr, S., Phillips, D., & Grajek, S. (1982). Environmental differences among day care centers and their effects on children's development. In E. Zigler & E. Gordon (Eds). *Day care: Scientific and social policy issues.* Boston: Auburn House.

McFadden, E.J. (1986). Helping the abused child through play. In Judy Spitler McKee and Karen Menke Paciorek. *Early childhood education* (11th Ed). Guilford, CT: Dushkin.

Meisels, S.J. & Shonkoff, J.P. (Eds) (1990). *Handbook of early childhood intervention.* New York: Cambridge University Press.

Miller, K. (1984). *Things to do with toddlers and twos.* Marshfield, MA: Teleshare Publishing.

National Academy of Early Childhood Programs (NAECP) (1984). *Accreditation criteria and procedures.* Washington, DC: National Association for the Education of Young Children.

National Association for the Education of Young Children (NAEYC) (1987). *Developmentally appropriate practice in early childhood programs serving children from birth through age 8* (Expanded Edition). Washington, DC: NAEYC.

National Center for Clinical Infant Programs (NCCIP) (1988). *Who will mind the babies?* Washington, DC: NCCIP.

Network of the Federal/Provincial/Territorial Group on Nutrition & National Institute on Nutrition (1989). *Promoting nutritional health during the preschool years: Canadian guidelines.* Ottawa: Health and Welfare Canada.

O'Brien Steinfels, M. (1973). *Who's minding the children? The history and politics of day care in America.* New York: Simon & Schuster.

Odom, S.L. & McEvoy, M.A. (1988). Integration of young children with handicaps and normally developing children. In S.L. Odom and M.B. Karnes (Eds). *Early intervention for infants and children with handicaps.* Baltimore: Paul H. Brookes.

Olds, A. (1982). Planning a developmentally optimal day care center. *Day care and early education, 8* (6).

Pence, A. (1990). The child-care profession in Canada. In I.M. Doxey (Ed). *Childcare and education: Canadian dimensions.* Scarborough: Nelson Canada.

Phenice, L. & Hildebrand, V. (1988). Multicultural education: A pathway to global harmony. *Day Care and Early Education, 16* (2), 15-17.

Phillips, D.A. (Ed) (1987). *Quality in Child Care. What does research tell us?* Washington, DC: National Association for the Education of Young Children.

Piaget, J. (1972). Development and learning. In C.S. Lavetelli & F. Stendler (Eds). *Readings in child behavior and development.* New York: Harcourt, Brace & Jovanovich.

Powell, D.R. & Stremmel, A.J. (1987). Managing relations with parents: Research notes on the teacher's role. In D.L. Peters and S. Kontos (Eds). *Continuity and discontinuity of experience in child care.* Norwood, NJ: Ablex.

Provence, S., Naylor, A., & Patterson, J. (1977). *The challenge of day care.* New Haven: Yale University Press.

Ramsey, P.G. (1987). *Teaching and learning in a diverse world: Multicultural education for young children.* New York: Teachers College Press.

Raver, S.A. (1991). *Strategies for teaching at risk and handicapped infants and toddlers: A transdisciplinary approach.* New York: Merrill.

Rogers, C.S. & Sawyers, J.K. (1988). *Play in the lives of children.* Washington, DC: National Association for the Education of Young Children.

Rubin, K.H., Fein, G.G., & Vandenberg, B. (1983). Play. In E.M. Hetherington (Ed). *Handbook of child psychology* (Vol. 4): *Socialization, personality and social development.* New York: Wiley.

Schwartz, S.L. & Robison, H. (1982). *Designing curriculum for early childhood.* Boston: Allyn & Bacon.

Schwarz, J.C. (1983). Effects of group day care in the first two years (Report No. PS 013 802). Paper presented at the Biennial meeting of the Society for Research in Child Development: Detroit, MI. (ERIC Document Reproduction Service No. ED 233 805).

Seedfelt, C. & Barbour, N. (1987). Functional play: A tool for toddler learning. *Day Care and Early Education.* (Spring).

Shapiro, K.A., Kaufmann, R. & Messenger, K.P. (Eds) (1988). *Healthy young children: A manual for programs.* Washington, DC: National Association for the Education of Young Children.

Shimoni, R. (1991). Parent involvement in early childhood education and day care. *Sociological Studies of Child Development, 5.*

Shimoni, R., Creighton, T., & Carnat, M. (1989). Parent involvement: An exploratory study. In Y. Benoit (conference booklet coordinator). *Seeds for tomorrow: Conference booklet 1989.* Calgary: Alberta Association for Young Children.

Shimoni, R., MacLean, D., & MacWilliams, C. (1990). Evaluating programs. *Day Care and Early Education, 17* (3), 42-46.

Sroufe, L.A. (1988). A developmental perspective on day care. *Early Childhood Research Quarterly, 3* (3), 283-293.

Thelen, E. & Fogel, A. (1989). Toward an action-based theory of infant development. In J. Lockman and N. Hazen (Eds). *Action in social context: Perspectives on early development.* New York: Plenum.

Thoman, E.B. & Browder, S. (1987). *Born dancing. How intuitive parents understand their baby's unspoken language and natural rhythms.* New York: Harper & Row.

Thomas, A. & Chess, S. (1977). *Temperament and development.* New York: Bruner/Mazel.

Thompson, R.A. (1988). The effects of infant day care through the prism of attachment theory: A critical appraisal. *Early Childhood Research Quarterly, 3* (3), 273-283.

Vandebelt Schulz, P. (1978). Day care in Canada: 1850-1962. In K. Gallagher Ross (Ed). *Good day care: Fighting for it, getting it, keeping it.* Toronto: Womens' Educational Press.

Vaughn, B.E., Egeland, B., Sroufe, L.A., & Waters, E. (1980). Individual differences in infant-mother attachment at twelve and eighteen months: Stability and change in families under stress. *Child Development, 50,* 971-975.

Weinstein, & Flynn (1982). In R. Lurie and R. Neugebauer (Eds). *Caring for infants and toddlers: What works, what doesn't.* Washington, DC: Child Care Information Exchange.

Weiser, M.G. (1991). *Infant/Toddler care and education* (2nd Ed). Toronto: Merrill.

White, B. (1984). Quoted in D. Cayley. The world of the child. *Canadian Society for the Prevention of Cruelty to Children 1,* 7-14.

Whitebook, M., Howes, C., & Phillips, D. (1990). *Who cares? Child care teachers and the quality of care in America.* Final Report, National Child Care Staffing Study. New York: Child Care Employees Project.

Widerstrom, A.H. (1986). Educating young handicapped children. *Childhood Education, 63* (2), 78-83.

Willis, A. & Ricciuti, H. (1975). *A good beginning for babies: Guidelines for group care.* Washington, DC: National Association for the Education of Young Children.

Wingert, P. & Kantrowitz, B. (1990). The day care generation. *Early Childhood Education 91/92: Annual Edition, 11,* 70-72.

Wolfensberger, W. (1972). *The principles of normalization in human services.* Toronto: National Institute on Mental Retardation.

Yeates, M., McKenna, D., Warberg, C., & Chandler, K. (1990). *Administering early childhood settings: The Canadian perspective.* Toronto: Merrill.

Index

Photo Credits